Introducing Blockchain Applications

Understand and Develop Blockchain Applications Through Distributed Systems

Joseph Thachil George

Apress®

Introducing Blockchain Applications: Understand and Develop Blockchain Applications Through Distributed Systems

Joseph Thachil George
Rome, Italy

ISBN-13 (pbk): 978-1-4842-7479-8   ISBN-13 (electronic): 978-1-4842-7480-4
https://doi.org/10.1007/978-1-4842-7480-4

Managing Director, Apress Media LLC: Welmoed Spahr
Acquisitions Editor: Spandana Chatterjee
Development Editor: James Markham
Coordinating Editor: Mark Powers
Copyeditor: Kezia Endsley

Cover designed by eStudioCalamar

Cover image by Shubham Dhage on Unsplash (www.unsplash.com)

Distributed to the book trade worldwide by Apress Media, LLC, 1 New York Plaza, New York, NY 10004, U.S.A. Phone 1-800-SPRINGER, fax (201) 348-4505, e-mail orders-ny@springer-sbm.com, or visit www.springeronline.com. Apress Media, LLC is a California LLC and the sole member (owner) is Springer Science + Business Media Finance Inc (SSBM Finance Inc). SSBM Finance Inc is a **Delaware** corporation.

For information on translations, please e-mail booktranslations@springernature.com; for reprint, paperback, or audio rights, please e-mail bookpermissions@springernature.com.

Apress titles may be purchased in bulk for academic, corporate, or promotional use. eBook versions and licenses are also available for most titles. For more information, reference our Print and eBook Bulk Sales web page at http://www.apress.com/bulk-sales.

Any source code or other supplementary material referenced by the author in this book is available to readers on GitHub (github.com/apress/introducing-blockchain-applications). For more detailed information, please visit http://www.apress.com/source-code.

Printed on acid-free paper

Table of Contents

About the Author

 **Joseph Thachil George** is a Technical Consultant for International Game Technology (IGT), Rome, Italy. Additionally, Joseph is pursuing his doctorate (PhD) in Computer Science and Engineering at the University of Lisbon, Portugal. He completed his M.S. in Cyber Security from the Università degli Studi di Firenze, Italy. He is also part of the research group (DISIA) of the University of Florence, Italy, and the research group (INESC-ID Lisbon) of the University of Lisbon, Portugal. His research interests cover dynamic malware analysis, automatic exploit generation for JavaScript-based web applications, and cyber security. At IGT, he has been a part of various projects related to game configuration and integration in various platforms. He specialized in Java and Spring Boot-based projects. He has also worked in various companies in India, Angola, Portugal, and the UK; he has seven years of experience at various IT companies.

About the Technical Reviewer

Prasanth Sahoo is a thought leader, an adjunct professor, a technical speaker, and a full-time practitioner in blockchain, DevOps, cloud, and Agile working for PDI Software. He was awarded the "Blockchain and Cloud Expert of the Year Award 2019" from TCS Global Community for his knowledge sharing within academic services to the community. He is passionate about driving digital technology initiatives through coaching, mentoring, and grooming.

Prasanth has a patent under his name and to date, he has interacted with over 50,000 professionals, mostly within the technical domain. He is a working group member in the Blockchain Council, CryptoCurrency Certification Consortium, Scrum Alliance, Scrum Organization, and International Institute of Business Analysis.

Acknowledgments

First of all, I would like to express my sincere gratitude to my mentor and adviser, Professor Nuno Santos (Department of Computer Science and Engineering at Instituto Superior Técnico—IST—University of Lisbon, Portugal) for his continued support and for providing research ideas and thoughts. His guidance has helped me throughout my research and writing of various technical books. Working with him has been a great experience, both professionally and personally. Furthermore, I would like to express my sincere thanks to Professor Tommaso Pecorella (Department Ingegneria dell' Informazione, UniFi, University of Florence, Italy) for his constant support as technical adviser.

Finally, I would really like to thank my father, Thachil Joseph George, my mother, Reena George, my wife, Meghna, and my brother-in-law, Sherline Poulose. All the people whom I love gave direct or indirect support so I could finish writing this book.

## CHAPTER 1

Introducing Blockchain Applications Through Distributed Systems

The primary objective of this book is to provide an in-depth understanding of blockchain technology and to demonstrate how to use it in a distributed setting or environment. The Blockchain technology employs several aspects of distributed networks and the distributed system is also connected to the majority of blockchain-based applications. As a result, you need a thorough understanding of emerging technologies in the distributed systems.

When you think of distributed systems, you must keep in mind that they are systems for which processing is distributed. This does not necessarily have to be physically distributed, but the processing components must be distributed and not united in a single block. This means that hardware and software architectures maintain the distributed system. Everything must be interconnected: the CPU through the network and the processes through the communication system. Distributed systems have infinite use cases, including electronic banking systems, massively multiplayer online games, and sensor networks.

1.1 Blockchain Use Cases

Since many blockchain applications are used in a distributed system environment, it is good to know about these technologies in depth. Let's look at a few examples.

- **Blockchain in the insurance sector:** In the insurance industry, blockchain enables safe and decentralized transactions, establishing a solid foundation for preventing fraud, providing more control, and improving data and reporting. Furthermore, insurance companies

1

© Joseph Thachil George 2022
J. T. George, *Introducing Blockchain Applications*, https://doi.org/10.1007/978-1-4842-7480-4_1

can have up-to-date, accurate notifications about changes, thanks to blockchain, which allows them to improve risk management and maximize capital and fund opportunities. It also allows for the possibility of implementing Big Data strategies, which are very useful for obtaining secure information about customers, priorities, and preferences.

- **Blockchain in digital payments:** Blockchain also has a lot of potential applications in digital payments. Obviously, there are still many issues to be resolved, such as transaction processing time, which is still extremely sluggish when compared to the demands of the market and a fast-paced world. The system's performance should be enhanced so it can be better absorbed by digital payments. Clear regulatory guidelines and a more thorough study of risks are two of blockchain's problems in the digital payments industry. Despite these difficulties, there is potential for this new technology to be used in digital payments.

- **Blockchain in agrifood:** The benefits of using blockchain in the agrifood industry are numerous. There are several uses of blockchain in the agrifood business, ranging from decentralization to shared control to immutability and information conservation. Blockchain's advantages appear to be particularly essential to the processing sector, as well as all operations and innovations linked to food certification. The blockchain allows users to establish open supply chains that include all of the players: raw material producers, logistics and transportation businesses, companies that work with raw materials at various stages of transformation, and companies that work with packaging and marketing. Finally, retail may pass along data and information to all other players while maintaining complete openness.

- **Blockchains in the energy industry:** Several projects aim to provide platforms open to all energy system stakeholders. For example, Power Ledger is an Australian startup involved in a variety of blockchain applications for renewable energy systems. The energy system operations and its markets and customers can all benefit from blockchain or distributed ledger technology. Blockchains provide disintermediation, transparency, and tamper-proof transactions, but they also provide unique ways for consumers and small renewable providers to participate more actively in the energy market and monetize their assets.

1.2 What This Book Covers

To implement blockchain effectively in a distributed system, you first need to understand the blockchain technology and its related components in depth. These are covered in Chapters 2-7. Since consensus algorithms are an important concept in a distributed system transaction, Chapter 8 includes a project related to this topic.

After that, the book discusses real-time systems and scheduling. These are key ideas in distributed systems that are covered in Chapters 9 and 10. (With real-time systems, the book explains how scheduling works. When many processes have the same demands and time restrictions and must be efficiently handled by the scheduling policy, this is known as *homogenous process scheduling*.)

The systems must first be modeled to develop a successful blockchain application. When modeling systems, the above-mentioned approach must be used. When using blockchain technology in a distributed system, you must model the blockchain layers as part of the distributed system modeling to get a clear image of the system architecture and the systems of systems (SoS) capabilities. The BLOCKLY 4SOS modeling approach is used to create all these models.

To model SoS systems, you must include BLOCKLY 4SOS as part of model-driven engineering. In Chapters 11 and 12, these topics are discussed in detail.

With the aid of cyber-physical systems projects, you might execute a mix of all of these approaches. The book presents five projects. They were created using a variety of programming languages, and Chapters 13-17 include source code and modeling languages. For each project, the components of cyber-physical systems are also discussed.

The book comes to a close with Chapter 18, which discusses worldwide regulations connected to blockchain and distributed systems, as well as the future of blockchain-distributed systems-related initiatives.

Let's start with the fundamentals of blockchain; the blockchain and its components are discussed in the next chapter.

CHAPTER 2

An Introduction to Blockchain

A *blockchain* is a sharable and immutable ledger that makes transactions and computations between systems easier and more secure and tracks assets across the business world.

It is important to understand that an asset can be tangible or intangible. This includes intellectual property, patents, copyrights, trademarks, and so on. The blockchain concept is widely used in the business field.

A blockchain (think of it as a "series of blocks") is a sharable and unchangeable data package. Generally, it can be defined as a digital registry whose entries are joined in a series/chains of "blocks" and strung together in sequential order, and whose integrity is ensured using cryptography. Although its size will grow over time, it is unchangeable because its contents, once written, cannot usually be altered or deleted without the entire architecture being invalidated. Tracking or trading assets on a blockchain system reduces risks and costs for parties on both sides of the transaction.

Note that these concepts belong to the broader group of distributed ledgers. (A *distributed ledger* is a shared ledger. It can be a public or private set of digital information that's synchronized and geographically distributed in multiple countries, sites, or institutions, without requiring an administrator or centralized data management.) This means that these systems are based on a distributed ledger that can be read and changed by multiple nodes in a network.

Moreover, the nodes involved do not need to understand each other's behavior or identity, nor do they need to trust each other. To ensure integrity and consistency between different copies, the addition of a new block is governed worldwide by a common rule or protocol. When a block is approved from the network or system, each node needs to update its own private copy. Hence, the data structure guarantees no future manipulation.

5

J. T. George, *Introducing Blockchain Applications*, https://doi.org/10.1007/978-1-4842-7480-4_2

Systems developed with the blockchain and distributed ledger technologies have digitalization of data, decentralization, disintermediation, traceability of transfers, and transparency.

Thanks to these characteristics, you can provide transactions in a centralized, monitored way and provide security for each transaction.

2.1 A Short History of Blockchain

According to Wikipedia, the first blockchain was presented in 2008 by Satoshi Nakamoto and was implemented the next year, with the aim of acting as a "ledger" (a register of all transactions) for the nascent digital currency Bitcoin. Nakamoto used the words *block* and *chain* differently in the original article. In 2009, Nakamoto's creation, Bitcoin, was used for the first time to purchase a physical asset: a pizza.

In August 2014, with Bitcoin having already achieved some notoriety globally, the size of its blockchain reached 20 gigabytes. In March 2018, it exceeded 162 gigabytes. In 2014, the term "Blockchain 2.0" began to be used to refer to a new way of using blockchain. The idea was to allow people excluded from the current monetization to be able to access a reliable and secure monetary deposit, protect their privacy, and monetize their information. According to some authors, it also has the potential to resolve the issue of social injustice by changing the way wealth is distributed.

In 2017, the Nevada senate completely liberalized blockchain. In particular, Section 4 of Senate Bill 398:

- Prevents local authorities from imposing taxes on blockchain.

- Prevents the request for any form of license for the use of blockchain.

- Prevents any other requests on the use of blockchain.

- Prevents local authorities from imposing taxes on blockchain.

In April 2019, during the International Handicraft Exhibition, the first product (made in Italy) was presented in which the production steps were entirely traced using blockchain technology.

The need to timestamp a digital document led to blockchain technology. You can, for example, write yourself a letter and send it through the mail. If you leave it unopened, you can guarantee that the letter was written before the envelope was postmarked. Businesses adopt increasingly complex processes into their daily operations to improve the credibility of their internal documentation in the event that they are questioned later. In the Internet world, transactions need to be done with digital stamps in a secure way. Secure time-stamped digital signatures can be created using Bitcoin or blockchain technology.

Hash functions are used in all digital signatures. These methods accept any file and generate fixed-length fingerprints, which is a code that uniquely identifies the file. Anybody with access to the file may produce the code; however, constructing the file from the code is very difficult.

2.2 Applications Using Blockchain

Blockchain has great potential to change business strategies and models in the long run. Moreover, blockchain is an enabling technology that could create new technologies and new foundations for the global economy and social environments, rather than a disruptive technology that attacks the traditional business model.

The use of blockchain promises an important improvement for worldwide supply chains, financial and marketing transactions, accounting, and distributed social networks. This new technology can be integrated into various sectors, and its protocols make it easier for companies to adopt new methods for processing and managing digital transactions.

Some examples include money payment systems and digital currencies that facilitate crowd sales, implementation of the prediction market, and generic governance tools. Blockchain can be used to certify the date of a document and verify that it has not been tampered with. This application of blockchain, obtained by inserting the hash of the documents to be certified, is called *notarization*. An example of this is the notarization of the movements of trucks that are transporting land from a construction site, in order to ensure compliance with environmental standards.

Blockchain can address the need for a fiduciary service provider and ensure that less litigation capital is incurred. It has the potential to remove systematic risk and financial fraud. It can automate various processes that previously had to be done manually for a long time, such as business integration.

In general, most blockchain applications involve cryptocurrencies such a Bitcoin, Blackcoin, Dash, and Nxt, and so on. Its center ledger system stores all the transactions. A decentralized voting mechanism is used to understand the transaction.

This new distribution method is also applicable and available in the insurance and bank sectors. These sectors are interested in this emerging technology, because the transactions are quick and very secure.

The collaborative economy and the Internet of Things (IoT) technologies can also benefit from blockchain technology by engaging many like-minded people in online collaborative voting applications.

Blockchain can also be used to build information systems for medical staff to increase their interoperability and security. Several blockchains have also been developed for storing data, publishing text, and identifying the origin of digital art. For example, a bank has opened research centers dedicated to blockchain to study the various implications of this new technology on financial services with the goal to improve efficiency and reduce costs. Another application has been proposed to share wireless networks.

2.3 Why Blockchain Matters

Businesses depend on information. In the business world, the faster and more accurate that information is, the better. Blockchain is ideal for providing this type of information because it provides instant, sharable, and fully transparent data that's stored in an unchangeable ledger. Only authorized individuals can view the data.

Additionally, a blockchain network can trace orders, money transactions, account ledgers, and production processes, among other things. Because members share a common information that is contained in the blockchain, it's also possible to see all the data of an end-to-end transaction (it's fully transparent to all the parties), leading to higher trust as well as new improvements and future uses.

2.4 Summary

In this chapter, you learned the basic concepts underlying blockchains, distributed ledgers, and timestamping documents. You also gained an understanding of why these technologies are important in the market, and how they've developed in recent years. The next chapter focuses on Bitcoin.

CHAPTER 3

Bitcoin

In the previous chapter, you saw how blockchain technology, without the need for a central authority, and thanks to the techniques and algorithms discussed, can establish trust between participants and certify the *immutability* of a distributed ledger. The blockchain lends itself to being an ideal model for digital currencies, where there is no need for intermediaries and third parties such as banks, insurance companies, and other central organizations. In fact, blockchain was born and spread thanks to Bitcoin.

In 2008, a person (or group of persons) named Satoshi Nakamoto released a research paper entitled "Peer-to-Peer Electronic Cash System in Bitcoin." This paper described a peer-to-peer cash system that permitted network transactions to be sent directly from one part to another without going through any intermediaries/banking organizations. It explains Bitcoins in great detail.

The term cryptocurrency describes all the systems, networks, and media that use cryptography to protect digital transactions, compared to those systems where transactions are managed through a common trusted entity.

This chapter covers the *Bitcoin protocol*. It analyzes in detail the main parts that compose it—the public and private keys, the Bitcoin addresses, and the blocks. The chapter then illustrates the network and consensus mechanisms, including the proof of work.

© Joseph Thachil George 2022
J. T. George, *Introducing Blockchain Applications*, https://doi.org/10.1007/978-1-4842-7480-4_3

3.1 The History of Bitcoin

Almost all of the technological parts of Bitcoin were born in academic publications of the 1980s and 1990s. "We need to emphasis that our aim is not to reduce the work and success of Nakamoto, but only to emphasize what the real leap of intuition was. Indeed, by tracking the initial of ideas present in Bitcoin, we can focus on the specific and complex way they come put together the underlying components".[1]

Bitcoin's history doubles as a case study, as it proves relationships between the academic world, external scientists, engineers, and professionals and shows on how these teams can gain knowledge from each other. Many professionals have studied Bitcoin and have produced numerous research papers.

Note that the ledger idea is the initial starting point for Bitcoin. If you understand the ledger, you will understand the system's structure and its communication. The ledger is the place where all the transactions take place. It's open and trusted by all parties and components in the system (see Figure 3-1).

---

[1] https://howieliux.github.io/assets/others/Mastering_bitcoin/Mastering_Bitcoin.html

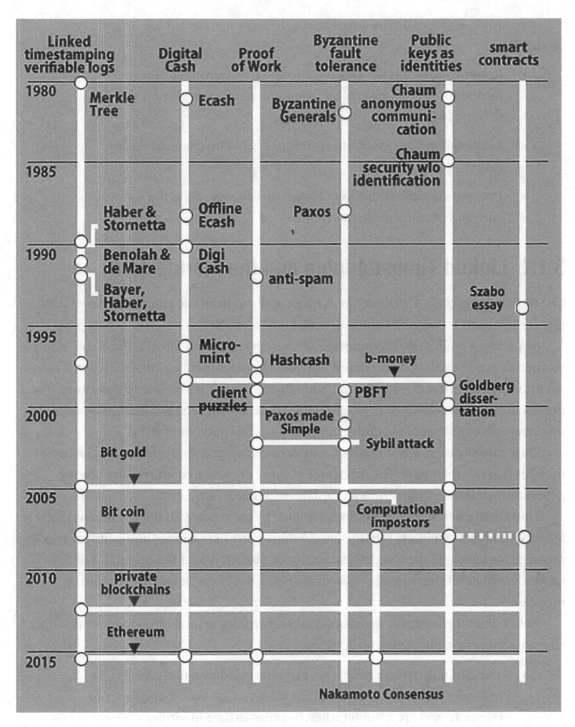

Figure 3-1. *The main ideas behind Bitcoin*

In order to support a digital currency, the ledger must have these fundamental properties:

- **Append-only:** It is only possible to add new transactions to the ledger. It is not possible to abandon, modify, or reorder the existing ledger.

- **Immutable:** The information present cannot be changed in the ledger.

- **Prevents double spending:** It is not possible to spend the same currency security more than once.

3.1.1 Linked Timestamping and the Merkle Tree

The Bitcoin ledgers data architecture is taken, with appropriate changes, from several articles by Stuart Haber and Scott Stornetta (1990 and 1997)

As we know well, since Nakamoto states it in the paper on Bitcoin, the Haber and Stornetta's paper dealt with the timestamp issue for documents. Note that when it comes to commercial contracts, patents, and other documents, it is possible to determine that the document was generated at given point of time. We understand that their notion of a documents are quite generic, and it can include different types of data.

They casually mentioned banking transactions as a possible application, but note that this was not their goal. The originator of every document confirms the time of generation and signs the document, its date, and time.

This initial document was approved/signed by the creator, so the document forms a lengthy chain with pointers into the past. A third-party user cannot edit a timestamped message because it is approved by its originator, and moreover the originator or the creator cannot edit the message without changing the entire subsequent chain of message.

Haber and Stornetta also mentioned in their articles several ideas to make this data structure more fast, effective, and accurate:

- The chain between documents can be created by using hashes instead of signatures; note that these hashes are easier and faster to compute and are stronger when it comes to data identifiers. We call such links *pointers*.

- Rather than timestamping documents separately , which could be inefficient if many documents are generated at once, the documents can be combined into batches or blocks, using the same timestamp in the documents.

- The documents in each block should be tied by a binary tree of hash pointers called the *Merkle tree*. Mr. Josh Benaloh and Mr. Michael de Mare presented these ideas independently in 1991, immediately after Haber's article.

Note that the Merkle trees are named after Ralph Merkle, who presented the asymmetric cryptography logic in his 1980 document.

Either way, Bitcoin takes the data structure from the work of Haber and Stornetta and redesigns its safety characteristics with the addition of the PoW scheme.

3.1.2 Distributed Consensus

A common authority is required for Internet money or currency transactions.

In the case of a distributed ledger, you can see that there will automatically be forks, which means that some nodes will conclude that block A is the last block, whereas all other nodes will conclude that it is block B.[2]

In this case, you need to understand that this is due to an opponent trying to interrupt the transaction of the ledger or because of the network delay, occasionally causing near-block generation together from different nodes, unaware of reciprocal blocks. The linked timestamp is not sufficient to rectify the forks, and this is expressed by Mike in 1997-1998.

The problem of how to reach consensus in situations where errors are possible is called the *Byzantine generals problem*. It was talked about informally in Chapter 2. Byzantine faults include both natural breakdowns and malicious behavior.

This idea was initially discussed in an article by Leslie Lamport, written with Robert & Marshall in 1982. In 1999, a document from Miguel Castro & Barbara Liskov presented the PBFT algorithm, and this enables you to solve the problem of Byzantine generals with excellent performance. (Note that the PBFT stands for Practical Byzantine Fault Tolerance.)

---

[2]https://www.oreilly.com/library/view/mastering-bitcoin/9781491902639/ch08.htm

The replication algorithm can manage the Byzantine defects. Byzantine fault-tolerant algorithms will become increasingly important in the near future, because as malicious attacks and software bugs become very common in the cyber world, this can cause faulty nodes to promote arbitrary behaviors.

But in the case of the previous algorithms, they needed a special synchronous system and were slow. The algorithm described in this book is very practical, because it works in asynchronous environments quickly.

Nakamoto doesn't cite the same article in his initial paper, nor does he utilize his phrasing. However, he employs some concepts, referring to his own protocol as a consensus protocol and taking into account both faults in the form of intruders, as well as nodes joining and exiting the infrastructure.

When asked about the connection between Bitcoin and the Byzantine generals problem on a mailing list, Nakamoto claims that the Proof-of-Work (PoW) chain fixes the issue.

Almost all failure systems assume that the majority of the nodes in the system are both trustworthy and honest (e.g., more than half or two-thirds). Nodes in an open peer-to-peer network are free to join and leave at any time.

As a result, a Sybil attack can be used to go around the system's consent or quality assurances. John Douceur defined the Sybil attack in 2002 and proposed a cryptographic breakthrough called Proof of Work to combat it.

3.2 Proof of Work

This section goes over the first phases of Proof of Work so you can get a better understanding of it. Cynthia Dwork and Moni Naor created the first proposal, which was titled "Proof of Work," in 1992. Their purpose at the time was to discourage spam.

For example, the Hashcash is a proof-of-work method that has been employed in a variety of systems as a denial-of-service countermeasure.

A hashcash stamp is a proof-of-work that takes the sender a parameterizable amount of time to compute. The recipient may quickly check the hashcash stamps he or she has received.

While hashcash was designed to add a penalty to sending email in order to prevent high-volume email spammers, it may now be introduced to any internet service to impose a computational cost on customers who might otherwise misuse a server's resources.

However, a spammer who wanted to transmit a million emails might need multiple weeks to do it using a similar approach.

Occasionally, the Proof-of-Work instance (also known as a *puzzle*) is required to identify the email and the recipient.

A spammer may otherwise send many messages to the same recipient (or the same message to multiple recipients) for the cost of only sending one message to one receiver. The second critical feature is that the recipient's computing cost should be as minimal as feasible; puzzle answers, no matter how complex to compute, should be straightforward to check.

Dwork and Naor's suggestion spawned an entire field of inquiry. Adam Back, a post-doc in the cypherpunk research community at the time, separately devised a similar concept called hashcash in 1997.

Cypherpunks were anti-government and anti-centralized institution activists who used encryption to bring about social and political change.

Hashcash is nothing more than a proof-of-work algorithm; it was used as a measure against spam and denial-of-service attacks in different systems.

It is based on a simple principle connected to the hash function: the only way to identify an input that has a hash on a given output is to test various inputs until the desired data is provided in a hash function. As a result, the only method to identify an input that hashes in one arbitrary series of outputs is to try hashing different inputs, one after the other.

3.2.1 Nakamoto's Genius

Understanding all of the predecessors that comprise elements of the Bitcoin design leads to an appreciate of Nakamoto's truly great discoveries.

Proof-of-Work (PoW) is used to protect the book master or ledger. Proof-of-work resolution is done by miners.

Each miner solves a slightly different form of the challenge; thus the odds of success are proportional to the fraction of the world's processing power that the miner owns. A miner who solves a problem can donate a new transaction block to the ledger, which is added to the ledger depending on the timestamp.

A prospector who contributes a block is paid with units of recently produced coin in exchange for maintaining the ledger. If a prospector contributes to an invalid block or a transaction, it will most likely be eliminated by the majority of other prospectors who contribute to succeeding blocks, invalidating the block reward for the wrong block.

Miners are mutually insured in this way, thanks to monetary incentives.

Instead of the sophisticated method used to bring the computer system, Nakamoto's genius is one of the individual components of Bitcoin.

Nobody thought of encouraging the knots to be truthful. No one has thought of using a consent algorithm to avoid the twofold cost.

To eliminate duplicate spending and ensure that the currency has value, Bitcoin requires a secure ledger. Miners must be rewarded in some way. The strength of the miner's power, in turn, is used to safeguard the ledger. Otherwise, an enemy with more than 51% the world's mining capacity may generate blocks quicker than the rest of the network, do double-spend computations or transactions, and completely rewrite history by avoiding the computer system.

As a result, Bitcoin is launched with a well-balanced reliance on these three components.

3.3 Key and Address

In order to have your own Bitcoins, that is, to spend them, it is necessary to have:

- A collection of digital keys, including a private key and a public key

- A Bitcoin address

- A digital sign

The Elliptic Curve Digital Signature Method is a cryptographic algorithm that underpins Bitcoin's private and public keys. It's used to make sure that only legitimate owners can spend money.

3.3.1 Private Key

In the context of Bitcoin, a private key is a secret number that allows you to spend Bitcoins. Each Bitcoin wallet comes with one or more private keys kept in the wallet file.

It is also used to make a digital signature.

A private key is just a number that is created at random. It's a signed 256-bit (32-byte) integer. Not all 256-bit unsigned numbers, however, are Bitcoin private keys. In fact, the standard secp256k1 used by Bitcoin limits the number of valid private keys.

Secp256k1 is described in the standards for efficient cryptography and corresponds to the parameters of the elliptic curve used in Bitcoin public key cryptography (SEC).

Keep in mind that the private key is utilized to generate the public key.

3.3.2 Public Key

The argument is that a public key can be used to verify the authenticity of a signature (that is, produced with the correct private key). In general, the public key is created by multiplying the private key by an elliptic curve. Bitcoin is defined in the `secp256k1` constant and uses a constant elliptic curve and a set of mathematical constants.

Starting with a private key << `privkey` >> and multiplying it by a predefined dot on the curve called the *generator point* G produces a different dot on the curve, which corresponds to the public key << `pubKey` >>. Usually, a public key can be defined by the coordinates of the point «`privkey`»*G=«`pubKey`» = (x,y) (see Figure 3-2).

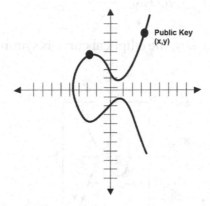

Figure 3-2. *Example of an elliptic curve cryptographic function for calculating the public key*

The generating point G is described as part of `secp256k1`, and it is the same for all keys in Bitcoin.

The private key << `privKey` >> multiplied by G will have the outcome with the same public key << `pubKey` >>. The connection between <<`privKey` >> and << `pubKey` >> is constant. However it can only be compute in single direction, from << `privKey` >> to << `pubKey` >>.

The (x; y) coordinates of a point on an elliptic curve can be used to describe the public key. Hexadecimal is the most commonly used format for storing data.

Hence, there are two formats for public keys:

- Uncompressed public key

- Compressed public key

Note that the uncompressed public key is the old format. It is generally no longer used in favor of the compressed format. Bitcoin originally used both x and y coordinates to store the public key. In this uncompressed format, the coordinates are simply strung together, and the prefix 04 is added to indicate that it is an uncompressed public key, as shown in Figure 3-3.

Figure 3-3. *Uncompressed public key*

With a compressed public key, the elliptical curve is symmetrical along the axis of X, as shown in Figure 3-4.

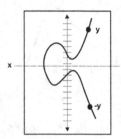

Figure 3-4. *Symmetry of the elliptical curve*

Hence, in the compressed public key format (see Figure 3-5), you only save the full x coordinates, along with a prefix indicating if y is even or odd.

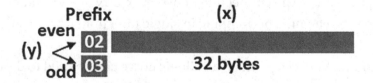

Figure 3-5. *Compressed public key*

This format saves a lot of space on the blockchain.

3.3.3 Bitcoin Address

A Bitcoin address, or simply an address, is an identifier of 26-35 alphanumeric characters, starting with the number 1, 3, or bc1, that represents a possible destination for a Bitcoin payment. Transactions in Bitcoin (cryptocurrency, BTC) can be made through an address, a bit like sending an email. However, unlike an email addresses, people have different Bitcoin addresses and at the same time a unique address should be used for every transaction.

A person can create an unlimited number of addresses, increasing the level of anonymity of payments. An address is created from three elements:

- A public key hash

- A prefix

- A checksum

Let's analyze these three components in detail.

The public key hash is nothing more than a double hash applied to the public key. In particular, it is the hash obtained through the SHA-256 and RIPEMD160, and therefore:

`<< PublicKeyHash >> = RIPEMD160 (SHA-256 (<< publicKey >>))`

It is sometimes referred to as `HASH160 (<< publickey >>)`, because it is simpler than writing `RIPEMD160 (SHA256 (<< publickey >>))`.

The prefix indicates the type of block to be created.

The most commonly used ones are:

- 00: For the P2PKH locking script (you will learn what it is later)

- 05: For P2SH locking script

Finally, the checksum is obtained by performing the SHA-256 hash twice on the public key hash and taking the first four bytes. So, you take these elements and put them in order to get a queue (see Figures 3-6 and 3-7):

1. `prefix`

2. `HASH160(«public key»)`

3. `checksum`

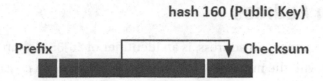

Figure 3-6. *Elements to form the Bitcoin address*

The Base58 function is then applied, which will finally provide the Bitcoin address, as shown in Figure 3-7.

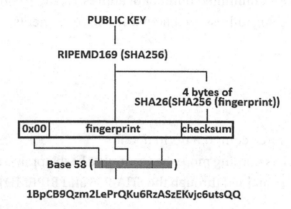

Figure 3-7. *Bitcoin address*

Base58 is a converter that you can use to represent large numbers in a shorter and more intuitive format, resulting in a text alphanumeric. Obviously, these operations are implemented at the application level, and it is not up to the user to carry out all these steps.

3.3.4 Digital Signature

The *digital signature* is a mathematical means of demonstrating that you are aware of the private key associated with a public key without revealing the effective private key. When making a transaction, you must first unlock the balances you want to use (UTXO, as you'll see in the next section). This can be accomplished by demonstrating that you "own" the balance and that you know the private key to the address where the balance is kept. Therefore, to unlock a balance without providing the private key you use the digital signature. In this way you show that you have the private key, without handing it over to the network. These are then used in transactions to prove you own the balances you are spending.

What stops someone from exploiting a transaction's digital signature to unlock other exits at your address? Each transaction has its own digital signature.

To put it another way, you employ not only the private key, but the private key and the transaction data to construct a digital signature. As a result, any digital signature is associated with the transaction in which it is employed. As a result, if someone tries to use a transaction's digital signature in a new transaction, it will clash with the data of the transaction in the digital signature shop and will be rejected by the Bitcoin network's nodes.

Consequently, the digital signature will also save against destroying the transaction in which it is used. A digital signature consists of two parts:

- A random part

- A part of the signature, consisting of

  - A private key

  - The data on which you are creating the digital signature

For the random part, let n be the order of point G of the second elliptic curve the standard secp256k1. You generate a random number 2 [1; n - 1] and call this random number.

You then multiply this random number by the point G (generator point) of the elliptic curve. This is the same G you used for the public key and indicated by the standard secp256k1. For the sake of brevity, you call the random number with the variable k.

$$k\, G = (xr; yr)$$

The random part of this digital signature is the point on the curve that you obtain (see Figure 3-8). But you only take the xr coordinate.

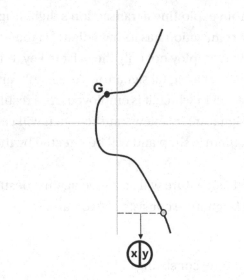

Figure 3-8. *Random number obtained on the curve, from which you take the X coordinate*

For the sake of brevity, you can call r the randomPart value obtained from

$$r = randomPart = xr\ mod\ n$$

For the signature part, you need to take the private key for the random part.

$$r * privKey$$

Then you include the data on which you want to create the signature.

In Bitcoin, this is represented by the hash of the transaction that contains the balance (UTXO) that you want to unlock. You define h (msg) = SHA-256 (<<transaction >>) and get:

$$[r * privKey] + h(msg)$$

The inclusion of the transaction hash binds the signature to a transaction (therefore it cannot be used in a different transaction). Finally, you divide this by the initial random number k:

$$s = sign = k\text{-}1\ (r\ privKey + h(msg))\ (mod\ n)$$

You have obtained the fundamental part of the digital signature. The digital signature is made up of an r and an s.

If someone asks you to prove that you know the key private for a public key, you can give them the signature digital (r; s) as proof.

3.3.4.1 Verifying a Digital Signature

To verify that a digital signature has been made using a correct private key, the person to whom you provide this digital signature must use both sides (r; s) to find two new points on the elliptic curve and check the signature.

From here on, the multiplication operator is used only when it is strictly necessary to divide the variables, otherwise yes assumes the implicit multiplication operation.

First, let's take the data on which the digital signature has been affixed. In this case, it is the SHA-256 hash that's applied to the transaction.

You divide this value by s (the core part of the digital signature) and multiply by G (the generator point), like so:

$$u1 = (x1; y1) = (h(msg)\ s\text{-}1\ mod\ n)\ G$$

You then find point 1 (see Figure 3-9).

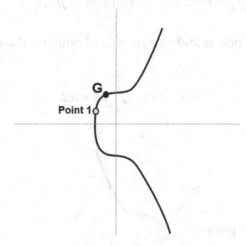

Figure 3-9. *Example of graphic representation of point 1*

Then you divide r by s and multiply by the < < publickey > >:

$$u2 = (x2; y2) = (r\ s\text{-}1\ mod\ n)\ pubKey$$

You then have point 2 (see Figure 3-10).

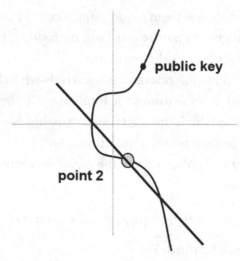

Figure 3-10. *Example of graphic representation of point 2*

Finally, add these two points and you get a third point on the elliptic curve. (See Figure 3-11.)

$$Rv = (xv; yv) = u1 + u2$$

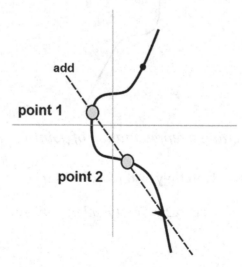

Figure 3-11. *Example of graphical representation of the sum between the point 1 and point 2*

If the value `c` = `xv mod n` of this point `Rv` = `(xv; yv)` obtained on the elliptic curve is equal to `r`, that is, `c == initial r`, then it's proof that the digital signature was made with the public key's connected private key.

3.3.4.2 Understanding the ECDSA Sign/Verify Math

The ECDSA signature has a simple description:

Note that the signing process signature encodes a random dot R (represented only from the X coordinate, you refer to `r = randomPart =xr mod n`) through transformations of the elliptic curve uses the private key `privKey`. It then encodes the hash of the message `h (msg)` in a number sign, which is proof that the signer understands the private key `privKey`. The signature `(random Part, sign)` may reveal the private key due to the complexity of the problem ECDLP.

Verification of the signature encodes the proof number sign using the public key `pubKey` and the message `hash h (msg)`. It then restores the original point R, used to create the signature, called `Rv`. Then compare the X coordinate `(xv mod n)` of the `Rv` retrieved with the `r = randomPart` value of the signature.

So how does the reported signature and verification scheme work? Let's consider the verification, then the equation to derive `Rv`. We then write the equation in the extended form.

$$Rv = (xv; yv) = h\,(msg)\,s\text{-}1\,(mod\,n)\,G + r\,s\text{-}1\,(mod\,n)\,pubKey$$

Replace `pubKey` with `privKey G`:

$$Rv = (xv; yv) = h\,(msg)\,s\text{-}1\,(mod\,n)\,G + r\,s\text{-}1\,(mod\,n)\,privKey\,G$$

Highlight G and `s-1 (mod n)`, obtaining:

$$Rv = (xv; yv) = (h\,(msg) + r\,privKey)\,s\text{-}1\,(mod\,n)\,G$$

We know that:

$$s\text{-}1\,(mod\,n) = (k\text{-}1\,(h\,(msg) + r\,privKey)) \text{ - } 1\,(mod\,n)$$

And so:

$$s\text{-}1\,(mod\,n) = k\,(h\,(msg) + r\,privKey)\,\text{-}1\,(mod\,n)$$

We substitute this in the equation of `Rv`:

$$Rv = (h\,(msg) + r\,privKey)\,k\,(h\,(msg) + r\,privKey)\,\text{-}1\,(mod\,n)\,G = k$$

The last step is to compare the point Rv with the point R. This is encoded by `privKey`. This algorithm compares the X coordinates of Rv with the X of R (where R = (xr; yr) e r = randomPart = xr mod n). More precisely, the signature is expected to be valid if given c = xv mod n, then c == r.

Figure 3-12 illustrates, at a high level, how the digital signatures in Bitcoin transactions work.

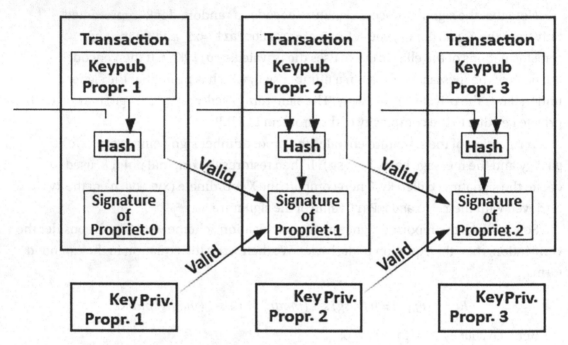

Figure 3-12. *Transactions and digital signatures*

3.4 The Transaction

The transaction is the most basic component of Bitcoin's blockchain. Transactions are verified and sent out. Many transactions combine to make a block. Furthermore, a chain of blocks is formed through a digital data link.[3]

---

[3] 2 Ante, L. A place next to Satoshi: foundations of blockchain and cryptocurrency research in business and economics. *Scientometrics* 124, 1305–1333 (2020). *https://doi.org/10.1007/s11192-020-03492-8*

To select the next block to be put to the chain, the blocks go through a consensus procedure. The chosen block is verified and added to the existing chain.

Miners are special peer nodes that perform the validation and consensus processes. It's important to note that they are unique or powerful machines that run blockchain protocol-specific software. Let's take a look at the specifics of a single Bitcoin transaction.

3.4.1 The Unspent Transaction Output (UTXO)

Unspent Transaction Output (UTXO) is a fundamental idea in the Bitcoin network UTXOs are a set of Bitcoins that are linked to a certain user. They can only be spent in a transaction if they are used entirely for that. A user can be associated with zero, one, or many UTXOs. Obviously, once a user has used a UTXO to complete a transaction, it cannot be used by another user. The sum of UTXOs associated with a user is the total balance of the latter.

In other words, Bitcoin stores data relating to transactions and balances of users in the form of UTXO, which are "unspent" Bitcoin amounts that have been sent to a user, and that are potentially expendable from that user.

The set of all the UTXOs in the network constitute the state of the blockchain Bitcoin. A Bitcoin transaction consists of inputs and outputs.

A transaction takes as input one or more UTXOs and, according to the request initiated by the sender, it generates one or more UTXOs to output the amount specified by the transaction request. As a result, an Unspent Transaction Output is the result of a transaction that a user receives and can spend later.

For example, suppose John has a UTXO with a value of ten Bitcoin and another five Bitcoin UTXO, and he wants to send eight Bitcoins to Sara, who has no UTXO in her portfolio. John can create a transaction, specifying the amount to spend on Sara, and enter ten Bitcoin UTXO as the transaction input.

The transaction will therefore look like this:

- **Input:** 10 Bitcoin Mario UTXO

- **Output:**

    – An 8 Bitcoin UTXO associated with Sara

    – A 2 Bitcoin UTXO associated with Mario (the rest of the transaction)

So, once the transaction is recorded, Mario will have in his wallet a 5 Bitcoin UTXO and a 2 Bitcoin UTXO, for a total balance of 7 Bitcoins. Sara will have an 8 Bitcoin UTXO, for a total balance of 8 Bitcoins. The anatomy of a UTXO is very simple. (See Figure 3-13.)

There are two sorts of scripts: locking scripts and unlocking scripts. Given the definition of the term, and the fact that unlocking ownership is the first step in transferring UTXO, the input value contains the phrase *unlocking script*. The output value, on the other hand, will be *locking script* as a result of the locking procedure. The term "script" means "stack structure," however we'll focus on the method rather than the definition.

A transaction output UTXO has the following structure (see Figure 3-13).

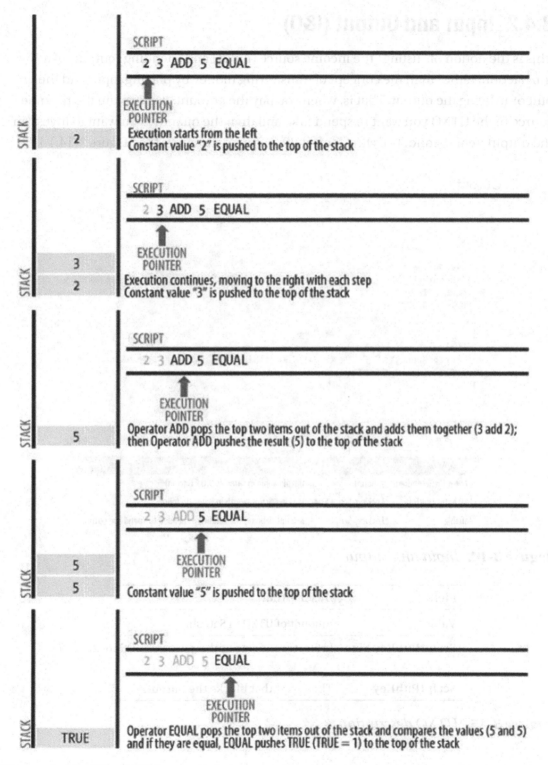

Figure 3-13. *The UTXO structure*

3.4.2 Input and Output (I&O)

This is the notion of "listing" the income source (input) and spending (output) of a transaction, rather than the concept of transferring money by placing input and the outcome being the output. That is, when you pay the amount, you explain the revenue source of the UTXO you want to spend first, and then the quantity you want to invest on the output item second. Let's first look at the output's structure. (See Figure 3-14.)

Output

```
"vout": [
  {
    "value": 0.01500000,
    "scriptPubKey": "OP_DUP OP_HASH160 ab68025513c3dbd2f7b92a94e0581f5d50f654e7
OP_EQUALVERIFY
    OP_CHECKSIG"
  },
  {
    "value": 0.08450000,
    "scriptPubKey": "OP_DUP OP_HASH160 7f9b1a7fb68d60c536c2fd8aeaa53a8f3cc025a8
OP_EQUALVERIFY OP_CHECKSIG",
  }
]
```

Size	Field	Description
8 bytes (little-endian)	Amount	Bitcoin value in satoshis (10^{-8} bitcoin)
1–9 bytes (VarInt)	Locking-Script Size	Locking-Script length in bytes, to follow
Variable	Locking-Script	A script defining the conditions needed to spend the output

Figure 3-14. *Input and output*

Field	Description
Value	Amount of UTXO in Satoshi.
ScriptPubKey Size	Indicates the size of the script UTXO block.
ScriptPubKey	The script that blocks the output.

Figure 3-15. *UTXO description*

When a transaction to transfer money is created, the transaction input must specify which UTXO will be issued. Simply put, the transaction's inputs are pointers to UTXO. They define a specific UTXO, which relates to the transaction's hash and the transaction output's index number. A transaction input additionally contains the unlock script that satisfies the output conditions given by UTXO in order to output UTXO (see Figures 3-15 and 3-16). The unlock script is usually a signature that verifies that the Bitcoin address identified in the block script belongs to the owner.

So, the structure of a UTXO input to a transaction is as shown in Figure 3-16.

Field	Description
Transaction ID	It is the unique identifier of the transaction that generated the UTXO. It is obtained through the SHA256 hashing of the transaction.
Index	UTXO index in the transaction output
ScriptSig Size	Indicates the size of the script unlocking the UTXO
ScriptSig	It is the UTXO unlock script
Sequence Number	deprecated function currently disabled. Set to 0xFFFFFFFF

Figure 3-16. UTXO description

This structure of transaction inputs and outputs leads to a transaction link design, as shown in Figure 3-17.

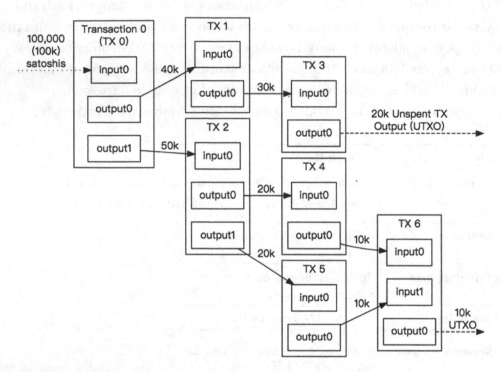

Figure 3-17. *Bitcoin transaction input and output*

3.4.3 Pay to Public Key Hash (P2PKH)

Given a high-level description of how a transaction takes place, this section covers the technical and structural details of it, to understand how it is implemented.

P2PKH (pay to a public key hash) is a script template for completing a Bitcoin transaction or sending money to someone. It is most commonly used script to lock an output on the key someone's public key. It ensures that only the UTXO beneficiary, or the person who owns the private key and therefore the public key relating the address Bitcoin beneficiary of UTXO, can spend it.

For greater understanding, let's analyze the output part of the Transaction process first, neglecting the details of the input. Then we will address the input aspect of the process, going into the process of check that it combines both parts.

3.4.4 Looking at the Output Side

Let's say Mario wants to send 20 Bitcoins to Sara. Sara, therefore, will have to generate a public key/private key pair associated with it. Then Sara will provide her Bitcoin address (see the "Bitcoin Address" section) to Mario.

The address could be transmitted in any way, including in a one-way manner that stops communication between the sender and receiver, and it can be further encoded in a different format, such as a QR code that includes a `Bitcoin:` URI.

Then, Mario, the spender of the transaction, will receive Sara's Bitcoin address and can specify it as the beneficiary/recipient of the transaction. This will be used to create the UTXO blocking script for the transaction, so that only Sara, or whoever can prove to have the associated private key to the public key relating to that Bitcoin address that Sara provided, can spend it.

Then Mario will transmit the transaction. Once the transaction is validated, added to the block, and reaches consensus, it will be part of the blockchain Bitcoin.

The network, therefore, classifies it as an Unspent Transaction Output (UTXO) and Sara's wallet software shows it as a spendable balance. In other words, Sara now has a 20 Bitcoin UTXO in her wallet received from Mario.

Therefore, in each UTXO there is the `PubKey` script, which blocks the use of the UTXO to the beneficiary, or to whoever owns the private key. It is then used in the transaction validation process. This is structured as shown in Figure 3-18.

Figure 3-18. *PubKey script structure*

The fields starting with OP denote an operation, while the others denote a value.

- `OP_DUP`: Performs a duplication operation; serves to copy the public key present in the `scriptSig` (which you will see later), which hash functions will be applied to compare the result obtained with the `pubKeyHash` of this `scriptPubKey`.

- `OP_HASH160`: First applies the SHA-256 hash function and then `RIPEMD160` to the public key of the duplicate `scriptSig`.

- PubKeyHash: The public Key hash; comes from decoding the Bitcoin address provided to the sender.

- OP_EQUALVERIFY: The operation that verifies that the two public key hashes (the one from the complete public key in scriptSig and the one in this PubKey script) are the same. Returns True if they are the same, False if they are different.

- OP_CHECKSIG: This operation is therefore carried out on the script. Mr. Check signature <sig> against public key <pub-Key>. If the signature joining the public key and has been generated using all the data required for the signature, OP_CHECKSIG returns True.

In order for this UTXO to be spent, there needs to be a resolved script. In order to solve this script and then use the UTXO to make a transaction, you must prove that you have the key private and the public key related to the Bitcoin address to which it was sent the UTXO.

3.4.5 Looking at the Input Side

Let's see how the process of creating a transaction works from the spender's perspective. Let's assume Sara wants to send 20 Bitcoins to Fabio. Sara, once Fabio has provided her with the Bitcoin address, will enter as a beneficiary of the transaction, together with the amount.

The Bitcoin address provided by Fabio will also be used for the PubKey script, which will therefore allow him to spend the output of the transaction exclusively to the owner of the relative private key.

Then Sara will fill in the transaction input, where for each UTXO, she must target and unlock the information shown in Figure 3-19.

Field	Description
«pubKey»	your complete public key
«sig»	your digital signature secp256k1

Figure 3-19. *The Script structure Sig*

3.4.6 Validation Process

The language used, Script, is stack-based and allows for limited operations to avoid loops in the code that would cause problems of execution. Because of their low complexity and predicted lead times, these languages are referred regarded as incomplete Turing languages. A stack is a data structure that resembles a stack of playing cards.

There are two procedures available: push and pop. Push puts a card to the top of the deck, whereas pop removes it. In this case, the cards are the data. Anyone who wants to send money to someone must prove they actually own that coin. The scriptSig of the input and the scriptPubKey of the referenced output are combined and evaluated.

Initially, the data entered in the Sig script is added to the stack of the transaction input (therefore, first sig and then pubKey).

The script extracts the public key from the stack, which coincides with the pubKey of the scriptSig, and applies it to it, hashed it first SHA-256 and then RIPEMD160. Then compare the result with the public key hash of the PubKey script. If it is successful, you proceed to verify the digital signature, otherwise the transaction is rejected.

So, if the signature common for the public key and has been generated using all the data required to be signed, then the transaction is valid.

You can see these operations, in more detail, through the diagrams in Figures 3-20 through 3-26.

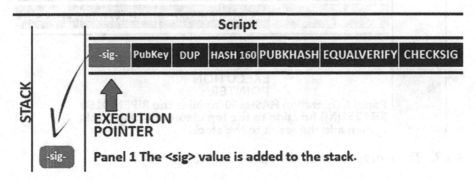

Figure 3-20. *Transaction validation process, Step 1*

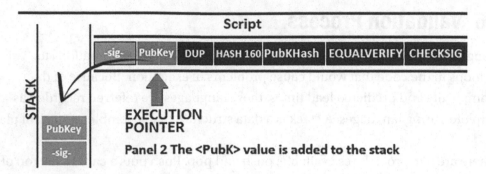

Figure 3-21. *Transaction validation process, Step 2*

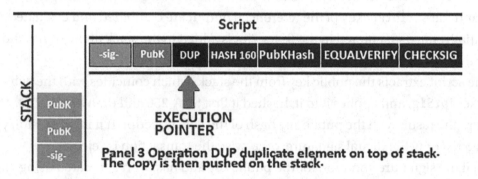

Figure 3-22. *Transaction validation process, Step 3*

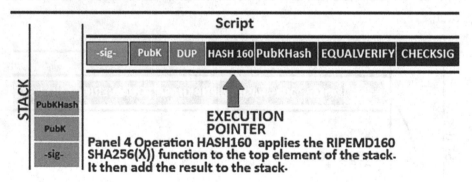

Figure 3-23. *Transaction validation process, Step 4*

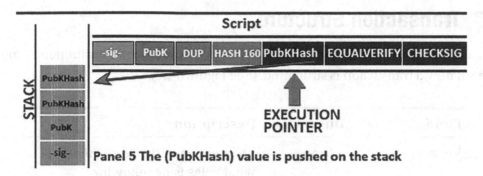

Figure 3-24. *Transaction validation process, Step 5*

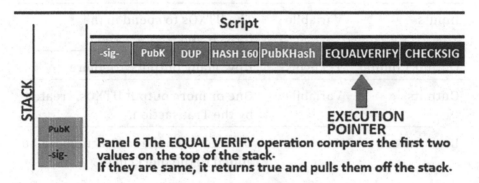

Figure 3-25. *Transaction validation process, Step 6*

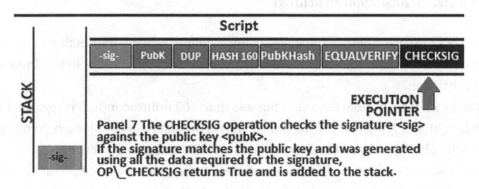

Figure 3-26. *Transaction validation process, Step 7*

So if False is not at the top of the stack after scriptsig and scriptPubKey were evaluated, then the transaction is valid.

In fact, the complete validation process of a transaction, in addition to being independent for each node that receives it, also includes other steps and checks that you will see later.

3.4.7 Transaction Structure

After learning about the operation and analyzing the fundamental components, you'll now learn how a transaction is structured. (See Figure 3-27).

Field	Dimension	Description
Version	4 bytes	The version of the Settlement. So what rules is he following.
Input Counter	1-9 bytes	How many inputs are included
Inputs	Variabile	The UTXOs to spend in the transaction.
Output Counter	1-9 bytes	How many outputs are there
Outputs	Variabile	One or more output UTXOs, created by the Transaction.
Locktime	4 bytes	Defines when the transaction can be added to the blockchain.

Figure 3-27. *Transaction structured*

The Locktime variable is a fascinating one. It defines when a transaction can be added to the blockchain for the first time. In most transactions, it is set to 0 to indicate instant execution.

If the block time is more than zero but less than 400 milliseconds, it is regarded as a block height, implying that the transaction is not included on the blockchain until the block height is reached. It is interpreted as a *UNIX timestamp* if it exceeds 400 milliseconds, and the transaction is not included in the blockchain before the required time. Locktime is the same as postdating a paper check.

3.4.8 Transaction Fee

By charging a modest fee for each transaction, transaction fees serve as an incentive to include a transaction in the next block, as well as a deterrent against "spam" transactions or other forms of system abuse.

The miner who mines the block and stores the transaction in the blockchain collects transaction fees. And, unlike the amount of a Bitcoin transaction, transaction fees are calculated depending on the size of the transaction in bytes.

- Note that Bitcoin blocks are limited to 1MB (1,000,000 bytes) of dimensions.

- Transaction data takes up space in a block.

So when a miner fills a block of transactions, they will want to maximize the amount of money they can raise in taxes. They do it selecting the transactions that give them the most money in commissions for the space they occupy in the block. Therefore, when processing the value of the transaction fee, the important metric is the commission per byte. The miners prioritize transactions based on a variety of factors, and in some cases, they may even process transactions for free.

Because transaction fees influence processing priority, a transaction with commissions is more likely to be included in the next block extracted, but a transaction with inadequate or no commissions may be postponed.

Transaction costs are not required in most cases, and transactions without them may be completed later; however, the inclusion of transaction fees encourages priority processing. A charge field is also missing from the transaction data structure.

Fees are implied instead as the difference between the sum of inputs and outputs.

There is no risk of losing Bitcoins because most wallets compute and account for transaction fees automatically. If the transactions are created programmatically or via the command line, however, the fees must be manually entered and accounted for.

Any excess amount left over after all expenses are subtracted from all inputs is the commission charged by the miners.

Therefore, if you do not want to lose Bitcoin, it is important to also specify the change in UTXOs of a transaction for your wallet.

3.5 Transaction Flow

Once a new transaction is made, it is forwarded to the Bitcoin network's nearby nodes to be spread throughout the network.

Each Bitcoin node that receives a transaction, however, verifies it first before sending it to its neighbors. Only legitimate transactions are sent over the network, and invalid transactions are discarded by the first node that encounters them.

If the transmitted transaction is genuine, that node forwards it to the other nodes with whom it is connected, and a success message is sent back to the sender synchronously. If the transaction is invalid, the node rejects it and sends the sender a synchronous rejection message.

Therefore, invalid transactions will be rejected, while valid ones are disseminated through the network and will form the *transaction pool*. The transaction pool is the set of validated transactions that await be confirmed and added to a new block.

As a result, it serves as a holding area for fresh transactions.

To produce a new block, miners choose transactions from the transaction pool. This new block is called the *candidate block*. Each miner then attempts to add their candidate block to the blockchain through the mining process.

Let's say a transaction A is the child of a transaction B when a UTXO spent. Transaction A is dependent on the output UTXO of the parent transaction (B). Transactions do not always arrive in the same order when broadcast over the network.

It is possible that the child will come before the parents. In this situation, nodes that view the child for the first time may notice that it belongs to an unknown parent. Rather than rejecting it, it places the child in a temporary pool until the parents arrive, after which the child is passed on to all the other nodes.

The orphan transaction pool, also known as the orphaned transaction pool, is a parentless transaction pool. All orphans referring to the parent's UTXO are freed from the pool and recursively revalidated once their parents arrive, allowing the complete transaction chain to be contained in the transaction pool, ready to be pulled into a block.

The orphan pool's detention mechanism ensures that otherwise acceptable transactions are rejected solely because their parent is late, and that the chain of belonging is finally rebuilt in the right order, independent of the order of arrival. The transaction chains can be as long as you want them to be. Each node checks each transaction it receives against a long list of criteria. Here is the fundamental verification criteria:

- The transaction's syntax and data format must be accurate.

- None of the input or output lists can be empty.

- `MAX BLOCK SIZE` is less than the transaction size in bytes.

- For each input, the referenced output must exist and cannot be spent (to prevent double spending).

- If the referenced output in any other transaction in the pool exists for any input, the transaction must be cancelled (to prevent double spending).

- To discover the referred output transaction for each input, scan the main branch and the transaction pool. Note that if the output transaction is absent for any input, the transaction will be orphaned. If a transaction match isn't already in the pool, add it to the orphaned transaction pool.

Each input's unlock scripts must be compared to the equivalent output blocking scripts. These are the most important verification rules, carried out by each node that receives the transaction. The list may vary based on an updated protocol. (See Figure 3-28.)

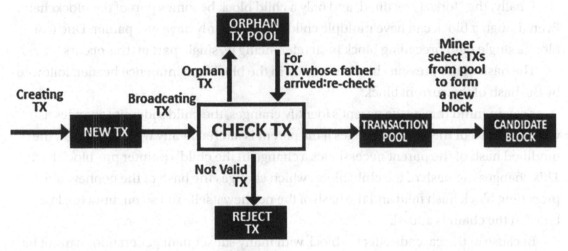

Figure 3-28. *Lifecycle of a transaction*

3.6 The Block

The blockchain's data structure is an ordered list with transaction block backlinks. The blockchain can be saved as a simple database or as a flat file. The blockchain metadata is stored in Google's LevelDB database by the Bitcoin Core client.[4]

The blocks are connected "backward," with each one referencing the block before it in the chain.

---

[4] `https://howieliux.github.io/assets/others/Mastering_bitcoin/Mastering_Bitcoin.html`

Every block in the blockchain is identified by a hash created by the SHA-256 cryptographic hash technique in the block's header. Additionally, each block uses the prior block's hash field in the block's header to refer to the parent block, which is the previous block.

To put it another way, each block's header contains the hash of its parent. The hash sequence that connects each block to its parent, known as the *genesis block,* generates a chain that extends back to the first block ever created.

A block has only one parent, although it can have multiple children at any time. Every child refers to the same block as its parent, and the "hash" field of the previous block includes the same hash (parent). During a blockchain fork, which is a transitory condition in which numerous blocks are mined almost simultaneously by several miners, more child blocks appear.

Finally, the "fork" is rectified, and only a child block becomes part of the blockchain. Even though a block can have multiple children, it can only have one parent. Due to a block's single field preceding block hash referencing its single parent, this occurs.

The hash of the previous block is located in the block and influence header, followed by the hash of the current block.

Keep in mind that as the parent's identify changes, the child's identity changes as well. The hash of the parent changes if the parent is altered in any way. As a result, the modified hash of the parent necessitates a change in the child's pointer pre-block hash. This changes the hash of the child block, which changes the hash of the nephew block's preceding block hash field and the hash of the nephew itself, and so on, until the last block in the chain is added.

Because of the cascade effect, a block with many subsequent generations cannot be altered without causing all subsequent blocks to be recalculated.

Due to the massive computer power required for such a recalculation, the existence of a long chain of blocks results in the blockchain's deep history, which is a major security element of Bitcoin. The first six blocks are taken as confirmation of the seventh block.

As you learn more about blockchain technology, you'll see that the blocks are becoming less and less likely to change. Finally, a block is a data structure that holds a collection of transactions uploaded to the blockchain.

3.6.1 The Structure of a Block

The block is made up of a header with metadata or a model, followed by a series of transactions that take up the majority of its space. A block's average size is set to 1MB. The block header is 80 bytes long, but the average transaction is at least 250 bytes long. (See Figure 3-29.)

Field	Dimension	Description
Block Size	4 bytes	Block size, expressed in bytes.
Block Header	80 bytes	Block header, consisting of several fields
Transaction Counter	1-9 bytes	Numbers of Transactions present in the block
Transactions	Variabile	Transactions stored in the block

Figure 3-29. *Structure of block*

3.6.2 The Block Header

There are three sets of block metadata in the block header:

- A reference to a previous block hash that connects this block to the blockchain's preceding block.

- The terms "target," "once," and "timestamp" all refer to Bitcoin mining.

- The market root is the root of the Merkle tree, which is used to effectively and securely summarize block transactions.

Merkle trees are a type of tree that grows in the Merkle. With Merkle trees, a node can only download a few block headers (80 bytes per block) and still detect the inclusion of a transaction in a block. It does this by recovering a small Merkle path from a full node without having to store or expand the vast majority of blockchains, which can be several gigabytes in size.

SPV nodes (simplified payment verification) are nodes that do not retain a full blockchain and use Merkle pathways to verify transactions without downloading full blocks. SPV nodes frequently employ Merkle trees. Only block headers are downloaded by SPV nodes, which do not hold full transactions or download all blocks.

They employ an authentication or Merkle path to check if a transaction is contained in a block without downloading all of the block's transactions. The block header's detailed structure is shown in the table in Figure 3-30.

Field	Dimesion	Description
Version	4 bytes	Version Number. Used in so that the nodes can read correctly the content of each block
Previous Block Hash	32 bytes	A reference to the hash of the block previous in the chain.
Merkle Root	32 bytes	Value of the root of transactions
Timestamp	4 byte	Expressed in Unix Epoch. It is the time block creation.
Difficulty Target	4 bytes	The difficulty of the PoW algorithm for this block.
Nonce	4 bytes	The counter used for the Proof of Work.

Figure 3-30. *Block header's details*

Figure 3-31 shows a graphic example of the structure of the blocks of the Bitcoin blockchain.

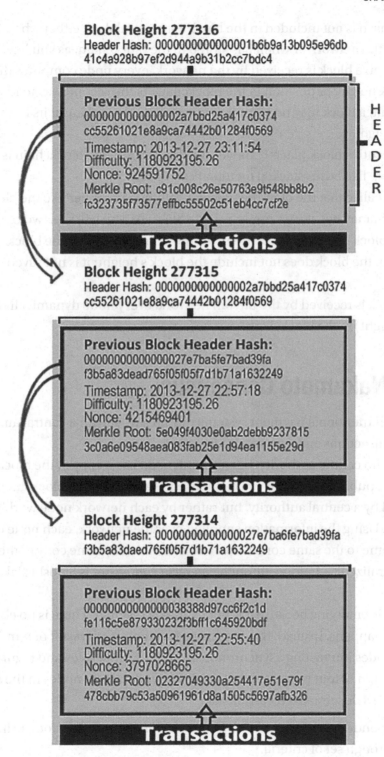

Block Height 277316
Header Hash: 0000000000000001b6b9a13b095e96db
41c4a928b97ef2d944a9b31b2cc7bdc4

Previous Block Header Hash:
0000000000000002a7bbd25a417c0374
cc55261021e8a9ca74442b01284f0569

Timestamp: 2013-12-27 23:11:54
Difficulty: 1180923195.26
Nonce: 924591752
Merkle Root: c91c008c26e50763e9t548bb8b2
fc323735f73577effbc55502c51eb4cc7cf2e

H
E
A
D
E
R

Transactions

Block Height 277315
Header Hash: 0000000000000002a7bbd25a417c0374
cc55261021e8a9ca74442b01284f0569

Previous Block Header Hash:
00000000000000027e7ba5fe7bad39fa
f3b5a83dead765f05f05f7d1b71a1632249

Timestamp: 2013-12-27 22:57:18
Difficulty: 1180923195.26
Nonce: 4215469401
Merkle Root: 5e049f4030e0ab2debb9237815
3c0a6e09548aea083fab25e1d94ea1155e29d

Transactions

Block Height 277314
Header Hash: 00000000000000027e7ba6fe7bad39fa
f3b5a83daed765f05f7d1b71a1632249

Previous Block Header Hash:
0000000000000003838d97cc6f2c1d
fe116c5e879330232f3bff1c645920bdf

Timestamp: 2013-12-27 22:55:40
Difficulty: 1180923195.26
Nonce: 3797028665
Merkle Root: 02327049330a254417e51e79f
478cbb79c53a50961961d8a1505c5697afb326

Transactions

Figure 3-31. *Bitcoin blockchain structure*

45

The block hash is not included in the block's structural data, either when it is broadcast over the network or when it is stored in the blockchain, as you have seen.

Instead, when a block is received by the network, every node computes the block hash. The block height, or position in the blockchain, is the second way to identify a block. As a result, a block may be identified in two ways: by looking at its hash or by looking at its height.

Each consecutive block placed "above" the first block in the blockchain is one position "higher," like boxes stacked on top of each other.

It's vital to realize that the block height isn't a unique identifier like the block hash. The block height may not always imply a single block. As you will see, two or more blocks with the same block height might contend for the same position in the blockchain. The data structure of the block does not include the block's height; it is not saved in the block.

When a block is received by the Bitcoin network, every node dynamically determines its position (height) in the blockchain.

3.7 The Nakamoto Consensus

Furthermore, all traditional payment systems rely on a trust with a central authority that administers transactions and, as a result, the ledger.

Bitcoin has no central authority, but each full node has a copy of the blockchain, complete with a public ledger that you can rely on as a record. The blockchain is not established by a central authority, but rather by each network node working independently. Using the information supplied over the network, each node of the network can come to the same conclusion and assemble the same copy of the ledger.

The decentralized technique, through *emergent consensus,* is Satoshi Nakamoto's key invention.

Consensus is emerging because it is not expressly reached. There is no election in which consent happens. Instead, the consensus is an emergent result of hundreds of independent nodes interacting asynchronously under simple rules and regulations.

The interaction of four processes that run independently on nodes in the network results in Bitcoin's decentralized consensus:

- Independent verification of each transaction for each full node using a thorough set of criteria.

- Autonomous grouping of these transactions into new blocks by mining nodes, as well as proved computations through a proof-of-work algorithm.

- Each node independently verifies new blocks before adding them to the blockchain.

- Independent selection of the longer proof-of-work chain for each node (i.e., proven to have higher computational power than the shorter one).

3.7.1 Miner

Some nodes are particular nodes, called mining nodes or *miner nodes*. They are responsible for creating and registering new blocks to the ledger. These nodes compete with each other to add a new block to the blockchain.

They are in contention with each other because who manages to win the block and add it to the chain receives a Bitcoin reward such as an incentive for contributing to the consensus of the Bitcoin network.

To form a new block, miners select transactions from the transaction pool, thus obtaining a candidate block to be registered to the ledger. To select transactions, miners apply a property metric transactions, giving higher priority to transactions with UTXO in older inputs and of a higher amount than the most recent ones and of smaller amount. In other words, given a transaction Tx. Let N be its UTXO number in input and for each UTXO i in input. We define the priority of TX as follows:

$$\text{PrioritàTx} = \frac{\sum_{i=1}^{N} \text{importo}_i * \text{età}_i}{\text{DimTx}} \tag{3.1}$$

At the same time, they will assign more weight to those with costs of commission per kilobyte higher than those that have commissions for lower kilobytes.

The average size of a Bitcoin block is set at 1MB. Hence, a miner will try to select the sequence of transactions which, respecting the priorities (of seniority and value) and the maximum block size, will allow you to have a greater income.

As a result, transaction commissions are usually valued based on the magnitude of the transaction.

3.7.2 Coinbase Transaction

The first transaction added to the block is a one-of-a-kind transaction that differs from regular transactions. Coinbase Transaction is the name given to it.

It is the transaction that allows the miner who extracts the block to receive:

- The incentive for having participated and contributed to the consent process adding a new block.

- The sum of all the commissions of all the transactions it has added to the block.

Obviously, the beneficiary Bitcoin address of this transaction is that of the miner who extracts the block. The difference between the total value of input and the total value of output for each transaction is used to compute the total commissions. That is to say:

- Take N as the total number of inputs, I as the index for each input, and Vi as the amount of input i.

- Let M be the total number of outputs, or the index for each output, and V be the amount of the output. Then:

$$\text{Commission} i \, \text{Total} i = \sum_{i=1}^{N} V_i - \sum_{0=1}^{M} V_0 \tag{3.2}$$

Instead, the miner reward is calculated from 50 bitcoin and by dividing this value by 2, every 210,000 blocks. That means Bitcoins are "minted" at a set and declining rate throughout the construction of each block. Each block, which is formed every ten minutes, comprises a new Bitcoin created from scratch. The currency issuance rate is reduced by 50% every 210,000 blocks, or about every four years. Each block included 50 new Bitcoins throughout the first four years of the network's functioning.[5]

The reward is based on the block height, with a beginning value of 50 Bitcoins per block and halving every 210,000 blocks. The proper reward is 25 Bitcoins because this block has a height of 277,316.

The computation may be observed in the Bitcoin Core client's `GetBlockValue` function, as demonstrated in Listing 3-1.

---

[5] `https://www.oreilly.com/library/view/mastering-bitcoin`

Listing 3-1. The GetBlockValue Function

```
int64_t GetBlockValue(int nHeight, int64_t nFees)
{
    int64_t nSubsidy = 50 * COIN;
    int halvings = nHeight / Params().SubsidyHalvingInterval();

        if (halvings >= 64)
        return nFees;

    // Every 210,000 blocks, or about every 4 years, the subsidy is
        decreased in half..
    nSubsidy >>= halvings;

    return nSubsidy + nFees;
}
```

3.7.3 Developing the Block Header

After calculating the transactions from the Transaction Pool and the Coinbase Transaction, the miner continues on to construct the block header in order to generate the Candidate Block. The following steps will then be taken:

1. Indicates the block's version number, which explains the block's architecture.

2. Adds the hash of the previous block that it accepted as a block parent.

3. Add the Merkle tree root value to the equation. So, after calculating the SHA-256 hash for each transaction, these are merged in pairs to form each level of the tree, until all transactions are summarized in a node at the "root" of the tree. As a result, the Merkle tree's root stores all transactions in a single 32-byte value.

4. Adds the timestamp in Unix Epoch format that it refers to now of block creation.

5. Defines the test difficulty of work required to make it a legitimate block by filling in the difficulty target.

6. The final field is the nonce, initialized to 0.

The block header is now complete, with all other fields filled in, and the mining operation may commence. The goal now is to discover a value for the nonce that transforms the difficulty target into a hash of the lower block header.

3.7.4 Difficulty Target

The target is used in mining. It is the number (expressed in hexadecimal) to which the hash value of a block must be reduced in order for it to be added to the ledger.

The target is adjusted every 2016 blocks (about two weeks) to ensure that blocks are extracted on average every ten minutes.

The complexity of the Proof of Work is determined by a moving average that aims an average number of blocks per hour to adjust for increasing hardware speed and variable interest in node execution over time. The difficulty increases if they are generated too quickly.

The target is calculated by each node of the network independently, but following the Bitcoin protocol rules.

The rule stipulates that every 2,016 blocks, all nodes automatically retarget the Proof of Work difficulty. The retargeting difficulty calculation compares the time it takes to find the remaining 2,016 blocks to the expected time of 20,160 minutes (which equals two weeks, based on a time of desired block of ten minutes).

The desired ratio between the actual period and the time period is then computed, and an adjustment based on the difficulty is made. The difficulty rises if the network finds blocks faster than every ten minutes. The difficulty decreases if block finding is slower than planned.

Let `RecentBlockTime` be the variable that indicates the time taken to find the latest 2016 blocks. The equation for calculating the *Difficulty Target* is:

$$\text{NewDifficultyTarget} = \text{OldTarget} * \left(\frac{\text{RecentBlockTime}}{20160} \right) \qquad (3.3)$$

The adjustment per cycle must be less than a factor of 4 to avoid significant volatility in the difficulty objective.

If the required difficulty adjustment exceeds a factor of 4, it is limited to the maximum allowed.

All remaining modifications will be performed in the next period. Because each node adheres to the same consensus rules and all blocks are identical, they will all arrive at the same difficulty value.

If a node miscalculates the goal (or lies about it) and then produces a block based on that value, the rest of the network will reject it since it does not match the target's requirements, and all of the work invested in mining that block will be lost.

3.7.5 Proof of Work

Once a miner node has created a candidate block, the block must be extracted by the node's hardware platform. It must solve the proof-of-work algorithm in order for the block to be valid. The SHA-256 hash function is utilized in the Bitcoin mining process.

Simply said, *mining* is the process of hashing the block header by modifying the "nonce parameter repeatedly until the resulting hash does not match a specific target.". "The hash function's result cannot be predicted in advance, nor can a pattern that generates a certain hash value be generated." Hash functions have this property, which means that the only method to achieve a hash result that matches a specific target is to repeat the input until the desired hash result arises randomly.[6]

As a result, we must understand that the miner computes the hash of this block's header to determine whether it is smaller than the current target. If the hash isn't smaller than the target, the minor increases the nonce (typically by one) and tries again. "Miners must try several million times to discover a nonce that results in a low enough hash of the block header at the present difficulty level of the Bitcoin network."

Furthermore, while it was possible to mine the blocks using a simple home computer in the early years, today you must utilize specialized and expensive hardware and share your processing power with other users by joining mining pools. When a mining node solves the problem, it sends the block to all of its neighbors so that it can propagate around the network, be validated, and ultimately be added to the ledger.

3.7.6 Validating a New Block

The third step in reaching consensus on the blockchain is independent validation, which is carried out by each node that receives a new block.

As the newly solved block propagates over the network, each node runs a series of tests to ensure that it is valid before forwarding it to its peers. Only legitimate blocks are propagated over the network as a result of this. Independent validation also ensures that honest miners are putting their blocks on the blockchain and profiting.

---

[6]https://howieliux.github.io/assets/others/Mastering_bitcoin/Mastering_Bitcoin.html

Those that act dishonestly have their blocks rejected, losing not only the reward, but also the effort of finding a proof-of-work solution, and therefore bearing the expense of electricity without reimbursement.

When a node receives a new block, it verifies it by comparing it to a large set of requirements that must all be met; otherwise, the block is eliminated.

These is a list of the most significant characteristics that can be summarized:

- The block's structure and syntax are correct.

- The target value is accurate.

- It's important to realize that the block header hash is easier than the target difficulty (proof of work check).

- The block timestamp is less than two hours in the future (holding timing faults).

- The block size follows the protocol's criteria.

- The initial transaction is made with coinbase.

- The transactions contained therein are valid (recheck transactions using the verification criteria outlined in the transaction flow).

As a result, independent validation ensures that miners cannot cheat. Miners must construct a complete block based on a shared protocol or set of rules observed by all nodes and extract it using a proper proof of work solution. They use a lot of electricity to do this, and if they cheat, all of the electricity and effort is squandered. Therefore, the validation not depended on is a key part of the decentralized consensus.

3.7.7 The Blockchain Forks

Different copies of the blockchain are not always constant because it is a decentralized data architecture. Blocks could arrive at different times on different nodes, giving nodes different perspectives on the blockchain. To tackle this problem, each node picks the most effective proof of work blockchain, also known as the highest chain or chain with the greatest cumulative difficulty, and tries to extend it as much as possible.

A node can calculate the total amount of proof of work used to form a chain by summing the difficulty recorded in each block.

The global Bitcoin network eventually converges to a coherent state by the time all nodes select the longest cumulative chain of difficulty.

The nodes manage three groups of blocks:

- The first is the one that is linked to the main blockchain.

- The blocks that do not have a known parent in known chains.

- The blocks that constitute the branches of the main blockchain (secondary chains) (orphans).

When any of the criterion validations fail, the invalid blocks are removed or rejected, and they are not included in the chain. You must realize that the main chain is the blockchain with the greatest or highest cumulative difficulty at any given time.

Unless there are two chains of equal length, one of which has a larger number of functioning proofs, this is usually the chain with the most blocks. When a new block is discovered, a node tries to incorporate it into the current blockchain.

The node examines the previous block's hash field, which contains the address of the new block's parent. The node will then search the current blockchain for that parent. The parent block is the "top" of the main chain in the most recent examples, implying that this new block extends the main chain.

Additionally, the new block may occasionally extend a chain that isn't the main chain. In this situation, the node connects the new block to the secondary chain, allowing it to compare the secondary chain's difficulty to that of the main chain.

If the secondary chain has a higher cumulative difficulty than the main chain, the node will fall back to it, making the secondary chain the new parent chain and the former main chain a secondary chain.

If a good lock is received but no parent is discovered in the current chains, the block is referred to as an *orphan*. The orphaned blocks are placed in the orphaned blocks pool and will remain there until their parent arrives.

The orphaned block can be retrieved from the orphan pool and attached to the parent once the parent has arrived or been received and joined to the existing chains. Keep in mind that orphaned blocks typically occur when two blocks mined within a short period of time are received in reverse order. By selecting the chain with the highest difficulty, all nodes reach network-level consensus in the end.

Temporary chain modifications are finally resolved by extending one of the existing chains with new proofs of work. Mining nodes use their mining power to "vote" for the next block to be extracted. The new block will represent their vote when they extract a new block to expand the chain.

3.8 Summary

When you think about the term "blockchain," the main concept that should come to mind is Bitcoin, which you learned about in this chapter. I explained the technical aspects of Bitcoin, the block structure of the Bitcoin blockchain, and the flow of transactions in the blockchain, with examples. To develop a blockchain application, you must understand these fundamental concepts.

The next chapter focuses on Ethereum, a blockchain-based software platform that is primarily used to support the world's second-largest cryptocurrency by market capitalization after Bitcoin.

CHAPTER 4

Ethereum

The Bitcoin blockchain model has proved to be a paradigm valid for cryptocurrencies, which has led to increased interest and study about blockchain in various fields of application.

Vitalik Buterin realized the potential of the blockchain model early on. He saw it as much more than a platform for cryptocurrencies.

A passion for Bitcoin led him to found, at the age of 17, together with Mihai Alisie, *Bitcoin Magazine*, a site and print magazine covering topics related to Bitcoin. Vitalik quickly realized that blockchain technology could do much more.

In 2013, he declared that Bitcoin needed a language of scripting for the development and creation of *decentralized applications*.

Failing to convince the community, he began developing a new distributed information platform, based on technology blockchain. Thus, Ethereum was born on July 30, 2015, and it introduced a new feature called *smart contracts*.

A new generation of blockchain was inaugurated, and to date it's still the most prominent—Blockchain 2.0.

Consider the image shown in Figure 4-1, in which Bitcoin and Ethereum are compared. On the left is Bitcoin, to which top of the stack is the Wallet application through which money transfer operations are made. To the right is Ethereum, which changed the blockchain into a computational system framework or architecture and opened a full world of opportunities in the decentralized realm. Note that Ethereum supports smart contracts and the machine virtual EVM on which these run. Smart contracts, in turn, enable decentralized applications that accomplish more of a transfer of value. In this way, a level of logic and calculation is added to the blockchain.

© Joseph Thachil George 2022
J. T. George, *Introducing Blockchain Applications*, https://doi.org/10.1007/978-1-4842-7480-4_4

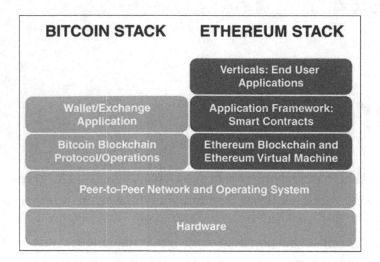

Figure 4-1. *Bitcoin vs. Ethereum stacks*

Ethereum users can not only transfer digital money through transactions, but they can develop smart contracts that allow them to perform transactions under certain conditions. For all intents and purposes, they can set conditions on the ways in which the value is transferred. Understandably, the idea of "programmable money" has attracted users, developers, and companies all over the world.

In addition, developers can implement and create applications that operate in the distributed network of the Ethereum blockchain, the DAPPs (decentralized applications).

With Ethereum, the blockchain becomes a decentralized IT platform where, in addition to transferring digital money, it is possible to distribute new applications and interact with other users of the network.

Anyone can write a new application to run on the network blockchain, instead of on a centralized server. This does not only require overcoming any kind of censorship by a central authority, but is also immune to changes and allows all users to check the code before interacting with it.

With Ethereum, blockchains are certainly not limited to the financial sector; they can also include electoral systems, registration of domain names, crowdfunding platforms, and intellectual properties, to name just a few examples.

In short, Ethereum is a revolutionary and far-sighted project, which in addition to being recognized as one of the best online investments, brought world fame to the young founder of the Ethereum network. This invention was awarded the prestigious World Technology Award in 2014.

This chapter goes into detail about the components and techniques that define the Ethereum blockchain.

4.1 Blockchain as a State Transition System

The *Ethereum blockchain* is an open-source public blockchain. The model implemented by Ethereum can be summarized by three definitions:

- **Cryptographically secure:** The information security present in the ledger is guaranteed by complex mathematical algorithms and difficult to break cryptography. In other terms, it is almost impossible to cheat the system.

- **Transactional singleton machine:** There is, by construction paradigm, a single canonical instance of the machine responsible for all transactions that are generated in the system. There is one global truth that everyone believes in.

- **With shared-state:** The state stored in this machine is shared and accessible by all.

Hence, the Ethereum blockchain paradigm is that of a cryptographically secure, shared-state transactional singleton machine. The Ethereum blockchain is essentially a state machine based on transactions.

A state machine is a graph of states and transitions.

- A state describes a period of time in the life of an object and is represented by vertices or *nodes*.

- A transition connects two states together and is represented with a oriented arc.

The exit from a state defines the response of the object to the occurrence of an event. An event is the recurrence of a phenomenon placed in time and in space.

Thus, a state machine is an automaton which, based on a series of input data, changes its internal state. (See Figure 4-2.)

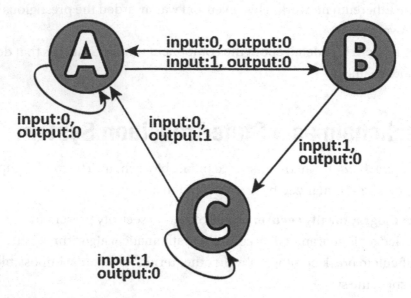

Figure 4-2.   *Example of a finite state machine*

From this, you can deduce:

- The status of the blockchain as the set of transactions present in the ledger.

- An event in the blockchain such as the creation of a transaction.

- A transaction function in the blockchain that takes on a state and new transaction and generates a new state.

So, let S be a state, TX a transaction, and APPLY the function of state transition. It can be formally defined:

$$APPLY\ (S;\ TX) \rightarrow S0\ or\ ERROR$$

Note that the Ethereum's state machine begins with a state of genesis, analogous to an empty list before transactions have been made on the network.

To cause a transition from one state to another, a transaction must be valid. When the various transactions are performed, this state of genesis passes from time to time to a subsequent state. (See Figure 4-3.)

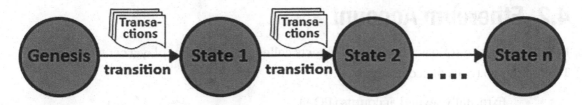

Figure 4-3. *Transitions of states based on transactions*

At any point in the junction, the final state represents the overall state of Ethereum.

The overall status of Ethereum contains transactions. Such transactions are grouped into blocks. Each block contains a number of transactions and is chained to the previous block. See Figure 4-4.

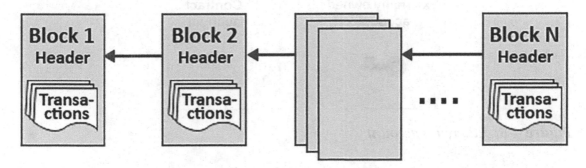

Figure 4-4. *Transaction flow*

From a technical point of view, the general ledger can be viewed as a state transition system in which there is a state that contains all of the general ledger transactions, as well as a transition function that takes a state and a transaction and returns a new state.

In a conventional banking system, for example, state is a balance sheet, a transaction is a request to shift X from account A to account B, and the state transition function decreases the value of X in account A and increases the value of X in account B.

The state transition function then gives an error if A's account has less than X at the start. Let TX = Send 70 from Luca to Sara.

APPLY ((Luca: e50; Sara: e50); TX) = ERROR

Or, *let TX = Send e20 from Luca to Sara*

APPLY ((Luke: e50; Sara: e50); TX) = Luke: e30; Sara: e70

4.2 Ethereum Account

In Ethereum, the state is a buildup of objects called *accounts* that play a central role. There are two types of accounts:

- Externally owned accounts (EOA)

- Contract accounts

In general, the EOAs are user accounts and are controlled by private keys and have no code associated with them. But contract accounts are controlled by their contract code and have an associated code. (See Figure 4-5.)

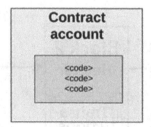

Figure 4-5. *Ethereum account*

4.2.1 The Account State

This account status is made up of four elements that are present regardless of the account type: (See Figure 4-6.)

- **Nonce (number only used once):** If the account is owned by a third party, this number indicates how many transactions have been sent from the account address. The nonce is then the number of contracts created by the account if it is a contract account.

- **Balance:** This is the Wei number that this address owns. One ether is equal to 10^18.

- **MemoryRoot:** A 256-bit hash of the root node of a Merkle tree Patricia (refer to Chapter 2). This tree encodes the hash of the storage account of this account and is empty by default. For contract accounts, this is smart contract storage.

- **CodeHash:** This is the hash code of an EVM (Ethereum Virtual Machine) account. For the contract account, this is the code that is hashed and stored as a `codeHash`. For external owned accounts, the `codeHash` is the hash of the empty string.

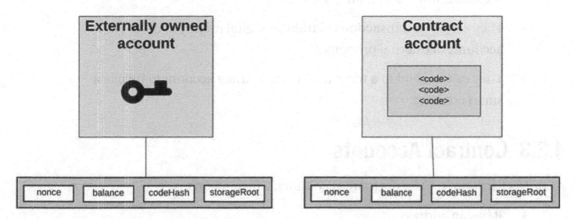

Figure 4-6. *Account status in Ethereum*

4.2.2 Externally Owned Accounts (EOAs)

Externally owned accounts:

- Have an Ether balance.

- Can send to the transactions (they either transfer or activate the code of a contract).

- Are controlled by the private key.

- Do not have an associated code.

Note that every account is defined by a key pair—a private key and a public key. Like Bitcoin, Ethereum also uses ECDSA (Elliptic Curve Digital Signature Algorithm). Ethereum also uses the curve dictated by standard `secp256k1`.

You should already know how private keys and respective public keys work. However, Ethereum differs from Bitcoin by the generation of an *Ethereum address*.

These, like Bitcoin, are derived from the public key. However, to this the hash function Keccak 256 is applied. From the result of this function, you have the *public key hash*. From this you take the 20 bytes farther to the right and you will get the Ethereum address. All Ethereum addresses start with the `0x` prefix.

- Accounts are indexed based on their address.

- Creating an external ownership account has no cost.

- An EOA uses transactions (or messages, as you'll see) to interact with the Ethereum blockchain network.

- They can send transactions to transfer digital money to other accounts of external property.

- They can be send to a transaction to a contract account to invoke a smart contract.

4.2.3 Contract Accounts

A contract account represents a smart contract, which means:

- It has an address.

- It has an Ether balance.

- It has an associated code.

- It is controlled by the associated code.

- The execution of the code is triggered/invoked by transactions or messages (calls) received from other accounts (EOAs or contract accounts).

- Once executed, it performs operations of arbitrary complexity (Turing complete) and manipulates its own persistent archive; it can have its own permanent state it can call other contracts.

The contract address is generated by hashing the SHA-3, also called Keccak-256, the address of the sender's account and their nonce, and taking the rightmost 20 bytes of this result. Contract accounts have a cost both in creation and in use (execution), because they use computational resource and network storage.

4.2.4 Differences Between Externally Owned and Contract Accounts

First of all, it is good to clarify that to participate in the Ethereum network, an external ownership account is required. Furthermore, any type of message sent through the Ethereum network has a cost because it uses computational and archiving resources.

That means an external owned account can send or deliver the messages to other account owned externally or to other contract creating accounts. (See Figure 4-7.)

Figure 4-7. *Transaction from EOA*

That means a message between two external owned accounts is simply a transfer of value.

However, a message from an owned account external to a contract account activates the contract account code, allowing it to perform various actions (examples include transfer tokens, write to internal memory, mint new tokens, run some calculations, create a brand-new contracts, etc.).

In other words, through a message from an ownership account external to a contract account invokes a smart contract. (See Figure 4-8.)

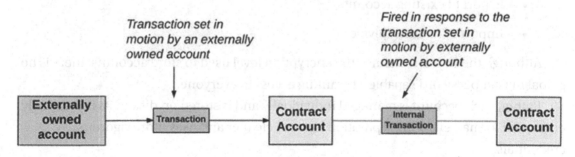

Figure 4-8. *Transaction example of account contracts*

Unlike externally owned accounts, the contract accounts won't be able to start new transactions. On the contrary, the accounts of the contracts can generate transactions only in response to different transactions received (from an external ownership account or another contract account). You will find out more about contract calls in the section entitled "Transaction and Message."

Hence, any action that occurs on the Ethereum blockchain is always activated by transactions activated by externally regulated accounts.

4.2.5 Storing Key: Encrypted Keystore

Every private key/address pair is encoded in a keyfile and the keyfiles are JSON text files. Additionally, the critical component of the keyfile, the private key of the account, is always encrypted with the password entered during the account creation.

The keyfile is located in the keystore subdirectory of the data directory Ethereum node that created the account or imported it.

The keystore uses the elliptic curve `secp256k1` as defined in the standards for efficient Encryption, implemented by the `libsecp256k` library and found at `github.com/ethereum/go-ethereum/accounts`. Accounts are stored on disk in the Web3 secret storage format.

After creating an encrypted keystore for Ethereum accounts, you can use this account manager for all cycle requirements account life. This includes the basic features:

- Creation of new accounts

- Elimination of existing ones

- Updating of access credentials

- Export of existing accounts

- Import to another device

Although the keystore defines the encryption level used to store accounts, there is no global master password capable of granting access to everyone.

Rather, each account is managed individually and is stored on disk in its individually encrypted format, ensuring separation is much cleaner and uses more rigorous credentials.

This individuality means that any operation that requires access to an account must provide authentication credentials required for that particular account in the form of a passphrase:

- When creating a new account, the caller must provide a passphrase with which to encrypt the account. This passphrase will be required for any subsequent access.

- When deleting an existing account, the caller must provide a passphrase to verify account ownership.

- When updating an existing account, the caller must provide both the current and the new passphrase. After completing the operation, the account will no longer be accessible via the previous passphrase.

- When exporting an existing account, the caller must provide both a current passphrase to decrypt the account, and a passphrase to reencode it before returning the key file to the user. This is necessary to allow the movement of the accounts between machines and applications without sharing credentials.

- When importing a new account, the caller must provide both the encryption passphrase of the keyfile to be imported and a new passphrase with which to store the account. This is necessary to allow the storage of accounts with different credentials than those used to move them.

Therefore, there are no recovery mechanisms for the loss of a passphrase. The cryptographic properties of the encrypted keystore ensure that the account credentials cannot be brutally forced in any way. For account management, various Wallet apps are available to manage them efficiently.

4.3 World State

The world state of the Ethereum blockchain is a mapping between the Ethereum address (160-bit identifiers) and the account state.

This mapping is maintained through a data structure called the Modified Merkle Patricia tree. Let's see what it is.

4.3.1 Trie

A Trie, also called a *digital tree* or *prefix tree*, is a data structure ordered tree used to store a dynamic set or array associative where the keys are generally strings.

In general, the position of a node in the tree defined the key that it is associated with. Nodes do not keep a copy of their own key, instead they depend on the position of the node in the tree. (See Figure 4-9.)

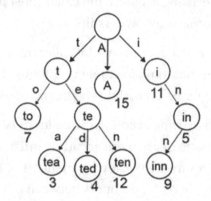

Figure 4-9. *Example of a Trie*

The root of the tree is associated with the empty string, and all the descendants of a node share the prefix associated with that node. Not all nodes necessarily represent a significant key, which typically is found instead in the leaves and possibly in some internal nodes.

4.3.2 The Radix Tree

Note that the Radix tree, also called a compact prefix tree or radix trie, is one data structure that represents a Trie in which space is optimized. In this tree, unlike the Trias, each leaf node is an only child and is joined with the parent node. (See Figure 4-10.)

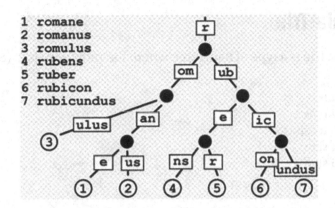

Figure 4-10. *Example of Radix tree*

Here the result is that the number of children of each internal node is at most the value r, a positive integer assigned to the radix variable of the radix tree. The value is a power of 2x, where x is greater than or equal to 1.

This makes radix trees much more efficient for sets where the keys are long strings, and for shared sets of keys with long prefixes. Thus, if radix equals 2, you get a binary Radix tree.

Let k be the length of the keys. Radix trees allow searching, insertion, and elimination in time O (k) This doesn't seem to be an advantage, but they can perform these operations with fewer comparisons and require many fewer nodes than balanced trees.

In general, Radix trees are useful for building associative arrays of keys that can be expressed as strings. They've particular application in IP routing, where the ability to contain large ranges of values with few numbers of exceptions is especially suited to the hierarchical organization of IP addresses.

4.3.3 Patricia Trie

Note that a Patricia trie is a type of Radix tree where the radix equals 2. (See Figure 4-11.)

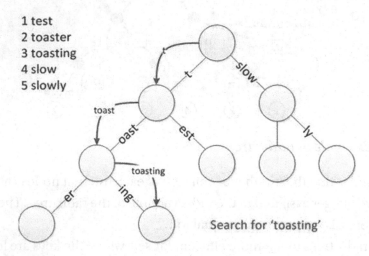

1 test
2 toaster
3 toasting
4 slow
5 slowly

Search for 'toasting'

Figure 4-11. *Tree radix, radix = 2*

In other words, it is a binary radix tree (radix = 2), where each node has two child nodes. So at each cross of the tree, for each node (which is not leaf) you have in front of a binary choice (two branches). This means that each bit of the key is compared individually and each node is a two-way branch (that's the left and right).

A Patricia trie is a special variant of the binary radix tree (radix = 2), where instead of explicitly storing every bit of every key, the nodes only store the position of the first bit that distinguishes two subtrees from each other.

During the intersection, the algorithm examines the indexed bit of the search key and chooses the appropriate right or left subtree. Among the notable features of Patricia trie is that it inserts only a single node for each stored key, making Patricia much more compact than a standard binary trie. We provide an example for a better understanding of a Patricia trie. Suppose you put three keys – smiled, smiles, and smile – in a Patricia Trie.

The binary representation of these three keys is shown in Figure 4-12.

Smile ⟶ 0111 0011 0110 1101 0110 1001 0110 1100 0110 0101 0000 0000

Smiled ⟶ 0111 0011 0110 1101 0110 1001 0110 1100 0110 0101 0110 0100

Smiles ⟶ 0111 0011 0110 1101 0110 1001 0110 1100 0110 0101 0111 0011

Figure 4-12. *Example by Patricia trie*

We note that smile is a prefix of smiled and smiles.

Analyzing the binary representation, we can see that the former bit that differs (from left to right) is 0 (highlighted in red in the second line). For this reason, smiled will be the left child of smile. Likewise, smiles will be smiled's right child because they share the same prefix up to a bit whose value is 1 (highlighted in red in the third line). The resulting Patricia trie after entering the three keys is shown in Figure 4-13.

PATRICIA Trie (radix = 2)

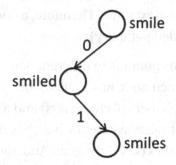

Figure 4-13. *Example of a Patricia trie*

Also, because the actual keys are no longer stored explicitly, you need to do a full comparison of the keys on the record indexed to confirm a match. About this, Patricia has a particular resemblance to indexing using a hash table.

4.3.4 Ethereum Modified Merkle Patricia Trie

This section explains how Ethereum changed the Merkle Patricia trie.

In the modified Merkle Patricia tree, the keys of the tree are represented by Ethereum addresses (20-byte, 160-bit addresses), represented in hexadecimal notation (16 characters). The values from the account state correspond to that Ethereum address.

In the case of a cryptographically secure Merkle tree, each node is referenced by its hash, and the root of the tree acts as a cryptographic imprint of the whole tree. In other words, the deterministic cryptographic hash of each node is used, precisely, as a pointer to the node itself.

This provides a form of cryptographic authentication to the data. If the root hash of a certain trie is publicly known, then anyone can provide evidence that the trie has a given value at a specific path providing the nodes go up every step of the way. It is impossible for an attacker providing proof of a pair (path, value) that they do not exist since the root hash is based on all the underlying hashes, so any changes would change the root hash. This is the *Merkle* part of the tree.

Additionally, there are three different types of nodes in the Modified Merkle Patricia trie:

- **Extension Node:** Contains a part of the common key for multiple nodes (encoded path) and contains a reference to a subsequent node (key), or the hash of the next node. Therefore, a constituted knot from these two fields (encoded path, key).

- **Branch Node:** Contains pointers to different nodes that have the same key prefix. A branch node has 17 fields, one for each character of the hexadecimal alphabet (16 characters) and a value field, to contain the final target value in case the path has been completely crossed, i.e., if a pair exists (key: Ethereum Address, value: Account State) where the key (Ethereum Address) terminates in the branch node. This node consists of 17 fields (v0 ... v15, value).

- **Leaf Node:** Contains a value and the remainder of the key (called key-end). A key to a leaf node (and therefore your Ethereum Address) is the concatenation of a prefix from all of its parents and the key-end of the leaf node.

An extension node only ever has one child node. For this reason, the child node is only ever a branch node. In fact if it pointed to a leaf node, they would be combined into a single leaf knot. If it pointed to an extension node, these would be combined into a single extension node. In Figure 4-14, you can see the structure of the various types of nodes.

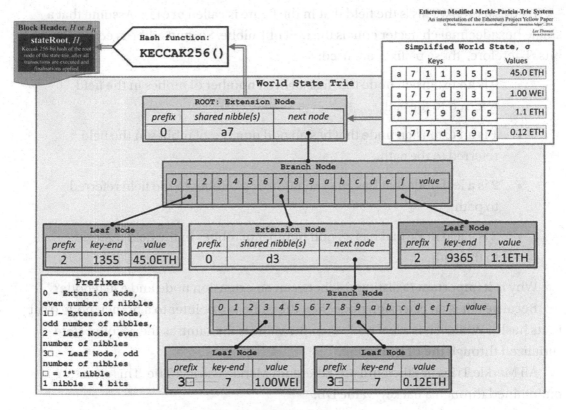

Figure 4-14. *Ethereum Modified Merkle Patricia trie*

For simplicity, the value field hosts the account balance. But in reality, it hosts the result of the RLP function (serialization function) applied to the Account State (which contains the four fields). Instead, the hash function used for nodes is SHA 3.

As you can see, both extension nodes and leaf nodes consist of two fields, a field dedicated to the path of the address and a field dedicated to the value. In the case of the extension node, this value is the hash of the node it points to. In the case of the leaf node, it is the account being serialized.

But how does Ethereum distinguish between the two nodes?

It adds a prefix. This is the field that in the figure is called `prefix`. Assume that a single hexadecimal character equals the unit of 1 nibbe. So, one nibbe is equivalent to 4 bits. Therefore, these prefixes are used:

- 0 is an extension node that has an even number of nibbes in the field referred to the path.

- 1 is an extension node that has an odd number of nibbes in the field referred to the path.

- 2 is a leaf node that has an even number of nibbes in the field referred to path.

- 3 is a leaf node that has an odd number of nibbes in the field referred to the path.

Why is it important to distinguish between an extension node and a leaf node?

Because if it is an extension node then the value is a pointer to a branch node (that is, its hash). While if it is a leaf node then the value is the same as the account state serialized through the RLP function.

All Merkle Tries in Ethereum are Ethereum Merkle Patricia Trie. This structure is maintained through a flat key/value DB.

4.3.5 Storage Root

A hash 256-bit root node or base node of a Merkle Patricia tree encodes the content of the account storage in the trie as a mapping from the Keccak hash to 256 bit to integer values encoded in 256-bit RLP. This, then, in the case of contract accounts, is the storage of the smart contract. Figure 4-15 illustrates the concept.

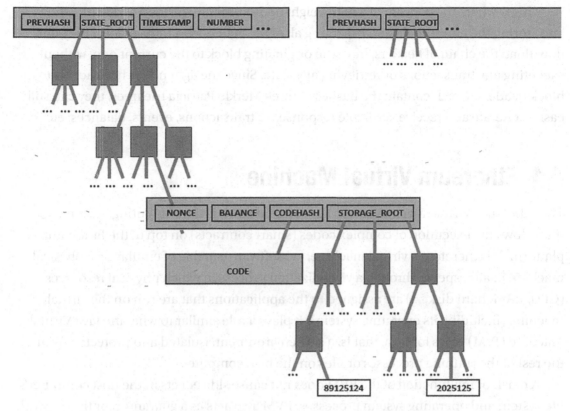

Figure 4-15. *Storage root is the root of or base of a Merkle Patricia Trie for storage of the account*

4.3.6 Why Merkle Trees?

The power to store all this information efficiently in Merkle trees is incredibly useful in Ethereum, and for those we call *light nodes*. A blockchain is handled by a group of nodes. Generally, there are two types of nodes: full nodes and light nodes.

A full node synchronizes the blockchain by archiving the entire chain, from the originating block to the last block, and performs all operations contained therein. Miners usually keep full nodes for the mining process.

It is also possible to download a full node without mining. Regardless, each full node contains the entire blockchain. But as long as a node does not need to execute every transaction or query historical data, it's not really necessary to store the entire blockchain.

This is where the concept of a lightweight node comes in. Instead of downloading and storing the entire chain and executing all of the light node's transactions, they only download the chain of headers, from the originating block to the current one, without executing any transactions or retrieving any state. Since the light nodes have access to the block headers, which contain the hashes of three Merkle Patricia trie trees, they can still easily generate and receive verifiable responses to transactions, events, balances, etc.

4.4 Ethereum Virtual Machine

The Ethereum Virtual Machine, often abbreviated EVM, is the computing center that allows the execution of complex codes (smart contracts) on top of the Ethereum platform. It is therefore a virtual machine, i.e. software capable of emulating a physical machine in all respects, through a virtualization process in which physical resources (CPU, RAM, hard disk, ...) are assigned to the applications that are run on the virtual machine (including its operating system). It plays a role similar to what the Java Virtual Machine (JVM) plays for Java, that is, a safe environment, isolated and protected from the rest of the running processes or files on the host computer.

A crash or malfunction of the EVM does not cause side effects in the host computer's file system and operating system processes. EVM also acts as a guarantor for the network nodes, which "offer" their own physical infrastructure for the storage and processing of potentially harmful smart contracts. The open and permissionless nature of the Ethereum blockchain (like that of Bitcoin), in fact, allows anyone to be part of it and deploy potentially malicious smart contracts.

4.5 What Is a Gas?

A very important concept in Ethereum is that of commissions. Consider that every node runs EVM as part of the verification and validation protocol. Every transaction and each smart contract is executed on the EVM for each node on the network.

Clearly this is not to optimize the efficiency of the calculation. This parallel processing is redundantly parallel. The goal is to offer a more efficient method of reaching consensus without the need for trusted third party. The fact that the *executions of smart contracts and transactions* are redundantly replicated through knots makes them very expensive.

This creates an incentive not to use the blockchain for computation, which can be performed off the platform. Any calculation that occurs because of a transaction on the Ethereum network comes at a cost.

Note that *gas* is the name of the execution commission that the senders of the transactions have to pay for each task carried out on the blockchain Ethereum.

The name gas is developed by the fact that this tax acts like crypto-fuel, driving the motion of smart contracts and of *transactions.* The gas and ether are purposefully dissociated since the gas units align to the calculation units having a natural cost, while the price of the ether generally fluctuates due to market forces. The gas is the unit used to count the fees required for a certain computation.

The price of gas is the amount of Ether we are ready to spend on every unit of gas and is counted in the gwei. Note that the Wei is the smallest unit of Ether, where 10^18 Wei denotes one Ether. One gwei is 1,000,000,000 Wei. With every computation/transaction, a sender sets a `gasLimit` and that means the gas cost or price *(gasprice)*. In this case, the gas limit refers to the full amount of gas that we are willing to spend on a particular computation or transaction. The Gas cost refers to the amount of Gwei we are ready to pay. The product of the gas cost and the gas limit represent the amount of Ether that the sender is ready to pay for the execution of a computation or transaction.

Here we will consider an example of a sender with a limit of gas cost. Suppose the sender gives the gas limit as 50,000 and a gas price of 20 gwei. This means that the sender is ready to spend a high amount of 50000 x 20 gwei = 1,000,000,000,000,000 Wei = 0. 001 Ether to execute that computation or transaction. (See Figure 4-16.)

Figure 4-16. *Example of payment of commissions for a transaction*

If a user has a large amount of Ether in their balance account to cover this, the transaction or computation can be executed. The sender is then refunded for the amount of gas not used during the final stage of the transaction or computation.

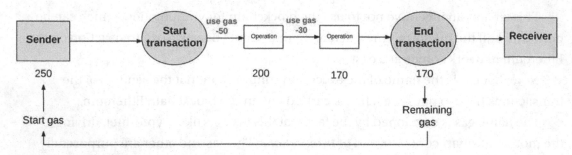

Figure 4-17. *Example of reimbursement for unused gas at the end of a computation*

If the sender will not give the gas needed to perform a transaction, the transaction will run out and would not be considered valid. In this case, the processing of the transaction would stop and any path changes that would be reverted in order to return to the Ethereum state prior to the computation. Also, a failed transaction would be logged to show which operation was attempted and where it failed. And since the car has already spent resources to perform the calculations before running out of gas, no amount is refunded to the sender. (See Figure 4-18.)

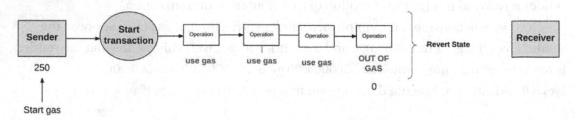

Figure 4-18. *Example of a failed transaction due to a lack of gas*

Note that the whole price spent by the sender for gas is sent to the address of the miner. As miners are spending their resources to run the calculations and identify the computations, they receive the gas tax as granted. (See Figure 4-19.)

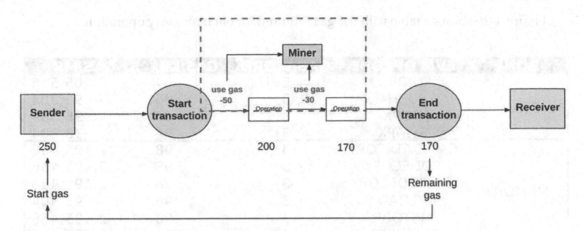

Figure 4-19. *Example of a miner receiving a commission*

So, it is clear that the higher the price of gas, the higher the mark the miner will get from computation. In this way, miners are free to select which computations to validate and which to avoid. To direct senders to a gas price they deem acceptable, miners have the option of advertising a cheaper cost for which they are willing to perform transactions. Miners will include transactions with the highest fees, so the more a user is willing to pay for gas, the more their transaction will quickly be included in a block. It is possible to see the gas required for each operation on this sheet.

4.5.1 Gas for Storing

Not only is gas used to pay for the calculation steps, but it is also used to pay for memory usage. The rates for archiving have some nuanced aspects. For example, since a major memory increases the size of the Ethereum state database on all nodes, there is an incentive to keep the amount of data small archived.

For this reason, if a transaction has a phase when it cancels an entry in the storage space, the execution commission of that transaction is canceled and a refund is granted to free up storage space. In addition, the storage costs are very high. When we develop a smart contract we have three ways to access memory:

- Stack: Access to the volatile stack.

- Memory: Access to volatile storage or memory.

- Storage: Access to non-volatile storage. The most expensive is non-volatile storage.

Figure 4-20 shows a table with the gas required for each memory operation.

ZONE	EVM OPCODE	GAS/WORD	GAS/KB	GAS/MB
STACK	POP	2	64	65,536
	PUSHX	3	96	98,304
	DUPX	3	96	98,304
	SWAPX	3	96	98,304
MEMORY	CALLDATACOPY	3	98	2,195,456
	CODECOPY	3	98	2,195,456
	EXTCODECOPY	3	98	2,195,456
	MLOAD	3	96	98,304
	MSTORE	3	98	2,195,456
	MSTORE8	3	98	2,195,456
STORAGE	SLOAD	200	6,400	6,553,600
	SSTORE	20,000	640,000	655,360,000

Figure 4-20. *List of gas costs for each operation on the memory*

In conclusion, storing data constantly on Ethereum is extremely costly. There is no point in using Ethereum to keep data. Only the data needed for the current operations should be stored; delegate archiving to another solution.

However, a great method would be to archive in Ethereum only the root or the base hash of the Merkle tree as proof of data tampering on an external service.

It is important to understand the smart contracts in terms of consumption or computation of gas to control operating price.

There are several APIs for estimating transaction costs as well as of smart contracts. But this goes beyond the objectives of this book. Ultimately, all operations, both computational and archiving, have a price explained in the gas units. When a user submits a transaction, they provide an ETH price per gas unit and the number of units of gas that they are willing to spend. The lower the code in the terms of gas, the more efficient it will be in terms of materials needed to execute the code.

4.5.2 The Purpose of Gas

An important aspect of how Ethereum runs is that every single operation performed by the network is performed together from every full node. But you have seen that the calculation steps on the Ethereum virtual machine can be more costly.

Hence, the Ethereum smart contracts are used for elementary activities, such as the execution of a simple business strategy, or verifying digital signs and another cryptographic objects, rather than for more complex uses such as file archiving, email machine learning, and in general operations that can strain the network.

The imposition of tariffs prevents users from overcharging. Note that the Ethereum is a complete or full Turing language and in a nutshell, it is capable of simulating any algorithm. This also allows you to create loops and it makes Ethereum sensitive to the problem of avoiding programs that are performed indefinitely.

In the absence of tariffs, an attacker could effectively try to distract the network by running an unlimited loop within an action or an operation without any repercussions.

4.6 Transactions and Messages

We have defined the Ethereum blockchain as machine states based on transactions. Therefore, a transaction is an event that can change the state of the Ethereum blockchain. A transaction can be created for different purposes:

- Digital money transfer between EOs

- Distribution of a smart contract in the Ethereum blockchain

- Execute a function on a distributed smart contract

A transaction can only be created and transmitted by EOs.

4.6.1 Transaction Structure

An Ethereum transaction is an array of bytes. The matrix is divided into fields, as shown in Figure 4-21.

Field	Size	Description
T_n	Up to 32 bytes	Nonce: number of transactions sent by the sender.
T_p	Up to 32 bytes	GasPrice: Price in Wei that the sender pays for each unit of Gas worn out
T_g	Up to 32 bytes	GasLimit: Quantity of Gas that the sender is willing to pay
T_t	20 bytes	To: Ethereum address of the recipient of the transaction
T_v	Up to 32 bytes	Value: Amount in Wei to be transferred from the sender to the recipient
T_i/T_d	Variabile	Date. Ti: Contract creation data / Td: message call data (we will see i messages)
T_w	1 byte	v: Recovery Identifier of the digital signature. v = chainId $*$ 2 + ((y mod 2) + 35).
T_r	32 bytes	*randomPart* of the digital signature, discussed in the section Signing in the chapter on Bitcoin
T_s	32 bytes	*signPart* of the digital signature, discussed in the Signing paragraph in the chapter on Bitcoin

Figure 4-21. *Transaction structure*

Transactions are maintained through the modified Merkle logic Patricia tree, which was discussed extensively in the section dedicated to the world state.

In this logic, the keys are represented by the Transaction IDs and the values are precisely the transactions.

4.6.2 Transaction Digital Signature Flow

We use the steps taken to sign a transaction, following the EIP (Ethereum Improvement Proposal) scheme proposed, after the hard fork that hit Ethereum, by Vitalik Buterin who protects against possible replay attacks. Using the old scheme also works; however the founder suggests using the new one to protect yourself from replay attacks. It is possible to see here :

github.com/ethereum/EIPs/blob/master/EIPS/eip-1155.md

This was proposed by the founder of Ethereum, with the list of IDs of all chains.

Once a transaction is created, it is serialized via the function RLP:

$$L_1 (T) = RLP (T (T_n; T_p; T_g; T_t; T_v; p; chainID; (); ())) $$

$$Dove\ p = T_i\ se\ T_t = 0,\ altrimenti\ p = T_d.$$

Once serialized, the cryptographic hash function called SHA-3 is applied, also called Keccak-256:

$$h_1 (T) = KEC (L (T))$$

Once this is done, you can apply the signature

$$ECDSASIGN (h (T); privKey) = (T_w; T_r; T_s)$$

In which:

- T_w is a recovery identifier and it is doubled plus 35 or 36

- T_r is the randomPart of the digital signature

- T_s is the sign of the digital signature

Therefore, T_r and T_s constitute the outputs of the ECDSA digital signature (randomPart; sign), while T_w is calculated according to EIP155, and has a dual purpose:

- Protects from replay attacks

- Allows you to retrieve information for the quick recovery of the public key

In fact, the sender's address is not present in the transaction. Once this is done, the T_w, T_r, and T_s fields are added to the transaction, getting $T(T_n; T_p; T_g; T_t; T_v; p; T_w; T_r; T_s)$

Then the RLP serialization function is applied to this:

$$L_2(T) = RLP(T(T_n; T_p; T_g; T_t; T_v; p; T_w; T_r; T_s))$$

And once again applied to the SHA-3 hash function:

$$h_2(KEC(L_s(T))$$

What you finally get is the Transaction ID.

4.6.3 Recovery Public Key from Digital Signature

For a digital signature, Ethereum, like Bitcoin, uses both the ECDSA algorithm that the standard secp256k1.

We deal here with the digital signature scheme in proposal EIP-155. In this example we will refer to the Ethereum Mainnet chain. But the procedure is the same for each chain that uses this scheme, just change the chainId to the appropriate one.

As you can see, there is no field for the sender's address of the transaction.

This information is in fact obtained. And it is for this reason that you have the variable v which gives you information about parity and the finiteness of curve point in which randomPart is the x value. The formula for calculating v is

$$v = chainId\ 2 + ((y \bmod 2) + 35)$$

- chainID is the ID of the chain used. For Ethereum Mainnet the value of this variable is 1.

- y is the y coordinate of curve point in which randomPart is the x value of the curve. It is part of the ECDSA signature.

Analyzing the formula proposed for the calculation of v, you see that the interesting part is y mod 2. Which assumes the role of recovery identifier?

It is used to speed up the process of retrieving the signer's public key. In fact, if the information is correct, this operation has two possible results:

- 0: -> the y coordinate is an even value.

- 1: -> the y coordinate is an odd value.

Consequently, we find that ((y mod 2) + 35) can have two possible values:

- 35: -> the y coordinate is an even value.

- 36: -> the y coordinate is an odd value.

Given a fixed value for the X coordinate and truncating the information relative to the Y coordinate, it is possible to have several possible pairs of points (x; y) with the same x.

To verify the signature, then, we would have to retrieve the public key, perform a loop, in which at each iteration, compare whether one of the possible pairs matches the signature.

Possible pairs match the signature. So, let's see the public key of the sender. We briefly explain how the ECDSA algorithm calculates the random part of a digital signature.

Given the curve `secp256k1`. Let G be the generator point defined by the standard `secp256k1`. Let n be the order of point G of the curve Then, we need to understand a that random number is generated in between the interval of [1, n-1]. And we call this `randomNumber` value. We find `randomPart` like this.

$$randomNumber\ G = (x1;\ y1)$$

Therefore,

$$random\ Part = x1\ mod\ n$$

Let h be the cofactor of an elliptic curve, then 2 (h + 1) gives us the information about how many possible points we have given to randomPart of the X coordinate. For `secp256k1` the cofactor is equal to 1. So, we have four possible points:

- Two because each X coordinate has two possible Y coordinates, one positive and one negative.

- Two because R.x = randomPart + j n with j 2 0; 1; 2; ... h (in our case h = 1);

However, R.x is uniquely recoverable from randomPart, as only one of the integers:

$$R.x = randomPart + j * n$$

for j 0; 1; 2; .....; h represents a valid x coordinate, that is, a multiple of G.

For this reason, [SEC2] encryption standards recommend elliptic curves with cofactor h = 1 or h = 2. For these curves recommended by [SEC2] the number of valid x coordinates is usually one, therefore this control is empty.

In the worst-case scenario, only log2 h + 1 bits are needed to find R.x from randomPart.

Therefore, given the fixed randomPart information of the X coordinate of point R and truncating the information relating to the Y coordinate, it is possible to have two possible pairs (x; y) with the same valid X coordinate. That is to say, the one with the positive Y coordinate (x; y) and the one with the negative coordinate (x; -y).

To verify the signature, then, you would have to run a loop in which, during each iteration, you determine if one of the possible pairs matches the signature. However, thanks to the information about the parity of the Y coordinate, we can obtain the yr value of point R to derive the public key corresponding to the signature in one fell swoop. In fact, since v gives us information about the parity of the coordinate Y for which randomPart is the information about coordinate X, we can calculate R = (xr; yr).

Let h (msg) be the hash of the transaction. We get, in this way, the corresponding public key Q:

1. For j ranging from 0 to h (for secp256k1 h = 1):

   a) Pony x_r = random Part + in

   b) From the information about the parity of y_r, derive point R. R = $(x_r; y_r)$

   c) Calculate the public key candidate

$$Q = \frac{signR - h(msg)G}{randomPart} \qquad (4.1)$$

   d) Verify the public key with the digital signature:

      i. $u1 = h(msg) * sign\text{-}1 \bmod n$

      ii. $u2 = randomPart * sing\text{-}1 \bmod n$

iii. Calculate:

$$R = (xr, yr) = u1G + u2Q$$

iv. Set c = xr mod n. So, if c == randomPart true, then the signature is verified. Returns True (valid).

Otherwise, if, after the loop, the value True was not returned then there is a disability in the information. In this way, the public key is derived from the ECDSA signature with standard secp256k1 and the signature is verified.

4.6.4 Three Types of Transactions

This section covers three types of transactions:

- *Fund Transfer Between EOA (Externally Owned Accounts):* This transaction is used when an EOA transfers funds to another EOA. This transaction has a blank Date field. (See Figure 4-22.)

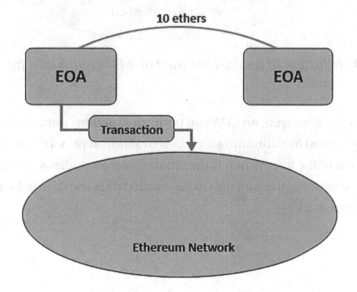

Figure 4-22. *Transfer of funds between EOs*

- *Storing Smart Contract on Ethereum Network:* In Ethereum, the distribution contract takes place through a transaction. This transaction has a blank destination address field. However, in the data field, there is the Smart Contract code in bytecode, plus some arguments if necessary. If successful, the sender receives a receipt with the contract address that they will need to use the smart contract (see Figure 4-23).

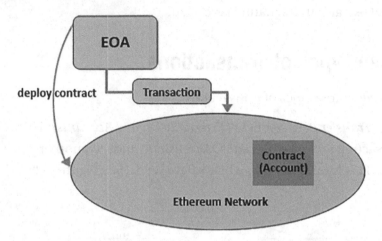

Figure 4-23. *Distribution of a smart contract of a Ethereum Run function on a deployed smart contract*

After a contract is deployed, an EOA can perform functions defined in this contract. Again, it is implemented by submitting an Ethereum transaction. In this case, the destination address of the transaction is the Smart Contract address. While in the data field, there is the selector of the function to be recalled plus the data to be input into the function. (See Figure 4-24)

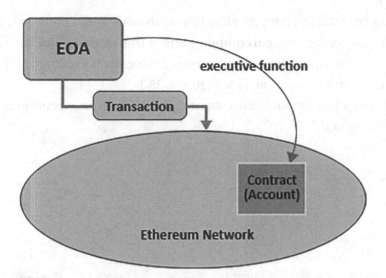

Figure 4-24. *Calling function on smart contract*

Obviously, the rights on a smart contract of those who can carry out operations are defined in the smart contract code, where there is the logic of the operations.

4.6.5 Messages

The message is a kind of virtual transaction sent by the EVM code from one smart contract to another. Note that transactions and messages in Ethereum are different. A *transaction* in the Ethereum language specifically refers to a digitally signed piece of data from a different source from the execution of the EVM code, to be registered in the blockchain. Messages can only be sent by the EVM code and are never represented in the data. They therefore express the ability of smart contract to send messages to different smart contracts.

These are the virtual objects, have never serialized, and only exist in the Ethereum run environment. They can also be conceived as a function call between smart contracts.

Basically, you need to understand that a message is like a transaction, except that it is developed by a contract and not by an outside actor. After a message is produced, and when a contract is currently executing, a code executes the main CALL or DELEGATE THE CALL codes, which develops a message.

Therefore, a contract can have relationships with other smart contracts, like external actors. They are also called internal computations or transactions, and when a contract sends a transaction internally to different contract, the code is executed and associated with the recipient contract account. (See Figure 4-25.)

In general, a message comes from a smart contract, and the execution triggers a transaction from an EOA.

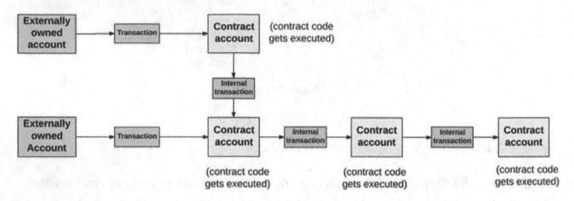

Figure 4-25. *Transactions and messages (internal transactions)*

The gasLimit is set by the external ownership account and therefore is sufficiently high to allow the execution of the overall operation, which includes any under-executions that occur because of operation itself, as messages between contracts.

For the overall chain of transactions a particular on execution of a message ends, then the execution of that message could be restored to its initial state, along with all messages subsequently activated by its execution.

4.7 Ethereum State Transition Function

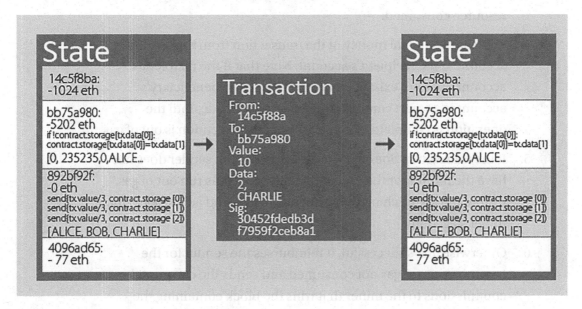

Figure 4-26. *State change and state transition function invoked by a new transaction*

This section discusses the validation of transactions and therefore the state transition function. This function allows you to transit to a new state if and only if the transaction is valid and you have arranged all the resources necessary to complete its execution. See Figure 4-26.

Let's look at the steps of the transition function of the Ethereum state:

APPLY (S; TX) -> S0 or ERROR is defined like this:

1.   Check the transaction for structure and syntax, verifying the validity of the signature and determine if the nonce of the transaction matches that of the sender. If unsuccessful, it returns an error.

2.   You can then compute the transaction cost as GASLIMIT GASPRICE and determine the address of the sender of the sign. If the sender's account is sufficient then it decreases by the value just calculated and increases the nonce; otherwise, it returns an error.

3. Initialize the variable GAS = GAS LIMIT. For each byte consumed it reduces the gas by a certain amount to pay for each byte of resource consumed.

4. Transfer the digital money of the transaction from the sender's account to the recipient's account. Note that if the recipient's account does not exist, it creates it. Then if the beneficiary's account is a smart contract, run the contract code until the operation is completed, or at least until the execution is out of gas.

5. If the transaction does not succeed because the sender does not have the money, or the execution of the code has run out of gas, restore full status changes, payment of taxes, and add taxes to the miner's account.

6. Otherwise, if it's successful, it reimburses the sender for the commissions for gas not consumed and sends the consumed commissions to the miner that wins the block containing the transaction.

The messages work in an equivalent route to the transactions in terms of recovery management: If a running message runs out of gas, and all other executions triggered by this, are restored, it's fine. In other cases, it gives an error or a STOP/RETURN statement.

As mentioned, a Smart Contracts developer has access to three types of storage memory:

- The LIFO (Last-in-first-out) stack (volatile) in which it is possible push or feed data (in a range from 0 to 1024).

- The (volatile) memory is an array of indefinitely expandable bytes.

- Ethereum's (nonvolatile) storage.

The code can also get the message's value and data incoming. It can block header data, and can also return an array of bytes of data as output.

The functional state of EVM can be defined by the set of data. In this case the block state is the global state that contains all accounts and budgets and storage.

Be sure to consider that at the beginning of each turn of run, the current instruction is identified taking the byte pointed to by the program counter. Each operation has its own definition in terms of how it interacts with the set of data.

4.8 Transaction Flow in Ethereum Blockchain

This section discusses the transaction lifecycle in the Ethereum blockchain. Let's take as an example a transaction that invokes a function of a smart contract—it's valid and applies to any type of transaction. Suppose you want to cast your vote in an election through a decentralized application distributed on the Ethereum network. Figure 4-27 shows a graphical interface of the application, which you have accessed it through your browser, and which has installed a plug-in to manage the Ethereum accounts.

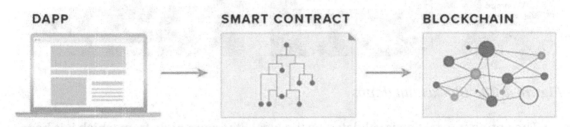

Figure 4-27. *Transaction that invokes a function of a smart contract*

The application gives us a list of elections, and we choose the one for which we have the right to vote.

The vote function we click is an event handled by JavaScript through an Ethereum communication library called Web3.js. It connects to a node of the Ethereum network, creates an instance of a proxy for the smart voting contract, and calls its `castVote()` function, passing the selected candidate. The function call is a transaction, since it alters the status of the voting app (through its function `castVote()`) and requires a digital signature that is generated on the spot. See Figure 4-28.

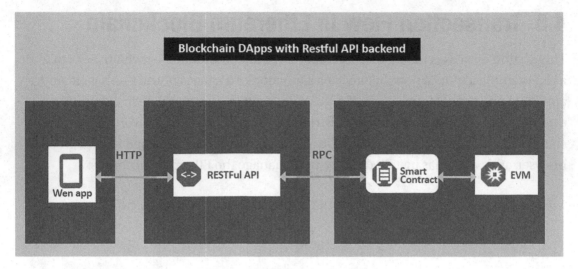

Figure 4-28. Blockchain dapps

The voting transaction is validated by the local Ethereum node from which it is been submitted. Validation involves checking various things:

- The structure and syntax is well defined.

- The digital signature is consistent with the sender's address and the content of the transaction.

- The nonce value of the transaction must be valid. Remember that the nonce of an account is the count of computations or the transactions sent by that account ledger or bill. To be valid, the nonce of a transaction should match the nonce of the sender's user account.

- The sender has enough ether to process the transaction.

- The data sent will not cause the castVote() function to fail.

So, if the validation is successful, the current node broadcasts the transaction to all its neighboring peer nodes. If the validation is not successful, the transaction is not transmitted and simply disappears. Then, the transaction is transmitted over the network through the various complete nodes, which in turn go through the previous validation process.

Then the transaction, spreading through the network, reaches the miner nodes. Each miner node, based on the transactions it receives, has its own transaction pool to add to the ledger. (See Figure 4-29.)

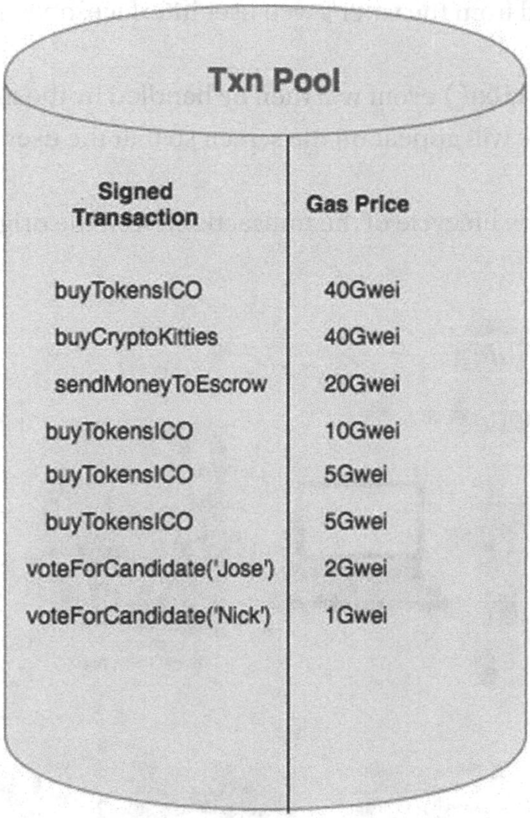

Txn Pool

Signed Transaction	Gas Price
buyTokensICO	40Gwei
buyCryptoKitties	40Gwei
sendMoneyToEscrow	20Gwei
buyTokensICO	10Gwei
buyTokensICO	5Gwei
buyTokensICO	5Gwei
voteForCandidate('Jose')	2Gwei
voteForCandidate('Nick')	1Gwei

Figure 4-29. *MemPool*

The miner node then chooses the transactions to include in the candidate block.

Hence, let's consider that n is the number of transactions and let `APPLI (S; TX)` be the function of state transition defined earlier.

Let `S [0]` be the state at the end of the last block.

$$For\ i = 0;\ 1;\ ...\ n\text{--}1\ S\ (i+1) = APP\ (S\ (i);\ TX\ (i))$$

If no application of the transition function returns an error, then they are valid and could be added to the block, otherwise it will discard those that are invalid.

Then to `S [n]` the miner adds the rewards obtained and defines the final state of the block. Then the miner will build the block, solve the algorithm of consensus and propagate it on the network to be added to the blockchain. Once the voting transaction is performed during validation of the block, the smart contract will publish the `VoteConfirmation()` event.

This will be received from the voter's web user interface, on which you are registered to hear that event.

The Vote Confirmation() event will then be handled by the interface's JavaScript web user, and a message will appear on the screen so that the user knows that the vote was successful.

Figure 4-30 shows the lifecycle of the transaction, from the origin to the confirmation event.

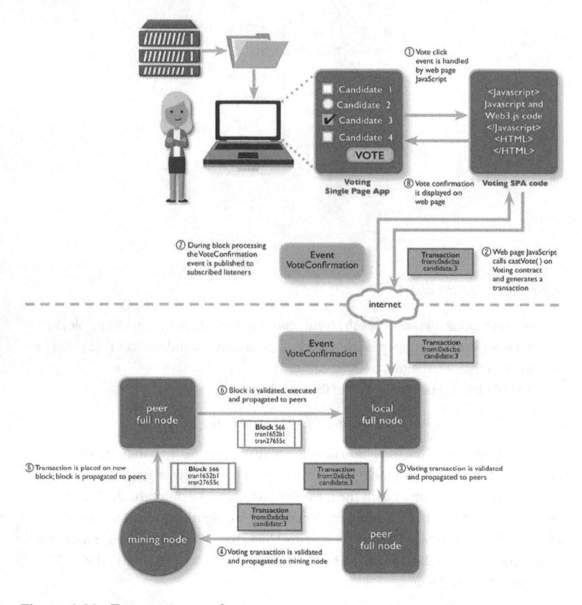

Figure 4-30. *Transaction pool system*

4.9 Transaction State

A transaction proceeds through a series of states until it is not confirmed in a block added to the ledger. (See Figure 4-31.)

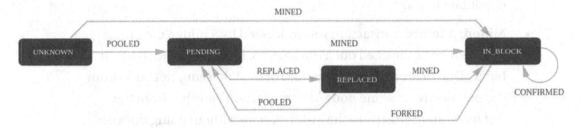

Figure 4-31. *Transaction state*

Let's analyze these states one by one:

- **Unknown:** A transaction that was neither viewed nor processed by the network.

- **Pending:** A transaction that is in the pending state and is waiting to be chosen and elaborated by the miners. It's in the so-called transaction pool.

- **In block:** A transaction moves into the block state when a miner has correctly selected the transaction and extracted it in a block. Once in the block, a transaction can roll back to the pending status if the block is forked.

- **Replaced:** A transaction can go to the replaced state from the pending state when one of these events occurs:

  - Another transaction from the same sender with the nonce itself enters the state of in block.

  - Another transaction from the same sender with the same nonce with a higher gas price enters the state pending.

95

So, let's see the state *transitions* of the transactions.

- **Pooling:** A transition from the unknown state to the pending state. It concerns the transactions that enter the transaction pool of somebody. They are therefore waiting to be selected to train a candidate block.

- **Mined:** A mined transaction was processed by a miner, creating a block. Once he checked out a transaction, he entered the status in block. Due to the *peer-to-peer* nature of the Ethereum network, from the perspective of some node, the transaction can shift from the *unknown* state directly to the in-block state without going through the pending state.

- **Replaced:** A transaction that moves from the pending state to replaced it is said to have been replaced. This happens when:

  - Another transaction from the same sender with the nonce itself enters the in-block state.

  - Another transaction from the sender state with the same nonce but with a higher gas price enters the pending status.

- **Forked:** This happens when a block transaction is part of a block that is inverted by the network. All transactions within that block will pass from the in-block state to the state pending.

- **Confirmed:** A transaction in block status is confirmed whenever a new block is extracted and added to the chain.

4.10 Block Structure

One block of the Ethereum blockchain is divided into the following:

- Block header

- List of ommer block headers

- Block data

The headers of the ommer blocks are in the same format as reported. (See Figure 4-32.)

Field	Description
H_p	**parentHash**: The Keccak-256-bit hash of the header of the parent block (of the block that precedes it)
H_o	**ommersHash**: The Keccak-256-bit hash of the ommers block list
H_c	**beneficiary**: The 160-bit Ethereum address of the miner benefiting all the commissions collected in the block.
H_r	**stateRoot**: The Keccak-256-bit hash of the State *Tree root*.
H_t	**transactionsRoot**: The Keccak-256-bit hash of the root of the Transactions Tree
H_e	**receiptsRoot**: The Keccak-256-bit hash of the root of the receipts tree of each transaction contained in the block
H_b	**logsBloom**: The Bloom Filter consists of the indexable information (logger address and log topics) contained in each logo entry from the receipts of each transaction contained in the block.
H_d	**difficulty**: A scalar value that corresponds to the difficulty level of the block.
H_i	**number**: A scalar that equals the number of ancestor blocks.
H_l	**gasLimit**: A scalar value that is equivalent to the gas limit that can be spent per block.
H_g	**gasUsed**: A scalar value that corresponds to the total gas consumed by the transactions of this block.
H_s	**timestamp**: A scalar in Unix Epoch format that coincides with the birth date of the block.
H_x	**extraData**: A byte array containing data related to this block. Maximum of 32byte
H_m	**mixHash**: 256-bit hash which, when combined with the none, shows that enough computations have been done for this block.
H_n	**nonce**: A 64-bit value which, combined with the mixHash, proves that enough computations have been done to extract this block.

Figure 4-32. Block structure

The list of *ommer block headers* is indicated with B_U, while the list of transactions is indicated with B_T. So, formally, we refer to block B as follows:

$$B = (B_H; B_T; B_U)$$

Remember that every tree in Ethereum is a Modified Merkle Patricia trie, which is extensively covered in the World State section.

The approach may seem very inefficient at first look, since the entire state must be captured at each block, but in fact only a low part of the shaft needs to be changed after each block. Since all the state information is a part of the final block, there is no need to record the full history of the blockchain.

In general, most of the tree between two adjacent blocks is the same, and therefore only one piece of information can be recorded once and referenced twice with hash pointers. Also, it is worth adding that the code execution process of the smart contract is generated by a transaction that is executed via the state computation or transition function.

In view of the block validation algorithm, if the computations or transactions are added to the block called X, the execution of the code generated by this transaction will be performed by all the nodes of the network, validating and adding the X block.

Figure 4-33 summarizes these Ethereum blocks.

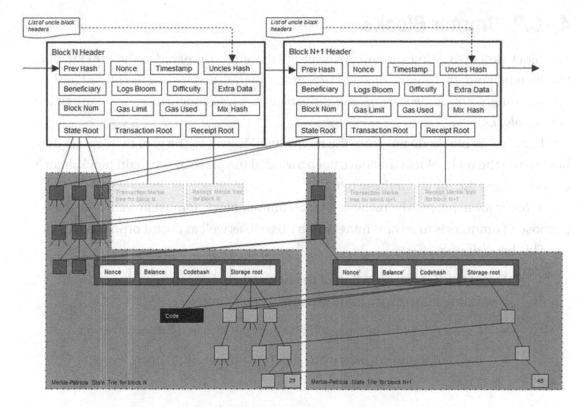

Figure 4-33. *Block structure in Ethereum*

4.10.1 Transaction Receipts

Each transaction, when executed and validated, changes the status of the blockchain. Therefore, every valid transaction has an outcome. Transaction receipts record the result of each transaction. Each computation or transaction receipt is a tuple consisting of four elements:

- Ru: The cumulative gas

- Rl: The set of registers developed through the execution of the transactions

- Rb: The Bloom filter composed of information in those registers

- Rz: The post-transaction status

Therefore, the transaction receipt is defined as follows:

$$R = (R_u; R_b; R_l; R_z)$$

4.10.2 Ommer Blocks

The block processing times are much lower in Ethereum compared to those of Bitcoin. On the one hand, this allows for faster processing of transactions, on the other hand, several miners simultaneously resolve more blocks. These concurrent blocks are called *ommer blocks.*

The ommer blocks do not enter the main chain. However, the goal to integrate these blocks into the main blocks that have been awarded the place in the main blockchain is to help reward the miner for these blocks.

In order for a miner to be rewarded for an ommer block, it must be valid. So, the purpose of ommers is to reward miners who do well, as well as award orphan blocks.

This has a double effect:

1. **Feeds the decentralization of the network.** In fact, even rewarding miners who mine orphaned blocks due to:

   - Greater network latency, which causes delays in data propagation

   - Less computing power, which leads to greater difficulty to extract a block

     - Reduces centralization and avoids pools of miners with greater computing power claiming most of the rewards without leaving anything to individual miners.

2. **Increases the safety of the chain by increasing the amount of work on the main chain.** So less work gets wasted.

The block that wins the place in the main chain is, generally, the one that has the largest share of proof of work. While the ommer blocks are those that usually share less than this test. Each block can have at most two ommer blocks.

4.11 Ethereum Simplified Ghost

The aim behind the *GHOST* protocol is to propose one solution for blockchains that had very fast block processing. In fact, chains with very fast confirmation times are affected by a "reduced" security as the work done by the miners mine blocks that spread more slowly in the network.

Basically, the solution is to include latent blocks in the computation of the main blockchain.

Also, blockchains that produce fast blocks strongly run the risk of centralizing toward a mining pool, which has a high percentage of hash power on the network, arriving thus to control the mining process.

To avoid this situation, Ethereum has adopted a "simplified" version of the GHOST protocol that's able to overcome both problems that plague blockchains that process blocks quickly.

The solution adopted by Ethereum is to provide a reduced reward for latent blocks. Not only that, but they also provide a reward for grandchildren blocks that include latent blocks.

The simplified version of Ethereum's GHOST protocol is defined like this:

- A block must specify a previous block, and 0.1 or 2 ommer block.

- An ommer block included in a block should have these properties:

  - It must be direct child of the k-generation parent of B, with k between two and seven.

  - So, it should not be a progenitor of B.

  - It should be a valid block.

  - The ommer block should be varied from all included ommers in the last blocks and by all the other ommers included in the same block.

There are two reasons that ommers can be included in up to seven generations:

- A GHOST with no generation limits would bring complications in calculating which ommers are valid for a certain block.

- An unlimited GHOST, moreover, as implemented in Ethereum, would eliminate the incentive of miners to mine the main chain, and not that of an attacker.

4.12 Ethereum Consensus

Let's see how, even here, it turns out to be an emerging consensus, and Ethereum bases its consensus on Proof of Work (POW).

The POW algorithm used by Ethereum is the Ethash, which is based on the Keccak-256-bit cryptographic hash function.

As you have already seen, when a transaction is created and signed, before being transmitted to the network, it is validated locally through the local Ethereum node.

This validation includes the following checks:

- The structure and syntax of the transaction is well formed.

- The digital signature is consistent with the sender's address and the content of the transaction.

- The nonce value of the transaction must be valid. To be valid, the nonce of a transaction must match the nonce of the sender's account.

- The sender has enough ether to finance the gas of the transaction.

- The data sent is consistent and well-formed and therefore does not cause failures of any operations invoked.

If one of these validation steps fails, then the transaction will fail and be transmitted to the network. Instead, if so, it is spread across the network through neighboring nodes. Each node that will receive a transaction is carried out in turn a verification of the validity of the transaction.

Again, if successful, this will be passed on through the network, otherwise ignored. This way you avoid clogging the network with invalid transactions that, therefore, would not lead to any change of state.

When these reach the miners, they validate them and add them to the transaction pool. In fact, miners, as in Bitcoin, keep a pool of transactions locally, waiting to be added to a candidate block.

Miners choose the transactions to add to the block based on various criteria, but primarily based on the fees that a transaction offers. Miners have a gas limit per block, which they cannot breach.

Then they choose a number n of transactions to add in block, and they apply the transition function for each of these status

```
APPLY (S; TX) -> S or ERROR
```

So the miner can finally build the block with the new state S0, fill in the fields, and solve the PoW puzzle we talked about in the Nakamoto Consensus section in the chapter dedicated to Bitcoin. Once the puzzle is solved, the miner can pass the block to the net. Each node that will receive the block will then validate the latter. The basic block validation algorithm in Ethereum works in the following way:

- Check if the previous reference block still exists and is valid.

- See if the timestamp of the block is larger than that of the previous and lower reference block of 15 minutes in the future.

- Verify whether the block number, difficulty, transaction origin, derivative transaction, and gas limit are valid.

- Verify if the POW on the block is still valid.

- S [0] can be the state at the end of the last block and TX can be the list of the computations or transactions of the block, with n steps.

For i = 0 ... n - 1, set S (i+1) = APPLY (S (i); TX (i)).

Then check if the application gives an error or if the final or total gas consumed in the block up to this point go beyond the GASLIMIT; this too gives an error.

- Assume that S FINALS (n), however adding the block reward paid to the miner block.

- Need to verify that the original state of the Merkle tree S_FINAL is the same in the original final step or state given in the header of the block. In such a case, the block is valid; on the other hand, it's not valid.

4.12.1 The Proof of Work Algorithm (PWA)

The PWA is formally defined as follows:

$$(n;\ m) = PoW\ (H;\ H_n;\ d)$$

Where

- (n; m)

  - M is a mixHash

  - n is the nonce

- H is the block header without the nonce and without mixHash.

- Hn is the nonce defined as a cryptographically pseudo-random number not independent on H and d.

- d is the DAG, and it is a large set of data required to compute the mix-hash. Simply put, a miner repeatedly spawns such mixHashes through the DAG, until the output has a lower nonce value than the desired value.

The relationship between the nonce and the difficulty of the block is formally defined here:

$$n \leq \frac{2^{256}}{H_d}$$

4.13 Ethereum 2.0

You have seen that, as with Bitcoin, Ethereum is an emerging consensus. The algorithm for extracting blocks used by Ethereum is the *Proof of Work* algorithm.

However, soon, there will be an upgrade from Ethereum 1.0 to Ethereum 2.0. This update will not be immediate but will proceed gradually through various stages.

One of the most important notes of this update is innovation of the algorithm used to extract the blocks. In fact, with the upgrade to Ethereum 2.0 there will be a transition to the Proof of Stake algorithm. The Proof of Work is an algorithm for extracting blocks that entails a computational burden no less. In order for it to be possible to win a block, you need the necessary computational power from expensive and specialized hardware.

This leads to a very high energy consumption with consequences on pollution. So, in summary, the problems related to PoW are:

- It is a very inefficient process due to the number of computational resources and the energy it requires.

- People and organizations who can afford more powerful hardware to carry out PoW are more likely to use it than the others, which means there is a risk of centralizing the mining process at organizations.

Figure 4-34 shows a statistical example of the distribution of mining power within the Ethereum network.

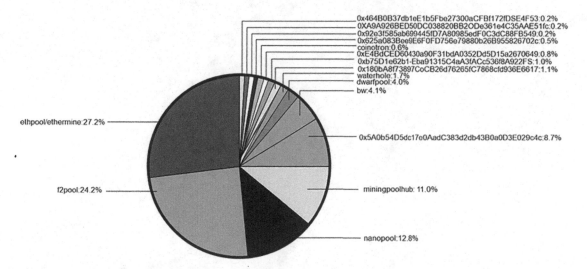

Hashrate distribution of mining pools

0x464B0B37db1eE1b5Fbe27300aCFBf172fDSE4F53:0.2%
0XA9A926BED50DC038820BB2ODe361e4C35AAE51fc:0.2%
0x92e3f585ab699445fD7A80985edF0C3dC88FB549:0.2%
0x625a083Bee9E6F0FD756e79880b26B955826702c:0.5%
coinotron:0.6%
0xE4BdCED60430a90F31bdA0352Dd5D15a2670649:0.8%
0xb75D1e62b1-Eba91315C4aA3fACc536f8A922FS:1.0%
0x180bA8f73897CoCB26d76265fC7868cfd936E6617:1.1%
waterhole:1.7%
dwarfpool:4.0%
bw:4.1%

ethpool/ethermine:27.2%

0x5A0b54D5dc17e0AadC383d2db43B0a0D3E029c4c:8.7%

miningpoolhub: 11.0%

f2pool:24.2%

nanopool:12.8%

Figure 4-34. *Distribution of the hash rate in Ethereum*

Therefore, from the image it is clear that more than 51% of the total mining power of Ethereum is in the hands of three organizations. To solve these problems, Ethereum considered Proof of Stake as a solution.

4.14 Summary

In this chapter, you learned about Ethereum and its structure (state and transaction functions). It explained how Ethereum was created to enable developers to build and publish smart contracts and distributed applications that can be used without downtime issues, fraud, or interference from a third party. The next chapter will focus on the consensus based on the Proof of Stake algorithm, on which research is deepening more and more. More blockchains are considering switching to this algorithm consensus, first of all Ethereum. The chapter ends by covering by Ethereum Casper, the proof of stake the developers of Ethereum are implementing.

CHAPTER 5

Proof of Stake: Consensus of the Future

The *Proof of Stake* algorithm replaces miners with validators and makes the mining process virtual. Ethereum developers have always wanted to switch to Proof of Stake, but it presents some problems that developers are still working to resolve.

The Proof of Stake algorithm is based on a different mining philosophy of blocks. In general terms, the algorithm is based on these facts:

- Any user who wants to be a validator must register on the network as validators through a stake of coins. The stake value is then blocked and frozen.

- This coin bet can never be less than a certain quantity. In fact the stake must be greater than the gain that they can derive from validating new blocks.

- In order to work correctly, the algorithm must punish dishonest validators by cutting their stake. This way, validators benefit more from behaving honestly than from attacking the blockchain.

At each time interval, a validator is chosen from the pool of validators for validating and providing another block to the blockchain. The choice of the validator is made at each time interval according to various criteria.

The odds bet by each validator affect the probability of being chosen. The greater the odds, the greater the likelihood of being chosen.

Each implementation of the Proof of Stake defines, as it sees fit, this choice. So it can vary from PoW to PoS.

© Joseph Thachil George 2022
J. T. George, *Introducing Blockchain Applications*, https://doi.org/10.1007/978-1-4842-7480-4_5

In general, there are two ways to make this type of selection:

- **Randomly chosen block:** The validator is picked through the pairs between the smallest hash value and the biggest stake value. However, since the stakes of each validator are public, this choice can be foreseen.

- **Coin age selection:** The validator is chosen based on how long their tokens have been held. Age is calculated based on the number of days the coins are held in the stake for the stake share. However, each time a validator adds a block, the age of the coin is reset to 0. So it has to wait for a certain time interval to validate a new block.

  - This allows decentralization.

  - This prevents large stake nodes from dominating validation and therefore the blockchain.

This obviously does not prevent new selection methods. On the contrary, everyone, through the choices of the project, can implement their selection.

In fact, each blockchain that uses PoS implements its own methods and its own techniques as it deems most appropriate. The chosen node will therefore validate the new block, sign it, and add it to the blockchain.

As a reward, the node receives transaction fees.

If a node wants to stop validating blocks, and therefore withdraw its stake, it can do so. However, it will have to wait a certain amount of time to allow the network to verify that it has behaved honestly. This algorithm allows you to reach:

- **Safety:** The stake acts as a financial incentive to validate only blocks and therefore valid transactions. It then rejects invalid ones. It also incentivizes validators to work on the canonical chain. In case of dishonest behavior, the penalty is that the episode is cut.

- **Energy efficiency:** No need for expensive and specialized hardware to carry out the complex calculations required, for example, by the PoW.

- **Incentive:** More and more users will be incentivized into managing validations.

- **Decentralization:** Thanks to the pseudo-randomness with which the validators are chosen, it avoids centralizing the validation to a restricted circle of organizations, as happens with the PoW.

- **Stability of the price of the coin:** Due to the fact that it no longer needs to release new coins as a reward to miners.

For this reason, as long as the stake is higher than the prize, the validator, in the case of dishonest behavior, will lose more coins than they can earn.

To effectively control the network and validate fraudulent transactions, a validator should hold 51% of the total stake amount in the network. However, if this is not mathematically impossible, it is practically unlikely. In fact, for this to happen, a validator must have control of the network, holding at least 51% of the current offer. There are two types of shareholder proof algorithms:

- **Proof of stake on a chain:** The algorithm pseudo-randomly picks a validator during every time band (each ten-second period could represent a time slot) and assigns to that validator the ability to generate a single block. This block must refer to some prior block (usually the block at the conclusion of the preceding longest chain, in most cases). As a result, as time goes, the majority of the blocks converge into a single chain that continues to grow.

- **Proof of stake in the style of BFT (Byzantine Fault Tolerance):** Validators are given the right to propose blocks at random, but a multi-round method determines which block is canonical. On that basis each validator submits a vote for some particular block at every round, and at end of the process all validators (honest and online) agree if the given block is linked with the chain. Note that the blocks can still be connected to the chain; the difference is that an approval on a block can occur within a block, and it is not dependent on the length or size of the chain afterward.

5.1 Chain-Based Proof of Stake

This section discusses a Proof of Stake algorithm combined with Proof of Work.

The first PoS technique proposed by developers of Bitcoin as an alternate block generation method to PoW was chain-based PoS. It is, in fact, a combined mechanism between PoS and PoW. It is within the context of the Nakamoto agreement within which the following principles are maintained:

- A communication in the style of gossip

- The rule of block validation

- The most extensive chain rule

- The logical goal

The first complete chain blockchain POS systems have been implemented and adopted by Nxt and Peercoin. The procedure of a chain-based POS can be stated by the algorithm that follows. PoS, unlike PoW, does not rely on useless hashes to create blocks. A miner can only find the solution once for a tick of the clock.

Since the complexity of the hashing puzzle reduces with the amount of the miner's bet, the estimated number of hashing attempts for a miner to solve the puzzle can be greatly reduced, even if their stake level is greater.

So, the PoS component avoids the use of force hashing concurrency, which would have occurred if PoW was used, resulting in a large energy savings.

We first propose the `BlockGen()` method and then the consensus algorithm. (See Figure 5-1.)

Thus, the PoS part avoids the brute force hashing competition that would have occurred if PoW had been used, thereby achieving a significant reduction in power consumption. We first propose the *BlockGen Method* () and then the consensus algorithm.

Algorithm 1: BlockGen()

Result: new Block

1. Evaluate and Package Transactions

2. Prepare a block header context C

3. Set a clock (whose ticking interval is a constant)

4. check the following condition for each clock tick

$$\text{Hash}(C|\text{clock\_time}) < \text{target} * \text{stakeValue}$$

return newBlock

Algorithm 2: Chain-Based Proof of Stake general procedure

Result: Consent

Join the network by connecting to known peers

Deposit your bet

Start *BlockGen* ()

while *running* **do**

    if *BlockGen() returns Block* **then**

        Block validation

        Write the block in the blockchain

        Update BlockGen () for the current blockchain

        Communicate the block to the Peers

    end

end

Figure 5-1. *BlockGen() and the chained-based proof of stake general procedure*

5.1.1 Committee-Based PoS

Chain-based PoS still depends on the hashing puzzle to create the blocks. As an alternative technique, committee-based PoS follows a more orderly procedure:

- Establishes a stakeholder committee based on the mail at stake.

- Allows the committee to create blocks in turn.

A safe multi-party computation (MPC) technique is frequently used to derive such a board in the global network. MPC is a kind of distributed computing where different parts starting with diverse inputs produce the same outcome.

The MPC process in committee-based PoS effectively achieves the functionality that takes the values from the present state of the blockchain targeted by all shareholders and produces a pseudo-random series of shareholders (sequence of leaders) that will then occupy the proposing committee. (See Figure 5-2.)

This leader sequence is the same for all parties involved and those with greater levels of authority can occupy multiple stitches in the sequence.

Algorithm 3: CommitteeElect()

Result: BlockGenSeq

1. Retrieve the current state of the blockchain

   - Participants and Stake of the members of the committee

2. Join the MPC that produces a pseudo-random sequence of block generation opportunities: *BlockGenSeq*

return BlockGenSeq

Algorithm 4: Committee-based Proof of Stake general procedure

Result: Consent

Join the network by connecting to known peers

Deposit your bet

while *running* **do**

  /* election of the candidate */

  if *new block cycle* **then**

    Participate in *CommiteeElect()*

    Check *BlockGenSeq* for my shift

  end

  if it's my turn to generate the block **then**

    Validate transactions

    Generate the block

    Write the block in the blockchain

    Report the block to the network

  end

  /* Longer chain & Validation */

  if block received & is valid & extends the longest chain **then**

    Write the block in the blockchain

    pass the block on to other members

  end

end

Figure 5-2. *CommitteeElect() and the committee-based proof of stake general procedure*

5.1.2 The Nothing at Stake Theory

There are no penalties or incentives in many early chain-based proof of stake systems. (See Figure 5-3.)

This has the undesirable consequence that, if multiple chains compete, the validator's incentive is to strive to make blocks on each chain. There are two basic reasons for this:

- Unlike PoW, validators can validate transactions across multiple branches for free. Because PoW is not required to build a block, it is computationally cheap to be produced on each fork.

- Validators work on all forks because it is profitable for them to do so. If validators validate blocks mainly on two (or more) chains, they will collect trading fees on any branch that wins. This increases the probability of collection.

The problem therefore is that if the validators point to every fork, the blockchain will become more susceptible to double spending attacks.

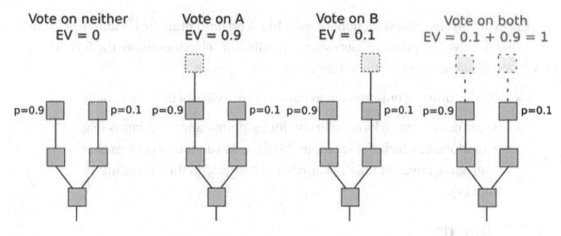

Figure 5-3. *Chain-based proof of stake systems*

In PoW, there is no incentive to mine on numerous chains at the same time. It will not boost a miner's chances of extracting a block if they split their hash power (computational power) between two chains.

This problem can be solved by two strategies—Slasher and Dunkle.

5.1.2.1 Slasher

This includes a punishment for validators that create blocks on numerous chains at the same time, as well as evidence of wrongdoing. The deposit of the wicked validator is cut in this situation. The incentive structure is altered as a result of this. (See Figure 5-4.)

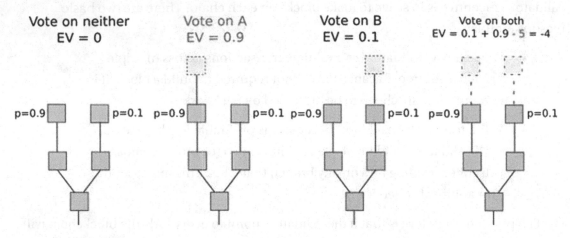

Figure 5-4. *Slasher*

However, the validator selection for each block on both branches is identical for this technique to solve the problem, necessitating validator selection before the fork. There are certain disadvantages to this solution:

- Nodes must be online often to have a secure view of the blockchain.

- Openness to the risks of collusion for medium-range validators (e.g., situations in which, for example, 25 of the 30 validators get together and agree ahead of time to launch a 51% attack on the preceding 19 blocks).

5.1.2.2 Dunkle

The second approach is to simply penalize validators who create blocks on the incorrect chain. Assume two opposing chains, A and B. A validator who constructs a block on A receives a reward of + R on A, but the block's header can be included in B, and the validator receives a penalty of -F on B. In other words, even validators trying to forge a chain (minor) "incorrectly" may be penalized. (See Figure 5-5.)

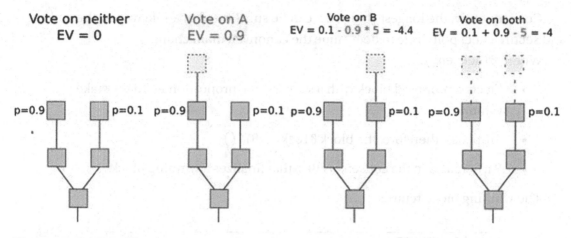

Figure 5-5. *Dunkle*

The insight here is that you can replicate the PoW economy within the PoS.

In PoW, there is a charge for making a mistake while creating a block on the chain, but this cost is hidden in the environment. Miners must spend more electricity and buy or rent additional hardware. Or alternatively, they must divide their computational resources, which is not convenient.

Here, the sanctions are simply stated. This technique has the downside of putting validators at greater risk.

For these reasons, Ethereum 2.0 is planning its own Proof of Stake, which takes the name of Casper, in the style of BFT (Byzantine Fault Tolerance).

5.1.3 BFT-Based Proof of Stake

Because the rule of the longest chain is still employed to ensure the probabilistic finality of the blocks, chain-based PoS and commission-based PoS substantially follow the Nakamoto consensus structure. In contrast, BFT-based PoS incorporates an additional layer of consent that gives a quick finalization that is deterministic of the blocks.

The blocking proposal can be made by any mechanism PoS (round-robin, committee-based, etc.) provided it injects a steady stream of fresh blocks into the BFT consensus layer.

Aside from the standard approach, a checkpoint mechanism can be employed to ensure that the blockchain's goal is fulfilled. (See Figure 5-6.)

Consequently, the longest chain rule can be substituted in a safe way by the current and secure checkpoint rule to determine the canonical main chain.

Where BlockGen():

- Elects a proposed block with a success rate proportionate to the stake value.

- Proposes, therefore, the block BlockFi BTC().

- Participates in the consensus BFT that finalizes a winning block.

The winning block returns.

Algorithm 5: BFT-based PoS general procedure

Result: Consent
Join the network by connecting to known peers
BlockGen()
/* Main loop */
while *running* **do**
    /* Block Proposing & Broadcast */
    if *BlockGen() returns block* **then**
        Add block to its tempBlockSet
        Broadcast block to the network
    end
    /* Block Validation */
    if *block is received & is valid* **then**
        Add block to its tempBlockSet
        Relay block to the network
    end
    /* BFT consensus layer */
    if *new consensus epoch* **then**
        Perform *BlockFinBFT()* on tempBlockSet
        Write the winning block to blockchain
        Clear tempBlockSet
    end
end

Figure 5-6. *Byzantine fault tolerance-based PoS general procedure*

5.2 Ethereum Casper

The FT approach (partially synchronous) allows validators to vote on blocks using proof of stake techniques, which deliver one or more forms of signed messages. The goal is to reach consensus and to identify and punish any dishonest validators.

Like the BFT consensus algorithms, the assumption is that if 2/3 of the validators follow the protocol properly, then, regardless of network latency, the algorithm will not be able to resolve conflicting blocks.

Vitalik Buterin states that one of Casper's targets is to reach the economic purpose. We can define this as follows:

B1 block is economically finalized, with margin $X crypto security, if a customer has proof that (i) B1 will be part of the canonical chain forever, or (ii) those actors who caused the restoration of B1 are guaranteed to be economically penalized by an amount of at least $X.

Obviously, the economic crypto safety margin must be high enough. In fact, if we think of X = $70 million, we understand that that block it is part of the chain and it is very expensive to change it. The PoW does not have these guarantees. It is a specific feature of the PoS.

The intention is to make 51% attacks extremely expensive, so most validators working together fail to restore the locks finalized without suffering an extremely great economic loss. The economic purpose is achieved by asking those who want to participate in the validation process to file a bet.

If the protocol determines that a validator acted dishonestly, violating the rules of the protocol, then they are punished, and their bet is cut.

The set of rules of the protocol are called *slashing conditions*. The slashing conditions make it possible to determine, beyond any reasonable doubt, when a validator has acted inappropriately (for example, voting for numerous different blocks at the same time).

On the other hand, there is a guarantee for validators who follow the rules of the protocol not to violate any rule and not to incur any sanction.

There are also the *finality conditions*, which describe when it is possible to consider a certain finalized hash. A hash is considered finalized when at least 2/3 of the total balances, deposited by the current set of active validators, are committed the hash. Slashing conditions must satisfy two properties:

- **Accountable safety:** If two conflicting hashes are finalized, then it must be demonstrable that at least 1/3 of the validators violated certain cutting conditions.

- **Plausible liveness:** A set of messages must exist so that 2/3 of the validators can transmit to complete some new hashes without breaching the slashing conditions unless at least 1/3 of the validators violated certain slashing conditions.

Accountable safety is what brings this idea of economic purpose: if two conflicting hashes are finalized (i.e., a fork), then you have mathematical proof that a large set of validators must have violated some cut conditions and you can present evidence of this to the blockchain and penalize them.

Plausible liveness basically means it "shouldn't be." It is possible that the algorithm remains blocked and is unable to finalize anything.

5.3 Casper Implementation

Blocktree, which is a tree data structure, is related to the blocks that have just been generated and received in Casper. The actual object of the consent is the *checkpoint tree*, which is a subtree of blocktree.

In particular, for each epoch of consent (every 100 in height of the blocktree or every 1 in height of the checkpoint tree), each validator transmits to its peers one vote for a block as a checkpoint.

A checkpoint is the genesis block and each block whose height in the blocktree is 100 or a multiple of 100. However, the "checkpoint height" of a block whose height is 100 k is simply k. In blocktree, the block's height has to be divisible by 100.

For a better understanding, see the checkpoint tree in Figure 5-7.

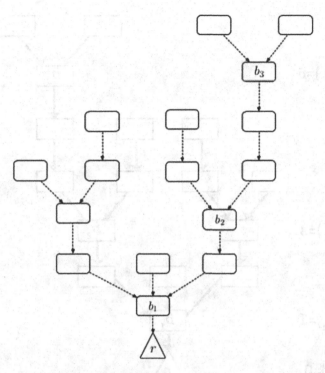

Figure 5-7. *Checkpoint tree: Dashed lines represent 100 blocks between checkpoints*

The height function is shown in Figure 5-8.

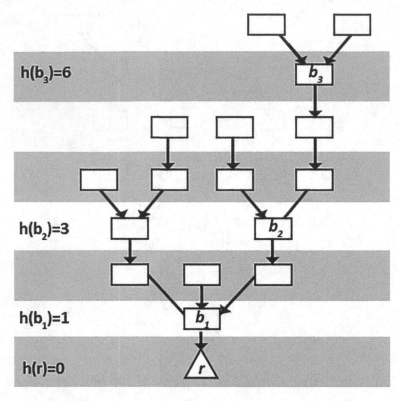

Figure 5-8. Checkpoint tree with the height function

The grade consists of justified source checkpoint (CPs) and their height h (s). A destination gates CPT and their height h (t) and the signature of the validator S. It must be h (t)> h (s).

Therefore <s; CPs; CPt; h (s); h (t)> is the vote of the validator.

Every vote is sent to the network and is weighted based on the value of participation of the signatory (from their stake).

If the pair of source-target control points <CP_s; CP_t> is voted from validators who have more than 2/3 of the total bets deposited, then CP_t is justified and CP_s are completed. All blocks between CP_s and CP_t are also completed.

Casper FFG depends on two so-called Casper commandments to ensure the security of consent:

1.   There can't be two votes for the same checkpoint height from the validator.

2.   The validator does not need to cast a new vote because the scope of its existing vote includes the source-target.

Violators face harsh penalties, including forfeiture of stakes and a temporary betting prohibition. Casper FFG can easily detect and apply the cutting rules since each vote is signed with the validator's private key, which is received by validators.

In addition, the following conditions apply:

- A supermajority link is defined as an ordered pair of checkpoints (a; b), also written a -> b, such that at least 2/3 of the validators (that is, the set of validators whose deposit sum is 2/3 of total) posted a vote with a sorgete and b target. The supermajority links can skip checkpoints. So it's okay if h (b)> h (a) + 1.

- Two checkpoints (a and b) are defined as conflicting if and only if they are nodes in distinct branches, that is to say, one is not an ancestor or descendant of the other.

- A checkpoint is said to be justified if:

    - It is the source

    - Link c0 - <c has a supermajority

A checkpoint c is said to be finalized if a supermajority link c-> c0 exists, and c0 is a significant child of c. In the same way, c is finalized if and only if c is justified. There must also be a supermajority link c - > c0, in which the checkpoints c and c0 are not conflicting, and h (c0) = h (c) + 1. (See Figure 5-9.)

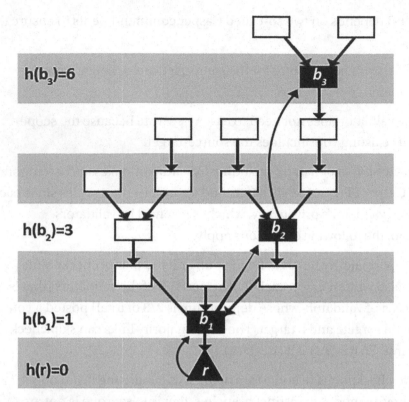

Figure 5-9. *The justified r -> b1 -> b2 -> b3 chain*

EIP 1011 contains information about Casper FFG's current smart contract. A stakeholder becomes eligible to participate by registering for the committed smart contract, which encodes Casper FFG e and can be accessed via Ethereum transactions.

Here we report the CheckpointTimes() function (see Figure 5-10), and then the Casper FFG (Casper the Friendly Finality Gadget) algorithm.

Algorithm 6: CheckPointVote()

Result: consensus

Broadcast a vote for a source-target checkpoint pair in
CheckPointTree;

Check received votes against the slashing rules and then evaluate
them by signer's deposit stake;

if *pair* (CP_s, CP_t)*'s votes cover more than* $\frac{2}{3}$ *of total deposited stakes*
then

| **return** (CP_s, CP_t);

end

Figure 5-10. *CheckPointVote()*

Then we report Casper FFG, as shown in Figure 5-11.

Algorithm 7: Casper FFG

Result: consensus

Deposit in the stake pool; Start *BlockGen()*

/* Main loop */

while *running* **do**

    /* Block Proposing & Broadcast */

    if *BlockGen() returns block* **then**

        Add block to its BlockTree

        Broadcast block to the network

    end

    /* Block Validation */

    if *block is received & is valid* **then**

        Add block to its BlockTree

        Relay block to the network

    end

    /* BFT consensus layer */

    if *new consensus epoch,* **then**

        Identify valid checkpoint blocks and attach them to *CheckPointTree*

        Participate in *CheckPointVote*

        It returns (CP_s, CP_t)

        Mark CP_s finalized

        Mark CP_t justified.

    end

end

Figure 5-11. *CheckPointVote()*

5.4 Summary

This chapter introduced the future scope of proof of stake, which replaces miners with validators and makes the mining process virtual. The chapter also discussed chain-based proof of stake, which uses a block system.

The popularity of public blockchains like Bitcoin and Ethereum has sparked interest in blockchain technology and its usage as a distributed system in the most cutting-edge commercial applications. To use blockchain in the distributed system, you need to understand the concept of *hyperledger fabric,* which serves as a foundation for application development or modular architecture solutions. The next chapter contains more details about hyperledger fabric.

CHAPTER 6

Hyperledger Fabric

The success of public blockchains, such as Bitcoin and Ethereum, has led to growing interest in Blockchain technology and its application as a distributed system in the most innovative business use cases.

However, corporate prerogatives are based on principles and characteristic that public and permissionless blockchains still cannot deliver.

For this reason, private and authorized blockchains were born, capable to satisfy business compromises.

In fact, private and authorized blockchains allow you to design systems in which:

- The networks are authorized

- Participants are identified and identifiable

- There is a guarantee of privacy and confidentiality of the data

- There is low transaction confirmation latency

There are therefore many different blockchain projects authorized for corporate use. Hyperledger Fabric is a free software enterprise accounting system based on distributed ledger, with certain important variations from other famous distributed ledgers as well as blockchain systems.

However, it is critical to distinguish Hyperledger from Hyperledger Fabric. The Hyperledger project is an open source blockchain program started by the Linux Foundation.

Hyperledger Fabric is aimed at serving as a foundation for application development or modular architecture solutions. Hyperledger Fabric enables plug-and-play components such as consent and membership services. Its modular and adaptable design accommodates a wide range of industry use cases. It takes a novel approach to consent, allowing full-scale performance while protecting privacy.

125

© Joseph Thachil George 2022

J. T. George, *Introducing Blockchain Applications*, https://doi.org/10.1007/978-1-4842-7480-4_6

It is an enterprise solution for the development of applications for a wide variety of use cases, as promoted by IBM, it allows innovation and versatility for various fields of application.

It is an *authorized* solution and therefore the participants are known, without the problems arising from a public network and without permits. So, there is trust among the participants.

This has a significant impact on consent. In one system authorized and managed by a trusted authority, consent is not required. Indeed, in these cases, it would be inefficient in terms of performance and speed.

This allows the Hyperledger Fabric platform high performance. This blockchain was specially designed to be highly modular, configurable, and customizable according to the various business needs.

6.1 High-Level Perspective

This section introduces Hyperledger Fabric by providing a high-level perspective. It includes the following components:

- A company move that establishes system consensus by determining the order of transactions and, as a result, transmits new blocks to peers.

- A subscription network operator is in charge of using cryptographic identifiers to validate network identities.

- An extra peer-to-peer gossip channel for broadcasting and ordering service result blocks to those other peers.

- The ledger may be configured to work with a variety of database management systems.

- The customizable endorsement policy for each application. Therefore, every aspect of the platform is modular and configurable.

- In Hyperledger Fabric, smart contracts are known to as *chaincode*. The execute-consensus architecture of Hyperledger Fabric is known as *execute-order-validate*.

Indeed, it divides the transaction flow into three stages:

- Carry out a transaction and verify its validity, approving it in this manner.

- Order the transactions using a programmable consensus protocol.

- Before registering transactions in the ledger, they must be validated according to the application blockchain's policies.

Hyperledger Fabric provides a channel structure. Let's say that each channel corresponds to one and only one blockchain. Therefore, a blockchain is associated only and exclusively to a channel. This means that only organizations that are part of a channel are authorized to the data of the channel itself, and therefore to the data of the blockchain of that channel.

This, together with the concept of private data, provides some guarantee of data security and privacy.

The task of categorizing entries is delegated to a modular component that is conceptually distinct from the peers who conduct the transactions and maintain the ledger. This is how the ordering process works.

Consent can be adjusted to the assumption of trust in a particular distribution or solutions as long as this is modular.

In discussing the concepts and mechanisms behind Hyperledger Fabric, the chapter follows and trusts the official Hyperledger Fabric documentation available on the web, when trying to summarize the concepts. So everything that is reported about Hyperledger Fabric derives from the study from the analysis of its official documentation.

6.2 Assets

Hyperledger Fabric allows you to construct any type of asset using *chaincode*, whether it's physical (property, goods, products, etc.) or intangible (contract terms, intellectual property, documents, etc.).

Assets are specified as a number of essential pairs in Hyperledger Fabric, with state changes being stored as transactions on a ledger (tied to the canal). Binary and/or JSON representations are available for assets.

6.3 Chaincode

Chaincode is a type of software that specifies business logic. In other words, it defines an activity or set of activities and the transaction instructions for changing the activities. The chaincode therefore defines the operations that alter the status of the activity. It uses rules to read or change key-value pairs.

A settlement proposal triggers the chaincode functions, which are performed on the current database ledger. When the chaincode is run, it creates a set of writing that can be broadcast over the network and added to all peers' ledgers.

6.4 Characteristics of the Ledger

The ledger keeps track of all network state transitions in a sequential order. Chaincode invocations (transactions) supplied by the parties produce state transitions. Every operation contains a set of session keys for the resources in the ledger which are created, updated, or eliminated in the ledger.

The ledger consists of:

- A chain to store unchangeable data in blocks.

- A state database that records the present position of the blockchain. Each channel has its own ledger, as previously mentioned. For each channel in which they participate, each peer has a copy of the data.

Here are some ledger features:

- Perform key-based searches and enquiries, as well as range and generally relied inquiries.

- Use a sophisticated query language to do read-only questions. (CouchDB).

- Perform read-only questions from history and query the ledger's record for a key, allowing options for where the data came from.

- Transactions contain the signatures of each peer who approves them before being forwarded to the service for placing orders.

- Transactions contain the signatures of each peer who approves them before they are forwarded to the ordering service.

- Entries are sorted into blocks and "distributed" to peers on the channel by an ordering service.

- Peers enforce approval policies by checking events against them.

- Before adding a block, a version check is conducted to confirm that the statuses of the read asscts have not changed since the chaincode code was executed.

- Once a transaction has been verified and committed, it is immutable. A configuration block in the channel ledger defines policies, access controls, and other relevant information.

Channels are membership provider instances that allow cryptographic materials to be obtained from multiple certifying bodies.

6.5 Privacy

I previously said that a ledger only exists in one channel and in a channel there is only one ledger. Only the members of a channel can therefore access the ledger of this channel. This allows you to do a lot of things while ensuring privacy and confidentiality.

For example, let's imagine the scenario in which there is a supplier company and various client companies. If the supplier company applies different prices depending on the client company, but does not want to reveal this detail, then the channel is the solution. In fact, it would be enough to implement a channel for each commercial relationship, and the confidentiality of any information is guaranteed.

Furthermore, within the channel itself it is possible to obtain an additional level of confidentiality. In fact, chaincode can define an asset the functions that alter the state of the latter. Well, in this area, only the peers who own the chaincode can read the asset related to that chaincode.

If a subgroup of organizations in that channel needs to keep financial data secret, they can gather (collect) the data and store it in a private database that is conceptually distinct from the channel registers and only accessible to a limited number of people inside the institution.

In this way, channels maintain private transactions for the rest of the network, and collections store private data between organizational subsets of channels.

Before submitting a transaction to the ordering service and adding the block to the account, the value of the chaincode can be encrypted with a cryptographic method to further obscure the data. Only a user with the key correspondent used to produce the ciphertext may decode encrypted data once it has been printed to the ledger.

6.6 Identity

Once the encrypted data has been decrypted, a blockchain is made up of multiple actors:

- Peers

- Orderers

- Client applications

- Directors

- Users

A trusted authority is required for an identity to be verifiable. A Membership Service Provider (MSP) is Fabric's most trusted authority. A MSP is an element that sets the rules that govern this organization's authorized identities. The standard PKI (Public Key Infrastructure) model is used in the default implementation, which employs X.509 identity certificates.

6.6.1 Infrastructure with Public Keys (PKI)

A *public key infrastructure* is one of the safety architectures that allows for the generation, management, and use of encryption keys and digital certificates. As a consequence, it's a set of technologies that allows for secure network connections. (See Figure 6-1.)

The elements of the PKI are:

- A certification authority (CA)

- Public key and private key

- Digital certificates

- Revocation of certificates

The certification authority (CA) issues the certificates. The MSP determines the benefits of the trusted members of a certain organization.

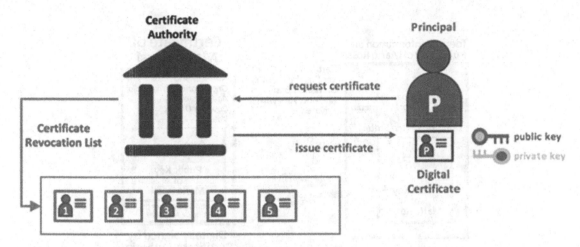

Figure 6-1. *Example of CA e-digital certificate*

6.6.2 Digital Certificates

A digital certificate is a collection of information about the certificate holder.

Among the elements of an X: 509 digital certificate are:

- Version

- Serial number

- ID of the algorithm

- Issuing body

- Validity

- Subject

- Information on the subject's public key

- Certificate signing algorithm

- Certificate signature

The certificate is encrypted and therefore proof against tampering. A change would invalidate the certificate. In fact, it is signed with the private key of the certification authority, and in this way, verifiable through the public key of the same authority. A change would invalidate the verification process. (See Figure 6-2.)

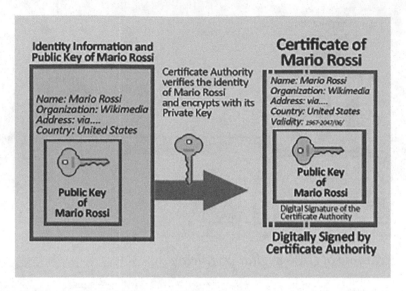

Figure 6-2. *Example of CA and a digital certificate*

It certifies the unique association between a public key and the identity of a subject.

The purpose of the digital certificate is to guarantee that a key public is associated with the true identity of the subject claiming it. In fact, the applied signature certifies that the public key declared is accurate.

In effect, the applied signature checks that the certificate's public key matches the topic specified in the certificate's contents.

In the beginning, therefore, if Mario Rossi wanted to digitally sign a document, he had to divulge his public key to the other actors of the communication. Any person who possessed it could receive from him documents signed with the private key and then verify the signature with the aforementioned public key; however any individual could disclose a different public key, of which he knew the relative private key, and declare that it was Mario Rossi's public key.

To avoid this problem, each user then enters their key in a certificate signed by a reliable third party (in the PKI case, the certificate authorities). All those who recognize this third party simply have to check its signature to decide if the public key really belongs to that user.

6.7 Certificate Authorities

Identity (public key pair and private key) and certificates are distributed by a certification authority to various actors. This certificate, which connects the plaintiff to the actor's public key, is digitally signed by the certification authority (and optionally with a complete property). As a result, if the CA is trusted (and the public key is known), the individual actor may be trusted. As a consequence, if one trusts the CA (and knows its public key), one may be sure that the identified actor is related to the public key supplied in the certificate and possesses the included characteristics, therefore verifying the CA's signature on the plaintiff's certificate. The CA is responsible for ensuring that all actors in an organization have a verified digital identity. (See Figure 6-3.)

Figure 6-3. Certificate authority

6.8 Membership Service Provider (MSP)

MSPs are able to verify identity. In other words, they determine whether an identity belongs to a certain organization or not, and the role it covers within the organization. So although the CAs can issue identities and digital certificates, MSPs can recognize these identities on the network.

MSPs also provide members with a variety of roles and permissions inside the network.

The MSP is the method through which an organization's identification is linked to its membership. The public key of a member (also called a certificate, certificate signature) is added to the organization's MSP to gain membership.

MSPs are also used to assign various roles and permissions to network participants. The MSP is the mechanism that connects identity to organizational membership. The member's public key (also called a certificate, certificate signature) is added to the organization's MSP to gain membership.

An MSP's capabilities, on the other hand, go beyond merely listing who is a network or channel member. By identifying an actor's unique rights on a node or channel, the MSP is responsible for converting an identity into a role. A user must be allocated a role when registering with a CA Fabric, such as administrator, peer, client, order, or member.

6.8.1 Local MSP

MSPs for clients and nodes are specified on a per-client and per-node basis (peers and orderers). Local MSPs control a node's permissions (the peer administrators who can run the node). At the MSP's client premises, the users can authenticate themselves as a member of a channel (for example, in chaincode transactions) or as the holder of a certain role in the system (as an administrator organization).

A customer local MSP is set in the system files of the node and only applies to that node. Because orderers, like peer nodes, are part of a single institution, they have a single MSP to identify the actors or nodes they trust.

6.8.2 Channel MSP

On the other hand, channel MSPs establish administrative and participation rights at the channel level. Peers and ordering nodes on an applications channel share the same viewpoint as channel MSPs, allowing them to authenticate channel guests properly. This implies that if a firm wants to join the channel, the channel setup should include an MSP who works with the organization's internal personnel. Therefore, transactions involving the identities of this organization will be rejected.

Local MSPs are documented in a channel configuration, whereas channel MSPs are represented on the file system as a folder structure. Channel MSPs determine who has power at the channel level. The channel MSP defines the connection between channel members' identities and the execution of channel-level rules.

The MSP channel links the MSPs of all participating organizations to a single ordering system. An ordering service will most likely have ordering nodes from many businesses, with the ordering service as a whole being handled by the businesses.

6.8.3 Storing MSP Data

Local MSPs are documented in a channel configuration, whereas channel MSPs are represented on the file system as a folder structure. Channel MSPs determine who has power at the channel level. The channel MSP defines the connection between channel members' identities and the execution of channel-level rules.

The MSP channel links the MSPs of all participating organizations to a single ordering system. An ordering service will most likely have ordering nodes from many businesses, with the ordering service as a whole being handled by the businesses.

As a result, a channel MSP logically resides and is handled from the channel or network, but each node's local file system contains a copy of every channel MSP.

6.9 Peers

A blockchain is mostly made up of nodes that communicate with one another. Because they have ledgers as well as smart contracts, peers are critical components of the network. The ledger records all smart contract transactions in an immutable manner. It is possible to add, remove, restart, reconfigure, and delete peers.

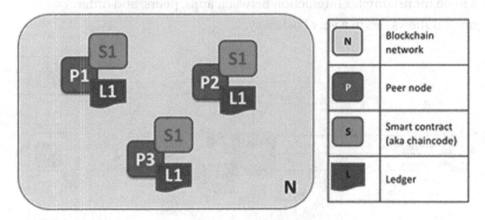

Figure 6-4. *Ledger and chaincode*

A peer therefore has one or more instances of the ledger and one or more instances of different chaincodes. (See Figure 6-4.)

In fact, a peer can participate in different channels, and therefore have different instances of the ledger (each channel corresponds to an independent ledger).

In addition, depending on how the network is configured and for what purposes it is designed, there can be multiple chaincodes. Consequently, a peer can host multiple instances of chaincode.

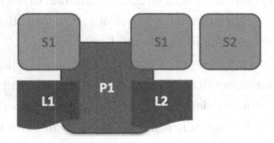

Figure 6-5. *Applications and peers*

Then, to obtain access to the ledger, you show how apps connect with peers. (See Figure 6-5.) Hyperledger Fabric makes the Fabric APIs available to developers Software Development Kits (SDKs), which allow them to interact with the peers, the chaincodes, and therefore the ledger.

Chaincode can be used by applications to query or update a ledger over a peer connection. A ledger query proposed transaction result is returned quickly, but ledger updates need more complex interaction between apps, peers, and orderers.

Figure 6-6 shows this in a very basic way.

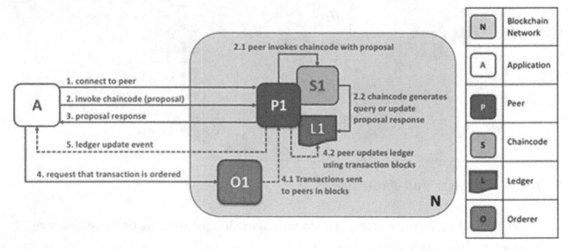

Figure 6-6. *Apps connecting to peers*

In Figure 6-6, application A links to P1 and uses the chaincode S1 to query or modify the L1 ledger. P1 requests a response from S1 with the outcome of the planned ledger query or update. Application A has received the proposal response, and the query phase of the procedure is now complete.

Application A generates a transaction from all update replies and sends it to O1 to sort. O1 gathers and distributes transactions in blocks from all peers, including P1. P1 verifies the transaction before committing it to L1. Once L1 has been changed, as received from A, P1 creates an event to signal completion.

In most cases, applications must connect to the peers they represent in order for the book update master to be approved. This is demonstrated in the "Transaction Flow" section.

6.9.1 Peers and Organizations

Different companies control blockchain networks, or a single company manages them all. Because they are owned by these companies, peers are crucial in the construction of this form of distributed network. Peers are also the connection points for an organization's network.

In this case, a network is formed by four contributing organizations and eight peers. The five peers in network N that are connected via channel C are P1, P3, P5, P7, and P8. Although the other peers of these companies have not entered this channel, they are generally members of at least one other channel. The applications developed by a company will link employees within that company as well as employees from other companies. For clarity, an ordering node is not shown in Figure 6-7.

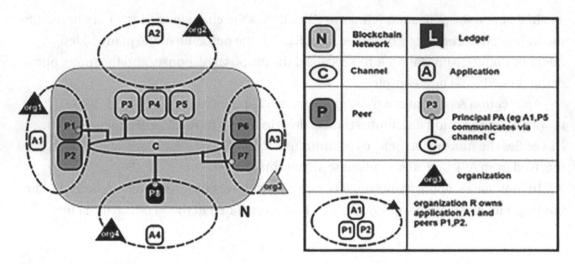

Figure 6-7. *Connecting organizations and peers*

Multiple contributing organizations with resources establish and administer the network. The resources in this topic are peers; however the resources supplied by an organization are more than just peers. The collaborative network would not exist without the organizations that offer their unique resources to it. The network grows and narrows as a result of the resources provided by these member entities.

6.9.2 Peers and Identity

Peers are assigned an identity through a digital certificate of one certain certification authority. When a peer connects to a blockchain via a channel, the peer's rights are determined by a rule in the channel configuration based on their identity.

Therefore, the (channel) MSP recognizes the organization to which it belongs through its *digital certificate.* (See Figure 6-8.)

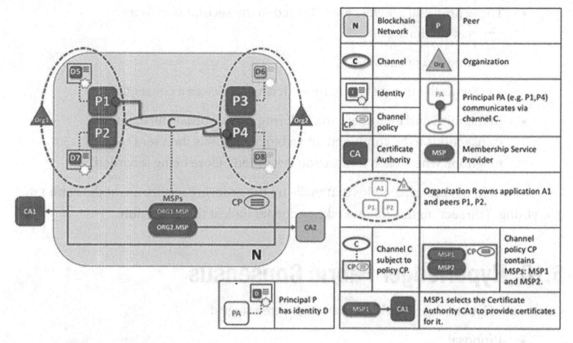

Figure 6-8. *Identity of the peers*

CA1 has provided identities to P1 and P2 in this case. The identities issued by CA1 are related with Org1 using ORG1.MSP, as determined by Channel C utilizing the MSP channel. ORG2.MSP also recognizes P3/P4 as Org2 components.

6.9.3 Peer, Consensus, and Order

To guarantee that almost all peers on a network blockchain retain their information in sync, applications that want to modify the ledger go through a three-step process.

- In the first step, the app connects with a limited set of supporting peers, who individually provide a proposed response that isn't yet applied to the ledger. The subset of endorsing peers that the application interacts with to update the ledger is determined by network policies.

- These proposal answers are collected in the second step by an application that:

  – Verifies its consistency.

  – Sends the transaction to the ordering service as a consequence.

- In the third and final stage, the ordering service orders all incoming transactions to be combined into a block, which is then sent to each neighbor, where each transaction is verified before being recorded.

As a result, the ordering nodes that make up the ordering service are at the center of everything. The section that follows takes a deeper look at this procedure.

6.10 Hyperledger Fabric Consensus

Consent in Hyperledger Fabric goes through three stages:

- Proposal

- Ordering and packing of transactions in blocks

- Validation and commit

6.10.1 Stage 1: Proposal

Initially, the program selects a set of peers to generate updates to the proposed ledger.

The approval policy (given for a chaincode) determines which organizations must approve a suggested ledger transaction before it can be accepted by the networks and therefore registered.

That's what it means to attain consensus: every relevant organization must agree the proposed ledger update before it can be accepted into any peer's ledger.

Applications develop transactions which are suggested, which they transmit to every one of the peer groups that must approve it. Each of these is unique. The supporting peer then generates a response to the settlement proposal by independently executing a transaction proposal-based chaincode. This update is not applied to the book master; instead, it is signed and returned to the application. (See Figure 6-9.)

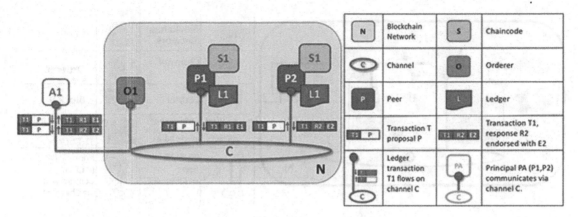

Figure 6-9. *Proposal*

A peer accepts a proposed answer by signing the whole payload with his private key and attaching its digital signature. This permission can later be used to demonstrate that a certain response was generated by a peer inside the company.

Phase 1 concludes when the application obtains a enough number of peer replies. Note that various peers can return to the application with different transaction answers, making the settlement proposal contradictory.

There are two possible causes for this. Because of the chaincode's nondeterminism (a feature to avoid in chaincodes), or because of peer inconsistency.

If an application tries to update the ledger with an inconsistent set of reply transactions, it will be refused. If the proposition is successful, each response is consistent and thus equivalent to the others.

6.10.2 Stage 2: Transactions Are Ordered and Packaged in Blocks

The transaction workflow continues with the packaging stage. Because he receives transactions comprising replies to settlement offers accepted by various applications and arranges them into pieces, the payer is crucial to this process.

Among other things, the authorizing officers have the responsibility of gathering proposed transaction changes, arranging them, and packaging them into blocks for delivery to peers. (See Figure 6-10.)

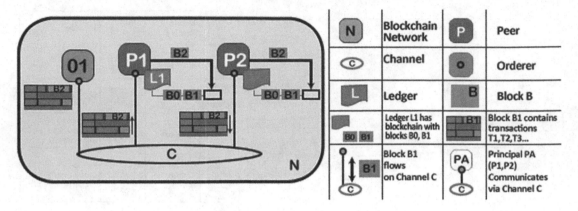

Figure 6-10. *Ordering transactions*

Stage 3 begins with the computer distributing the blocks to all peers connected to it. When a new block is produced, the peers are linked to the orderers via channels in such a way that a copy of the new block is disseminated to all peers connected to the originator. Each peer will process this block individually, but in the same way as every other peer on the channel. Figure 6-11 illustrates how to keep the ledger constant in this way. It's also worth noting that not all peers need to be connected to a computer: peers can connect to cascade to other peers via the gossip protocol.

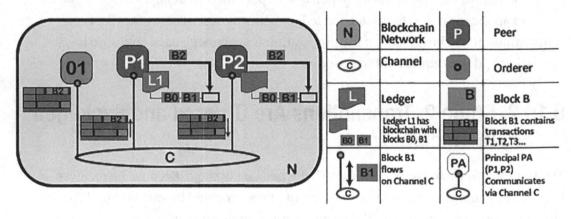

Figure 6-11. *Verification and finalization*

When a peer gets a block, it processes each transaction in the block in the order that it occurs. For each transaction, each peer will check if the transaction has been authorized by the organization requested according to the approval rules of the chaincode that started the transaction. (See Figure 6-11.)

A few transactions, for example, may just require clearance from a single organization, while others may necessitate several approvals before being declared genuine.

This validation procedure ensures that all relevant companies produced the same outcome. This validation is distinct from the approval check in Stage 1, in which the application receives answers from the peers it authorizes and chooses whether or not to transmit the proposed transactions. If the application violates the approval rules by submitting erroneous transactions, the peer might still refuse the transaction at Stage 3, validation.

If the transaction has been correctly accepted, the peer will seek to enforce it on the blockchain. To do so, a peer must conduct a check ledger consistency to confirm that the current state of the book master corresponds to the ledger state at the time the proposed update was created.

Even though the transaction has been fully approved, this may not always be doable. Another transaction, for example, the identical resource in the ledger, may have been changed to the point that the transaction update is no longer applicable and so cannot be implemented. Because all peers in the channel follow the same standards for validating transactions, the ledger is kept constant.

6.11 Ledger

Hyperledger Fabric's IA ledger is made up of two separate but interconnected parts: a blockchain and a global state. (See Figure 6-12.)

Both represent a bundle of information on a group of business items.

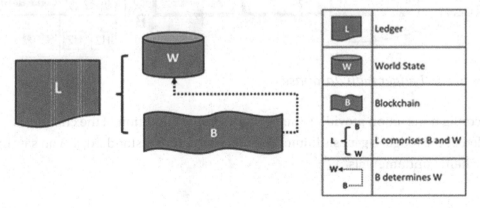

Figure 6-12. *Ledger*

The first step is to use the blockchain. A transaction log records all of the events that have led to the world's present state. Transactions are collected in blocks that are added to the blockchain, which allows you to view the path of events that led to the present situation. Because it is immutable once written, the blockchain's data structure varies considerably from that of the rest of the world.

Second, a global state exists. The current values of a set of business object states are stored in a database. Instead of having to calculate the current value of a state by crossing the entire register of transactions, a program can directly access it using the world state. By default, accounting states are expressed as key-value pairs. States can be generated, updated, and eliminated, so the world state can change frequently.

As a consequence, the global state is generated from a subset of the blockchain.

6.11.1 Blockchain

The blockchain keeps track of the events that led to the current status of assets.

The blockchain has always been implemented as a file, unlike the state, which utilizes a database. (See Figure 6-13.)

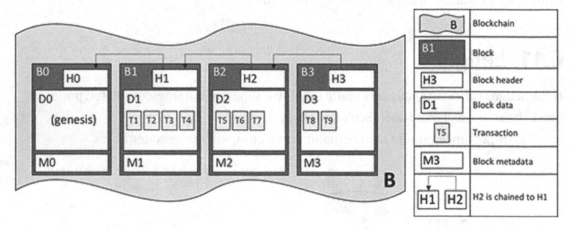

Figure 6-13. *Ledger with database*

A config transaction providing the network's initial condition of the channel is included in the ledger's genesis frame. The block structure is standard, as you saw in "Blockchain Fundamentals."

6.11.2 Transaction

The structure of transactions, on the other hand, is fascinating. Their design is depicted in Figure 6-14.

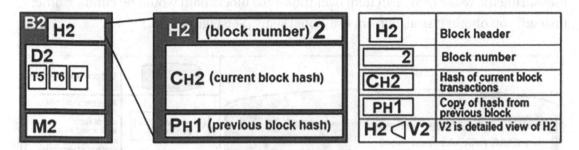

Figure 6-14. *Ledger with a transaction*

In this example, you can see the following fields:

- **Header:** Contains some critical transaction metadata, such as the transaction's chaincode name and version.

- **Signature:** The application client generates a digital signature, which is provided. This feature is used to verify that the transaction information has not been altered because it requires the application's private key to create.

- **Proposal:** Encodes an application's input parameters into the chaincode that generates the proposed ledger's update.

  When chaincode is executed, this proposal offers a set of input variables that, when coupled with the existing world state, produce the new world state.

- **Response:** Encompasses the values of the world before and after. Is the outcome of a smart contract, and if the transaction is correctly validated, it will be added to the ledger to update the global system.

- **Endorsements:** This is a list of all approved transaction answers that must adhere to the approval policy for each company. There will be no change in global status if enough people sign a transaction.

6.11.3 World State

The *World State* reflects the primary value of a business object's characteristics as a single accounting state. Most applications demand the current value of an object; measuring the real worth of an item over the whole blockchain would be cumbersome; instead, you obtain it straight from the global state. (See Figure 6-15.)

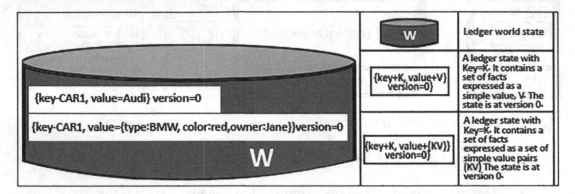

Figure 6-15. *State*

A database keeps track of the present status of the planet. This is understandable because a database provides a wide range of archiving operators as well as fast state recovery.

For the global state database, there are two options: LevelDB and CouchDB. Each chaincode has its own global status, which is unique from the status of all other chaincodes. This means that the world's states are stored in a namespace, which can only be accessed by contracts intelligent from the same chaincode. As a result, a chaincode can't see another chaincode's world state.

6.12 Ordering Service Implementations

The ordering service in the latest version of Hyperledger Fabric is a crash fault-tolerant provider. It's called *Raft*.

The "leader and follower" paradigm is used by Raft, in which the ordering nodes of a channel dynamically elect a leader, who then duplicates messages to the channel's follower nodes. Raft is crash fault-tolerant because it can withstand the loss of some nodes, such as leader nodes, as long as the bulk of the ordered nodes are still operational (CFT).

6.13 Summary

This chapter discussed Hyperledger Fabric in detail. It started with Hyperledger Fabric features and then deepened your understanding of Hyperledger Fabric. The hyperledger concept is important for the following reasons:

- Permissioned blockchain

- Good performance and low transaction latency

- Modular and configurable according to your needs

- Database abstraction to speed up interactions with the World State

- Ability to create different channels and therefore ledgers

- Ability to develop applications and chaincode in different languages programming

There are no particular drawbacks to this platform. When discussing hyperledger, you must also consider the distributed system and how the hyperledger can be used in a distributed system. That's where the concept of a consensus algorithm comes in. The next chapter focuses on the consensus algorithm in a distributed environment.

CHAPTER 7

Consensus Algorithms for Blockchains

A *consensus algorithm* is a mechanism that enables humans or machines to cooperate in a distributed setting. Even if some agents fail, the system must be able to agree on a common source of truth for all agents. To put it another way, the system must be tolerant to failures.

In a centralized design, the system is controlled by a single entity. That system can make adjustments in most circumstances because there isn't a complicated governance mechanism in place to obtain consensus among multiple administrators.

It's a different story with a decentralized setup. Say you're working with a distributed database; how do you decide which entries to add?

The most crucial development that opened the way for blockchains was overcoming this difficulty in an environment where strangers do not trust one other. This chapter looks at how consensus algorithms are crucial to the operation of cryptocurrencies and distributed ledgers.

7.1 Consensus Algorithms and Cryptocurrency

The blockchain is a database that stores the balances of cryptocurrency users. It's critical that everyone (or, more precisely, every node) have a duplicate of the database. Otherwise, you'll soon find yourself with contradictory information, undermining the cryptocurrency network's very purpose.

Users can't spend each other's currencies, thanks to public-key cryptography. However, network participants must still rely on a single source of truth in order to ascertain whether funds have been spent.

© Joseph Thachil George 2022
J. T. George, *Introducing Blockchain Applications*, https://doi.org/10.1007/978-1-4842-7480-4_7

To coordinate participation, Satoshi Nakamoto, the creator of Bitcoin, suggested a Proof of Work method. We'll delve into how PoW works later; for now, we'll look at some of the common characteristics of the various consensus algorithms.

To begin, you need people who want to contribute blocks (referred to as *validators*) to provide a stake. The stake is a monetary amount that a validator must present, which deters them from acting dishonestly. They will lose their stake if they cheat. Computing power, cryptocurrency, and even reputation are examples.

Why would they jeopardize their own assets? There is a monetary incentive. This is typically comprised of fees paid by other users, freshly minted cryptocurrency units, or both, and is typically comprised of the protocol's native cryptocurrency.

Transparency is the last thing you need. You must be able to recognize when someone is lying. It should be expensive for them to create blocks, but inexpensive for anyone to validate them. This guarantees that regular users keep validators in check.

Individual members of a group make and support the best option for the group as a whole using consensus algorithms. It is a decision-making system in which individuals must support the overall choice regardless of whether they agree with it.

Simply put, it's a method for a group of people to make decisions. As an example, consider a team of 10 people who want to choose a project that will benefit all of them. Each of them can make a suggestion, but most will opt for the one that will best benefit them. Others will be affected by this decision, whether they agree with it or not.

Consider doing that with tens of thousands of participants. Isn't it going to make things a lot harder?

Consensus algorithms agree not just with the popular vote, but also with a solution that benefits everyone. As a result, the network is always victorious.

Consensus models on the blockchain are ways to establish equity and fairness in the online world. A *consensus theorem* is the name given to the consensus mechanisms that were utilized to get this agreement.

7.2 Objectives of Consensus Models

These blockchain consensus models have a number of specific goals, including:

- **Reaching an agreement:** As much as possible, the mechanism collects all of the group's agreements.

- **Collaboration:** Each party aims for a more favorable agreement that benefits the entire group.

- **Collaboration:** Everybody works as a group, putting their individual goals aside.

- **Equal rights:** Each voter has the same value in the voting process and each person's vote is important.

- **Involvement:** The voting must be done by everyone in the network. No one will be left out, and no one will be able to abstain from voting.

7.3 Different Types of Consensus Algorithms

Another very difficult aspect of Byzantine is reaching an agreement. Nodes will be unable to reach a compromise or have a greater difficulty value if even one defect occurs.

With consensus algorithms, you do not have to deal with this issue. Their major purpose is to achieve a given aim by any means necessary. The Byzantine consensus structure is substantially less trustable than the blockchain consensus models.

Because of this, in a distributed system with potentially contradicting outputs, it's good to employ consensus techniques for a greater or higher result.

A consensus algorithm is a computer engineering method that allows dispersed processes or systems to agree on a *single data value.* Consensus methods are used in networks with numerous faulty nodes to ensure dependability. In distributed computing and multi-agent systems, resolving this issue, known as the *consensus problem,* is critical.

Consensus algorithms must assume that certain processes and systems will be unavailable and that some communications will be lost, in order to handle this reality. Consensus methods must be fault-tolerant as a result.

Consensus methods are used in networks with numerous faulty nodes to ensure dependability. They must ensure that the system's agents can agree on a single source of truth.

7.4 Types of Blockchain Consensus Algorithms

There are a number of blockchain consensus algorithms with varying features (see Figure 7-1). The following sections cover many of them.

7.4.1 Proof-of-Work (PoW)

Satoshi Nakamoto invented PoW, which is the earliest consensus mechanism in the blockchain world. Mining is another name for it, and the nodes involved are called *miners.*

The miners must resolve complex math riddles employing a large amount of computing power in this technique. They employ a variety of mining techniques, including Graphical Processing Unit (GPU) mining, Application Specific Integrated Circuit (ASIC) mining, and Field Programmable Gate Array (FPGA) mining. The person who solves the problem first gets a block as a prize.

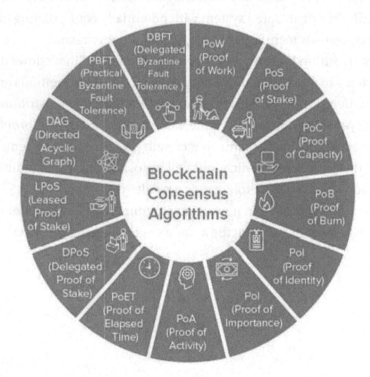

Figure 7-1. *Types of consensus algorithms*

Several cryptocurrencies—including Bitcoin, Litecoin, ZCash, Primecoin, Monero, and Vertcoin—utilize the Proof of Work mechanism.

PoW has had an impact on not only the finance industry, but also on healthcare, governance, management, and other fields. In fact, it has provided the option of multichannel payments and multi-signature transactions over an address in order to improve security.

7.4.2 Proof of Stake (PoS)

The simplest and most ecologically friendly alternative to the PoW consensus mechanism is Proof of Stake (PoS).

The block creators in this blockchain system do not act as miners, but rather as validators. They can construct a block over everyone, which will save energy and time. In order to validate the block , they must invest a certain amount of money or stake.

In addition, unlike PoW, miners are given the option to keep their transaction fees in this algorithm because there is no reward mechanism in this consensus model.

As a result, companies like Ethereum were pushed to upgrade their paradigm from PoW to PoS in their Ethereum 2.0 release. It also aided the correct functioning of several blockchain ecosystems such as Dash, Peercoin, Decred, ReddCoin, and Piv X.

While PoS addressed some of the flaws that previously plagued PoW, the market still faced numerous challenges. Several types of PoS were created to address these issues and provide a better blockchain ecosystem. The two major variations of Proof of Stake (PoS) are PoSD and LPoS, discussed next.

7.4.2.1 Proof of Stake Delegated (PoSD)

In PoSD, players stake their coin and vote for a certain number of delegates, with the amount they invest determining how much weight they receive. For example, if user A invests 10 coins in a delegate while user B spends 5, A's vote is more important than B's.

Delegates are also paid in interchange fees or a set number of bitcoins.

Due to its stake-weighted voting method, PoSD is commonly considered a digital democracy and one of the fastest blockchain consensus algorithms. Some of the real-world uses of the blockchain consensus mechanism include Steem, EOS, and Bit Shares.

7.4.2.2 Leased Proof of Stake (LPoS)

LPoS is updated variant of the PoS consensus mechanism on the Waves platform.

Unlike the traditional proof-of-stake approach, which allows users to lease their cryptocurrency balance to full nodes, this consensus process enables users to rent their remaining balance to complete nodes.

Those who rent the most have the best chance of creating the block. In addition, the leaser gets paid a share of the transaction charge collected from the entire node.

This Proof-of-Stake variation offers a fast and secure way to build public cryptocurrencies.

7.4.3 Byzantine Fault Tolerance (BFT)

The Byzantine Error is a situation in which the system's participants must agree on a suitable approach to avoid catastrophic failure, yet some of them are unsure. PBFT and DBFT are the two most common BFT consensus models in the blockchain industry.

7.4.4 Practical-BFT

Practical-BFT is a simple method that tackles the Byzantine Common's difficulties by permitting users to agree to the messages that have been delivered to them by completing a computation to verify the validity decision.

The party then informs other nodes of its decision, which are then required to make a decision. The final choice is then based on the information gathered from the other nodes.

7.4.5 Delegated Byzantine Fault Tolerance (dBFT)

The dBFT technique was introduced by NEO and NEO coin holders have the ability to elect delegates as well.

This is true regardless of the amount of money they invest. Anyone who meets the minimum requirements, which include a verified identification, adequate equipment, and 1,000 GAS, can serve as a delegate. After that, a speaker is chosen at random from among the delegates.

7.4.6 Direct Acyclic Graph (DAG)

DAG is a simple yet important blockchain consensus mechanism that every mobile app development business dealing with blockchain should be familiar with.

In this type of blockchain consensus architecture, each node prepares to become a "miner." If miners are removed from the equation and transactions are validated by users, the cost associated with them is lowered to $0. The process of validating transactions between any two nodes becomes easier, making it lighter, faster, and more secure.

Despite the fact that these are the most common consensus models in the development environment, several other blockchain consensus mechanisms have begun to gain traction, including the following.

7.4.7 Proof of Capacity (PoC)

The method that is followed is plotting. Two cryptocurrencies that use this blockchain consensus technology are Burstcoin and SpaceMint.

How does it work? First you need to grasp two ideas—charting and mining—in order to appreciate the essence of the consensus theorem.

- The PoC algorithm uses nonces that are different from those used in Bitcoin. Until the nonces are solved, you'll have to hash your ID and data.
- Hard drive "mining" is the next concept. As previously indicated, you can get zero to 4095 scoops at one time and then you can store it in our storage space. You will be given a strict timeframe to resolve the nonces. This timeline mentions how long it will take to create a block.

You will receive a block as a reward if you can resolve the nonces faster than the other miners. Burst is a well-known example of a company that has embraced the PoC algorithm.

7.4.8 Proof-of-Burn (PoB)

PoB consensus architecture is an alternative to PoW and PoS in terms of energy consumption. It operates by letting miners burn/ruin virtual cryptocurrency tokens, allowing them to produce blocks proportional to the currencies. They are more likely to win a new block for each coin they get if they burn more coins.

However, in order to burn money, they must transmit it to an address where it cannot be used to verify the block. This is often utilized in the situation of distributed consensus. The best example of this consensus mechanism is Slimcoin.

7.4.9 Proof-of-Identity (PoI)

PoI is similar to the idea of authorized identity. It's a piece of cryptographic confirmation for a user's private key, which is associated with each transaction.

Each identified user can create and manage a data block that can be shared with others in the network.

This blockchain's methodology ensures the data's validity and integrity. As a result, it's a good candidate for use in smart cities.

7.4.10 Proof-of-Activity (PoA)

PoA combines the benefits of the PoW and PoS consensus models.

The miners compete to solve a cryptographic puzzle as quickly as possible, using special hardware and electric energy, exactly as they do in PoW. However, the blocks that come together only have the information on the block successors' identity and the prize transaction.

Proof-of-Activity (PoA) is a combination of the Proof-of-Stake (PoS) and Proof-of-Work (PoW) consensus techniques. It allows legitimate transactions and consensus among miners to take place. In both PoS and PoW, PoA seeks to solve centralization concerns. It also aspires to do it in a resource-conserving manner.

7.4.11 Proof-of-Elapsed Time (PoET)

PoET is based on the principle of evenly distributing and increasing the odds for a larger percentage of participants. As a result, each participating node is required to wait for a specific time to begin the next mining process. The member who has been waiting the least amount of time is requested to propose a block.

At the same time, each node chooses how long it will wait before entering sleep mode.

7.4.12 Proof-of-Importance (PoI)

PoI is a NEM-developed variant of the PoS protocol that takes into account the roles of validators. This is influenced not only by the quantity and likelihood of their shares, but also by other factors, such as reputation, total balance, and the number of transactions done through each specific address.

The table shown in Figure 7-2 compares the different consensus algorithms.

	PoW	PoS	PoET	PBFT	Stellar
Type	Permissionless	Permissionless and Permissioned	Permissionless and Permissioned	Permissionless	Permissionless
Finalization	Probabilistic	Probabilistic	Probabilistic	Immediate	Immediate
Throughput	Low	High	Medium	High	High
Adversary	<=25 %	Depend on the implementation	Not Known	<=33 %	<=33 %

Figure 7-2. *Algorithm comparison table*

7.5 Consensus in Distributed Systems and Blockchain Technology

The two primary forms of blockchains are authorized, which is called authorization of blockchain. Nodes are anonymous on the permissionless blockchain.

A fork can be caused by adding a new modified transaction block. When a valid transaction disagrees with an invalid one, a fork occurs. The consensus algorithm's main purpose is to obtain consensus across the nodes so that each node may agree on a true value. Nodes are not anonymous in the authorized blockchain and are considered known entities.

In addition, the communication paradigm, whether synchronous or asynchronous, is taken into account when defining the consensus system. Crash errors, transient errors, omission mistakes, security errors, software errors, Byzantine errors, time errors, and environmental problems are all examples of errors.

Crash failure occurs when a process comes to an abrupt halt. In a synchronous context, timeout measures will help reveal this failure, however in a non-synchronous atmosphere, failure is difficult to recognize.

- **Passage failure:** Non-inevitable and long-lasting failures are referred to as *transient* failures. Low batteries or a power surge might create a hardware issue. These software flaws might be defects in internal codes that arise infrequently and go unnoticed during testing.

- **Reliability failure:** Reliability failures arise because of safety assaults and impersonation. As a result, it's conceivable that data will be corrupted.

- **Software failure:** Software failures occur as a result of faults in design and modeling. Other types of failures, such as crash or omission, can be caused by this type of failure.

- **Byzantine failure:** A byzantine failure is a fault that manifests itself differently in each member of the system. It makes it difficult for all members to establish an agreement or reach a consensus.

These mistakes perplex the system, making it harder for it to accept them. A server, for example, may seem to be down to one viewer while being functional to another. Because of their conflicting viewpoints, both observers will be unable to reach a consensus, and the server cannot be deemed failed.

- **Temporal failure:** Temporal failures happen when a deadline is missed. That is, accurate results may be obtained, but they are too late to be considered useful. In real-time systems, this category is extremely important.

- **Environmental perturbations:** If the solution is not made adaptive to changes in the environment, it will fail. A change in the environment could cause a right result to be incorrect.

Blockchains are decentralized ledgers that are not administered by a central authority. Malicious individuals could be rewarded handsomely for attempting to cause faults. As a result, thinking about the Byzantine problem and its solutions is important for blockchain.

A Byzantine error manifests itself differently in each member of the system. It inhibits all participants from reaching an agreement or forming a consensus. These errors perplex the system, making it difficult for it to accept the errors.

7.6 Review Questions

1. "Consensus is a fundamental concept in distributed systems, but it is unique to blockchain." Is this statement correct or incorrect?

2. Which statement is true?

   a. A consensus algorithm is a method that allows companies or machines to cooperate in a dispersed setting.

   b. A consensus algorithm is a method that prevents users or machines from cooperating in a distributed environment.

   c. A consensus algorithm prevents users or machines from cooperating in a distributed environment.

   d. You can show equivalence relations using a consensus procedure, which is a mechanism.

3. Which of the following statements about the concept of Proof of Work is correct?

   a. PoW systems allow players who know a secret, usually a public key, to perform faster computations.

   b. PoW systems allow players who know a secret, usually a private key, to perform faster computations.

   c. With this process, miners must use extensive computation capacity to solve complicated mathematical challenges.

   d. With this process, miners must use algorithms to solve complex mathematical challenges.

4. Which of the following statements about Proof of Activity is correct?

   a. Miners compete, much as in PoW, to solve a cryptographic problem as soon as possible using specialized hardware and electricity.

   b. Miners resolve a cryptographic challenge using specific hardware and electric energy as quickly as possible, much like in PoW.

   c. Miners use it to resolve a cryptographic challenge using special software and electric energy as quickly as possible, much like in PoW.

   d. Miners compete to resolve a cryptographic challenge using special software and energy as quickly as possible, much like in PoW.

5. "In its functioning, PoI is a PoS version that considers the role of shareholders and validators." Do you think this statement is true or false?

7.7 Review Answers

1. Answer: Incorrect. Consensus is a major idea in distributed-systems, not just in blockchain.

2. Answer: A, A consensus algorithm is a method that allows companies or machines to cooperate in a dispersed setting.

3. Answer: C, Miners must solve complicated mathematical riddles employing a large amount of computing power in this technique.

4. Answer: A, Miners compete, much as in PoW, to solve a cryptographic problem as soon as possible using specialized hardware and electricity.

5. This statement is true.

7.8 Summary

The blockchain can be a distributed ledger, which has sparked interest across a wide range of industries. Blockchain technology is already being used in a variety of sectors to create goods and services. It is important to grasp blockchain's core components, functional characteristics, and architecture in order to appreciate its affect and applicability to various applications.

Bitcoin, a cryptocurrency, is the most well-known application of blockchain. Because a blockchain network is a distributed ledger, it requires a consensus mechanism among peer nodes to ensure that it functions properly.

To comprehend blockchain's influence and applicability to diverse applications, it's critical to understand its fundamental components, functional features, and design. Several consensus algorithms have been proposed in the modern world, each with its unique set of reliability and scalability features. To fulfill the needs of all businesses, a single consensus algorithm will be inadequate. It's essential to assess the strengths, weaknesses, and applications of the various consensus algorithms.

Parameters related to blockchain consensus, privacy, and scalability were identified and discussed. The consensus techniques are compared and contrasted in terms of these factors. There are research gaps in the development of efficient consensus algorithms as well as the assessment of current algorithms. Developers and researchers will be guided through the process of assessing and creating a consensus algorithm in this book.

Due to the obvious consensus algorithms, the nature of blockchain networks is extremely flexible. There is no such thing as a "perfect" blockchain consensus algorithm. But, we guess, that is the allure of technology: it is always improving. Since this chapter explained blockchain and consensus algorithms in detail, you should now be ready to start a project based on these technologies. The next chapter explains the first project of this book.

## CHAPTER 8

The Consensus Algorithms for Blockchains Project

This project is a basic blockchain written in Python. It is a set of blocks that are linked together in such a way that the information they store is impossible to modify (and more and more difficult as more blocks are joined to the blockchain).

The PoW (Proof of Work) algorithm is used to mine every block in this blockchain. Its purpose is to find a hash of all the data saved in the blocks that meets certain criteria. For this purpose, each block has a variable data called nonce that must be modified until the desired hash is discovered.

The desired hash in bitcoin, for example, requires the first X digits to be zeros. The amount X determines how difficult mining is (the larger the X, the greater the difficulty). In this blockchain, X is a property of the blockchain that can be set in its constructor. However, this is dependent on the mining capacity of the nodes that support the network in Bitcoin and the majority of other coins.

8.1 Starting the Project

This project has one dependency, called hashlib, which secures the hashes and message digests the import hashlib.

To run the project, open a terminal and type the following:

```
python3 project1.py
```

© Joseph Thachil George 2022
J. T. George, *Introducing Blockchain Applications*, https://doi.org/10.1007/978-1-4842-7480-4_8

The Create Transaction method is used to generate transactions. Required inputs include the sending address, the receiving address, and the number of FDCs (*Federated Data Collaborations* in the Internet of Things). To add the transaction to the blockchain, use the Mine Pending Transactions function after it has been created. As an argument, this method requires the address of the block's miner, i.e., the address that will be rewarded in the future. You may also use the Show Address Balance method with the address name you want to verify as an argument to check each address balance.

8.2 The Python Code

Listing 8-1 shows the TransactionProject.py Python file. The python file TransactionProject.py will help us do following tasks:

1. Create transaction in blockchain

2. Mining of transaction

3. Validate Transaction

4. Creating blocks in blockchain

Listing 8-1. TransactionProject.py

```python
import datetime
import hashlib
from pprint import pprint

class Transaction(object):

    """Transaction class
    """

    def __init__(self, fromAddress, toAddress, amount):
        self.fromAddress = fromAddress
        self.toAddress = toAddress
        self.amount = amount

class Block(object):

    """Block class
    """
```

```python
    def __init__(self, timestamp, transactions, previousHash=""):
        self.timestamp = timestamp
        self.transactions = transactions
        self.previousHash = previousHash
        self.nonce = 0
        self.hash = self.calculateHash()

    def calculateHash(self):
        info = str(self.timestamp) + str(self.transactions) + str(self.
        previousHash) + str(self.nonce)
        return hashlib.sha256(info.encode('utf-8')).hexdigest()

    # Proof of work algorithm
    def mineBlock(self, difficulty):
        self.hash = self.calculateHash()
        while(self.hash[:difficulty] != "0"*difficulty):
            self.nonce += 1
            self.hash = self.calculateHash()

class BlockChain(object):

    """Blockchain class
    """

    def __init__(self):
        self.chain = [self.createGenesisBlock()]
        self.difficulty = 4
        self.pendingTransactions = []
        self.miningReward = 100

    def createGenesisBlock(self):
        return Block("20/03/2018", [], "0")

    def getLatestBlock(self):
        return self.chain[-1]

    def minePendingTransactions(self, miningRewardAddress):
```

```
        newBlock = Block(datetime.datetime.now(), self.pendingTransactions)
        newBlock.previousHash = self.getLatestBlock().hash
        # you can check if transactions are valid here
        print("mining block...")
        newBlock.mineBlock(self.difficulty)
        print("block mined:", newBlock.hash)
        print("block succesfully mined.")
        self.chain.append(newBlock)

        self.pendingTransactions = [Transaction(None,
        miningRewardAddress, self.miningReward)]

    def createTransaction(self, transaction):
        self.pendingTransactions.append(transaction)

    def getBalanceOfAddress(self, address):
        balance = 0
        for block in self.chain:
            for transaction in block.transactions:
                if transaction.fromAddress == address:
                    balance -= transaction.amount
                if transaction.toAddress == address:
                    balance += transaction.amount
        return balance

    def isBlockChainValid(self):
        for previousBlock, block in zip(self.chain, self.chain[1:]):
            if block.hash != block.calculateHash():
                return False
            if block.previousHash != previousBlock.hash:
                return False
        return True

    def showBlockChain(self):
        print("blockchain: fedecoin\n")
        for block in self.chain:
            print("block")
            print("timestamp:", block.timestamp)
```

```
            pprint("transactions:", block.transactions)
            print("previousHash:", block.previousHash)
            print("hash:", block.hash, "\n")
    def showAddressBalance(self, address):
            print(address, "balance:", self.getBalanceOfAddress(address))

fedecoin = BlockChain()
fedecoin.createTransaction(Transaction("address1", "address2", 100))
fedecoin.createTransaction(Transaction("address2", "address1", 50))
fedecoin.minePendingTransactions("fede_address")
fedecoin.createTransaction(Transaction("address1", "address3", 100))
fedecoin.createTransaction(Transaction("address2", "address1", 50))
fedecoin.minePendingTransactions("fede_address")
fedecoin.showAddressBalance("fede_address")
print("fedecoin is valid?", fedecoin.isBlockChainValid())
fedecoin.chain[1].transactions = Transaction("address1", "address2", 1000)
print("fedecoin is valid?", fedecoin.isBlockChainValid())
fedecoin.chain[1].calculateHash()
print("fedecoin is valid?", fedecoin.isBlockChainValid())
```

8.3 Example 2: Using Flask in Python

We utilized the Python Flask framework to create this blockchain application.
The following are the requirements for this application.

```
Python 3.0+
Flask and requests
for Install
pip install Flask == 0.122 requests==2.18.4
```

Here are the steps:

1. Put in place a basic proof of work.

2. Create an API interface for the blockchain.

3. Construct a blockchain miner.

4. Use the blockchain to interact.

8.3.1 Step 1: Create a Simple Proof of Work

The goal of PoW (Proof of Work) is to provide a number that solves a problem. It must be difficult to track down the number, but anyone else on the network should be able to verify it. Because the number is made up of cryptographic signatures, it will be denied access if it is supplied incorrectly elsewhere. The PoW approach allows you to send money without having to trust anyone or any institution because the blockchain only cares about cryptographic signatures. This is the foundation of PoW.

Bitcoin is based on PoW. Listing 8-2 illustrates an example.

Listing 8-2. ProofOfWork.py

```
from hashlib import sha256
x = 10
y = 0   # We don't know what y should be yet...
while sha256(f'{x*y}'.encode()).hexdigest()[-1] != "0":
    y += 1
printf('The solution is y = {y}')

 @staticmethod
    def hash(block: Dict[str, Any]) -> str:
        """

        Creates a SHA-256 hash of a Block
        :param block: Block
        """

        # We must make sure that the Dictionary is Ordered, or we'll have
          inconsistent hashes
        block_string = json.dumps(block, sort_keys=True).encode()
        return hashlib.sha256(block_string).hexdigest()

        def proof_of_work(self, last_proof: int) -> int:
    """

        Simple Proof of Work Algorithm:
         - Find a number 0' such that hash(00') contains leading 4 zeroes,
           where 0 is the previous 0'
         - 0 is the previous proof, and 0' is the new proof
    """
```

```python
    proof = 0
    while self.valid_proof(last_proof, proof) is False:
        proof += 1

    return proof

@staticmethod
def valid_proof(last_proof: int, proof: int) -> bool:
    """

    Validates the Proof
    :param last_proof: Previous Proof
    :param proof: Current Proof
    :return: True if correct, False if not.
    """

    guess = f'{last_proof}{proof}'.encode()
    guess_hash = hashlib.sha256(guess).hexdigest()
    return guess_hash[:4] == "0000"
```

8.3.2 Step 2: Create an API Endpoint for Blockchain

Place the code shown in Listing 8-3 at the end of your Python file. Your file will then be an API endpoint thanks to this code. This will enable you to use Postman to transmit and receive requests in your blockchain.

Listing 8-3. Apiendpoint.py

```python
class Blockchain(object):

# Instantiate our Node
app = Flask(__name__)

# Generate a globally unique address for this node
node_identifier = str(uuid4()).replace('-', '')

# Instantiate the Blockchain
blockchain = Blockchain()
```

```
@app.route('/mine', methods=['GET'])
def mine():
    return "We'll mine a new Block"

@app.route('/transactions/new', methods=['POST'])
def new_transaction():
    return "We'll add a new transaction"

@app.route('/chain', methods=['GET'])
def full_chain():
    response = {
        'chain': blockchain.chain,
        'length': len(blockchain.chain),
    }
    return jsonify(response), 200

if __name__ == '__main__':
    app.run(host='0.0.0.0', port=5000)

@app.route('/transactions/new', methods=['POST'])
def new_transaction():
    values = request.get_json()

    # Check that the required fields are in the POST'ed data
    required = ['sender', 'recipient', 'amount']
    if not all(k in values for k in required):
        return 'Missing values', 400

    # Create a new Transaction
    index = blockchain.new_transaction(values['sender'],
    values['recipient'], values['amount'])

    response = {'message': f'Transaction will be added to Block {index}'}
    return jsonify(response), 201
```

8.3.3 Step 3: Create a Blockchain Miner

The code shown in Listing 8-4 will establish a miner for your server that will mine transactions and add them to the blockchain block. Use this code with the help of your IDE (Eclipse or PyCharm).

Listing 8-4. Miner.py

```python
@app.route('/mine', methods=['GET'])
def mine():

    last_block = blockchain.last_block
    last_proof = last_block['proof']
    proof = blockchain.proof_of_work(last_proof)

    blockchain.new_transaction(
        sender="0",
        recipient=node_identifier,
        amount=1,
    )

    block = blockchain.new_block(proof=proof, previous_hash=0)

    response = {
        'message': "New Block Forged",
        'index': block['index'],
        'transactions': block['transactions'],
        'proof': block['proof'],

    }
    return jsonify(response), 200
```

8.3.4 Step 4: Run Your Blockchain Project

Make sure that the server is up by using the following IP and port address:

http://127.0.0.1:5000/

(To exit, press Ctrl+C.) Now launch Postman and look for the search bar at the top of the screen. Make sure the GET button is selected to the left of it.

Then type this address into the address bar:

http://127.0.0.1:5000/mine

8.4 Review Questions

1. "An orphan block is produced only when a 51% attack succeeds."
   Is this statement correct or incorrect?

2. What does a ledger in blockchain do?

   a. Identifies the owners.

   b. Identifies the objects owned.

   c. Maps between the owner and the object.

   d. Identifies the owners' names.

3. Which of the following is the most common method of keeping
   bitcoins?

   a. The pocket

   b. The wallet

   c. The box

   d. The stack

4. What is the structure of a blockchain block?

   a. Transaction data

   b. Hash point

   c. Timestamp

   d. All of these

5. "In the case of Bitcoin, after 10 minutes, a new block is created
   with the most recent transactions." Is this statement correct or
   incorrect?

8.5 Review Answers

1. Answer: Incorrect, this is restricted to blockchain.

2. Answer: C, Maps between the owner and the object.

3. Answer: B, The wallet.

4. Answer: D, All of these.

5. Answer: Correct.

8.6 Summary

This chapter provided two examples that illustrate consensus algorithms. These examples are provided in the Python language. These examples also help illustrate the blockchain's PoW system. With the help of these examples, you can build your applications according to your needs.

When you think about blockchain technology, you need to understand distributed system management, because blockchain technology is widely used in distributed systems. The main purpose of this book is to implement blockchain in the distributed system. The next chapter covers time management in the distributed system.

CHAPTER 9

Real-Time Systems

A distributed real-time system (DRTS) is made up of self-contained computing nodes that are linked together by a real-time network. These nodes work together to achieve a common goal within predetermined time limits. For a variety of reasons, distributed real-time systems are required.

Any real-time computer control system must be able to measure the time between events in real time and react to a stimulus in a predetermined real-time interval. This chapter discusses some of the implications of including this real-time metric in real-time distributed systems.

The term "real-time system" refers to a system that is subjected to real-time constraints, i.e., the response must be guaranteed within a certain time restriction, or the system must satisfy a specific deadline. Examples include flight control systems, real-time monitoring systems, and so on.

9.1 Understanding Real-Time Systems

Real-time systems with timing constraints are characterized as either hard or soft. *Hard real-time systems* are incapable of missing a deadline. The implications of missing the deadline might be disastrous. If tardiness increases, the utility of a hard real-time system's result declines abruptly, and it may even become negative. Tardiness refers to how late a real-time system does a task in comparison to its deadline. One example of a hard real-time system is a flight controller system.

Soft real-time systems, on the other hand, can occasionally miss deadlines with a low enough chance to be acceptable. There are no negative consequences to missing the deadline. With increasing delay, the utility of a soft real-time system's result rapidly reduces. Telephone switches are an example of a soft real-time system.

J. T. George, *Introducing Blockchain Applications*, https://doi.org/10.1007/978-1-4842-7480-4_9

9.2 Real-Time System Reference Model

Three components characterize this reference model:

- **A workload model:** This identifies the applications that the system supports.

- **A resource model:** This describes the resources that the program has access to.

- **Algorithms:** They describe how the software application will use resources.

Real-time system terms include:

- **Job:** A tiny task that can be assigned to a processor and may or may not necessitate the use of resources.

- **Task:** A collection of related jobs that work together to offer system functionality.

- **A work's release time job:** The point at which the job is ready to be executed.

- **Job execution time:** This is the time it takes for a job to complete its execution.

- **Job deadline:** This is the deadline by which a job must be completed. There are two types of deadlines: absolute and relative deadlines. (A job's **relative deadline** is the maximum permissible response time. A job's **absolute deadline** is the sum of its relative deadline and its release time.)

- **Job response time:** This is the time from when the time a job is released to the time it is completed.

- **Active resources:** Another name for processors, these are required for the successful completion of a task. In order to execute and progress toward completion, a job requires one or more processors. Computers and transmission links are two examples.

- **Passive resources:** During the execution of a job, a resource may or may not be required. Memory and mutex are two examples. Also called resources. If two resources may be used interchangeably, they are identical; otherwise, they are heterogeneous.

Characteristic	Hard Real Time	Soft Real Time
Response Time	hard	soft
Peak-Loadd	perform.predictable	degraded
Error Detection	system	user
Safety	critical	non-critical
Redundancy	active	standby
Time Granularity	millisecond	second
Data Files	small/medium	large

Figure 9-1. *Hard real-time versus soft real-time systems*

Figure 9-1 depicts the key distinctions between hard and soft real-time systems. Hard real-time systems have response time requirements of milliseconds or less, which if not reached, can result in disaster. Soft real-time systems, on the other hand, have higher and less rigorous reaction times. Peak-load performance in a harsh real-time system must be expected and not breach specified deadlines. A degraded function at a rarely occurring peak load can be accepted in a soft real-time system. In all circumstances, a hard real-time system must remain synchronized with the state of the environment.

9.2.1 Fail-Safe vs. Fail-Operational Systems

If there is a good state in the environment that can be reached in the event of a system failure, the system is considered fail-safe. One example is a train signaling system.

High error-detection coverage is required in a fail-safe application. The application's failure safety is a feature. A system must be fail-operational if the application does not provide for the identification of a safe state, and such systems, such as a flight control systems on airplanes, must remain operational in the event of a failure.

9.2.2 Guaranteed Timeliness vs. Best Effort Systems

Even if there is a malfunction, the computer system must deliver a minimal level of service.

9.3 RT System Categorization

On the basis of the requirements from the outside, consider these categories:

- Soft real-time vs. hard real-time

- Fail-safe vs. fail-operational

- Timeliness guaranteed vs. best effort

- Adequacy of resources

- Time triggered vs. event triggered

If the temporal accuracy can be proved by analytical reasoning (within the stipulated load- and fault-hypotheses), a system implementation guarantees assured timeliness. If such an intellectual case for temporal correctness cannot be presented, a system implementation is best effort.

Even within the defined load- and fault assumptions, the temporal validation of best effort systems relies on probabilistic considerations. Guaranteed timeliness should be the foundation of hard real-time systems.

9.3.1 Resource Adequacy

A system's processing resources must be capable of managing the stated peak load and fault scenario if it is to deliver assured timeliness. There have been several applications in the past where resource adequacy was thought to be prohibitively expensive.

Because hardware costs are falling, implementing resource-appropriate designs is becoming more cost-effective. In challenging real-time applications, resource-adequate designs are the only option.

9.3.2 Predictability in Rare Event Situations

A rare event is a significant occurrence that seldomly occurs throughout the course of a system's lifespan, such as a burst pipe in a nuclear reactor. A uncommon event can result in a slew of associated service requests (e.g., an alarm shower).

The value of a system in a number of applications is dependent on predictable performance in uncommon event scenarios, such as a flight control system. Workload testing, in most circumstances, will not address the uncommon occurrence scenario.

9.3.3 The State and Event

Figure 9-2. *State event*

A *state* is a condition that lasts a specific amount of time in real time, such as a part of the timeline. An instantaneous occurrence is referred to as an *event*. See Figure 9-2.

State information describes the characteristics of states at the observation site (itself an event). The change in the qualities of the states immediately before and after the occurrence of the event, as well as an estimate of the moment in time when the event occurred, is provided by event information.

9.3.4 Time Triggered vs. Event Triggered Systems

The control signals in a real-time system are said to be event triggered (ET) if they are obtained purely from the occurrence of events, such as the completion of a task, the reception of a message, or the incidence of an external interrupt.

A real-time system is time triggered (TT) if the control indicators, such as message sending and receiving, are generated purely from the development of a (global) notion of time.

9.4 Temporal Requirements

For real-time systems, the data pieces that the operator sees must be accurate in terms of time. The greatest real-time gap between a stimulus and a reaction must be determined and limited. Even though it's a rare occurrence, the temporal behavior should also be predictable. See Figure 9-3.

How long is the observation: "The traffic light is green" temporarily accurate?

Figure 9-3. *Temporal parameters associated with real-time data*

9.5 Classification of the Scheduling Algorithm

9.5.1 Hard Real-Time and Soft Real-Time Scheduling

In hard RT systems, the deadline of critical tasks must be guaranteed in advance in all possible ways and with anticipatable scenarios. This requires careful design of the system resources. If you are designing a soft real-time system instead, you can accept a low-cost scheduler design.

9.5.2 Dynamic and Static Schedulers

A scheduler is called dynamic (online) if it bases its running decisions on the basis of current requests. Dynamic schedulers are therefore flexible and adapt with the evolution of the system. A scheduler is called static (pre-runtime) if decisions are made before its scheduler is running and cannot be changed. This requires a profound and complete knowledge of the task to be performed (maximum execution time, priorities, mutual exclusion constraints, deadlines, etc.). Such a scheduler has a low cost in phase execution precisely because no decision calculations are made.

9.5.3 Scheduler With/Without Preemption

In schedulers with preemption, a task can be interrupted following the request of a higher priority task. However, the preemption is authorized if some assertions are not violated (see mutual exclusion). In non-preemptive schedulers, tasks are not interrupted until their completion.

9.5.4 Static Scheduling

In static scheduling, the order of execution of tasks is calculated offline. Static scheduling is typical in time-triggered applications and with periodic tasks.

9.5.5 Dynamic Scheduling

Dynamic schedulers determine which task is to be executed when an event arrives, based on the current state of the system. The various dynamic scheduling algorithms differ according to the assumptions that are made.

9.5.6 Independent Task Scheduling

This category assumes that the tasks do not have any dependencies (e.g. mutual exclusion).

9.6 Review Questions

1. "A distributed real-time system (DRTS) is made up of self-contained computational nodes linked by a real-time network." Is this statement correct or incorrect?

2. Which of the following describes a hard real-time system?

   a. Can miss its deadline on a regular basis with a low possibility.

   b. Can miss its deadline from time to time, with a reasonable chance of doing so.

    c.   Can occasionally miss its deadline due to some unacceptably low probability,

    d.   Can miss its deadline from time to time, but with a low probability.

3.   Which of the following statements is correct for *state*?

    a.   A state is a condition that lasts for a certain amount of time in real time.

    b.   A state is a condition that lasts for a non-real time span.

    c.   A state is a condition that does not last for a period of time.

    d.   A state is an unpredictably changing condition that lasts for a period of time.

4.   Which of the following statements about an *event* is correct?

    a.   An event is a happening that occurs in a particular state.

    b.   An event is a one-time non-occurrence.

    c.   An event is a one-time occurrence.

    d.   All of these.

5.   Three pieces define a reference model:

    a.   Workload model

    b.   Resource model

    c.   Algorithm

Is this statement correct or incorrect?

9.7 Review Answers

1.   Answer: Correct. A distributed real-time system (DRTS) is made up of self-contained computational nodes linked by a real-time network and consists of autonomous computing nodes connected by a real-time network. The nodes in such a system cooperate to achieve a common goal within specified deadlines.

2. Answer: D, Can miss its deadline from time to time, but with a low probability.

3. Answer: A, A *state* is a condition that lasts for a certain amount of time in real time.

4. Answer: C, An *event* is a one-time occurrence.

5. Answer: Correct. The main parts of the RT system model are the workload model, the resource model, and algorithms.

9.8 Summary

This chapter explained the time management of distributed systems. In addition, soft real-time and hard real-time systems were discussed, which illustrate the reference models. In order to implement a distributed system, it is necessary to understand this time management system. Scheduling algorithms are also an important concept of distributed systems, so the next chapter explains dynamic and static scheduling algorithms in the distributed system.

CHAPTER 10

Scheduling in Real-Time Systems

The task state determines the milestone of a task in a process. The default states are as follows:

- The job has been received and is waiting to be accepted in the system.

- The task has been accepted by the allocated user (or system). Other users and systems cannot modify or complete the work since it is locked.

- The task has been completed.

- A user has been assigned to the job. (Manual tasks only.)

- The task attempted to generate a work order in the activation system, but was unsuccessful. (Activation tasks only.)

These conditions must be met and cannot be changed. To support your business processes, you can define extra states (user-defined states). You can set a task's state to suspended if it can't be completed on time.

In the absence of other operations, the processor executes a series of instructions until they are completed. A task is a sequence of instances (jobs).

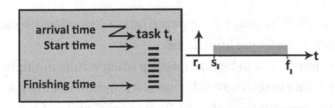

Figure 10-1. *State even*

185

© Joseph Thachil George 2022
J. T. George, *Introducing Blockchain Applications*, https://doi.org/10.1007/978-1-4842-7480-4_10

Jobs that are ready are kept in a queue known as the waiting list (QUEUE). The scheduling algorithm is a method for selecting a task to run on the CPU.

10.1 The Concept of Scheduling

The process is composed of the scheduling algorithm:

- **Preemptive:** Work can be briefly paused so that a more critical task can be completed.

- **Non-preemptive:** The task can't be interrupted. A schedule is a list of tasks allocated to the processor in a certain order to the processor. A processor's process is a set of tasks that have been allocated to them.

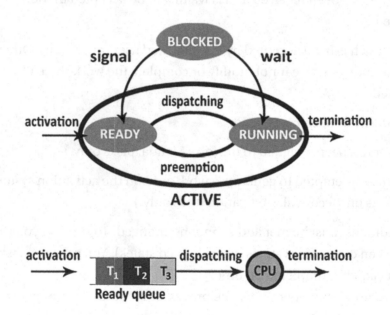

Figure 10-2. *State transition and ready queue*

Processes may need to be swapped or paged out to secondary memory in applications with severe real-time limitations.

An operating system is said to be *multitasking* when it runs multiple programs at the same time. It is important to distinguish between a program intended as a "container of instructions" and a program intended as an "in progress" entity. A running program is called a process (or task).

So while a *program* is a static entity that describes the actions to be performed, a *process* is a dynamic entity that represents the execution of those actions. The mechanism that the OS adopts to execute several processes "in parallel" (concurrent processes) is called *time sharing*.

It consists of assigning the CPU for a time slice called `time-slice`, which is set for each process. When that time expires, the execution of the process is suspended and the CPU is assigned to another process. This technique is called *preemptive multitasking*.

The most important problem with multitasking systems is the allocation of the resources required by the various processes. In fact, it may happen that several processes simultaneously request a specific single resource that cannot be shared (e.g. the printer). In this case, the process requestor is suspended immediately and the requesting process is placed in a wait queue. Only when the resource is released and no other process in the queue precedes it, can it acquire the resource and resume execution.

Another problem concerns access to peripherals. Because device I/O operations are extremely slow relative to processor speed, a process's request for an I/O operation causes the process to suspend until the operation is complete (the hardware mechanism at stake is obviously the interrupt).

A process can be in one of these three states:

- Running. The process has the CPU and is running (ready).

- The process was suspended because the time expired.

- Blocked (blocked, waiting, suspended). The process cannot advance because it needs a resource that is not yet available or because it is waiting for I/O.

Managing ready jobs is implemented by a set of queues, each with a defined priority. Each process is assigned a priority so that when the process goes to the ready state, it is placed in the queue with the corresponding priority.

The process that runs is the first in the queue. If there are no jobs waiting in it, the first job in the queue is executed, and so on.

10.2 Types of Constraints

A transition restriction prevents the data from entering an impossible state as a result of a prior state. For example, a person should not be able to switch from being "married" to "single, never married." "Divorced," "widowed," or "dead" are the only allowed states after "married."

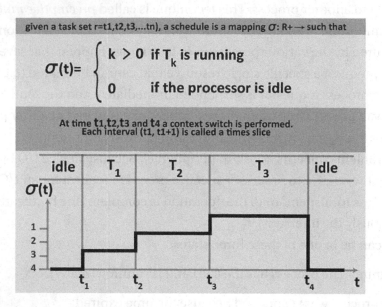

Figure 10-3. *Task processor*

A transitional constraint is a characteristic that governs every legitimate transition from one state of the model to its successor state in the formal model of information security. It can be thought of as a supplement to state criteria, which applies to states as a whole but has no influence on transitions between them.

Once its destination address has been written to secondary storage and it is not waiting for a particular task, the process is executable and switchable. If a process is waiting for a task, it is put to sleep and its whole address space is written to secondary storage.

Note the following about constraints:

- Types include jitter, trigger, completeness, and deadline.

- They can be explicit (included in the system activities specification) or implicit (not included in the system activities specification).

- They impose a logical order on the execution limits of resources.

- They ensure that access to mutually exclusive resources is synchronized.

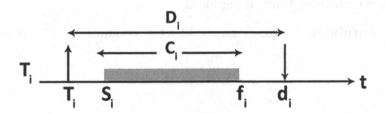

Figure 10-4. *Real-time tasks*

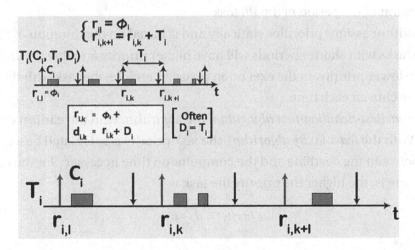

Figure 10-5. *Tasks activation*

10.2.1 Independent Task Scheduling Constraints

This category assumes that the tasks do not have any dependencies (e.g. mutual exclusion).

The *rate monotonic algorithm* is a dynamic algorithm with preemption based on static priorities with the following assumptions:

1. Requests for all tasks belonging to a specific task set for which you have hard real-time constraints are periodic.

2. All tasks are independent (absence of mutual exclusion or dependencies).

3. The expiration of each task (Ti) corresponds with the duration of its period (pi).

4. You know a priori the maximum computation time for each task.

5. Context switching times are ignored.

6. The sum of the utilization factors of the n tasks is limited at the top by:

$$\mu = \sum \frac{c_i}{p_i} \leq n\left(2^{\frac{1}{n}} - 1\right)$$

Where:

c_i = Computation time of the i*th* task

p_i = Duration of the period of the i*th* task

The algorithm assigns priorities statically and is based on the duration of the task period. The tasks with shorter periods will have higher priority and those with longer periods have lower priority. In the execution phase, therefore, the task with the shortest period will be chosen each time.

With the *earliest-deadline-first algorithm,* the algorithm with the earliest expiration is selected. With the *least-laxity algorithm,* the task priority is calculated based on the difference between the deadline and the computation time necessary for the task. The lower this value is, the higher the priority the task is

$$laxity_i = d_i - c_i$$

10.2.2 Scheduling Dependent Tasks

In this category, which is closer to reality and therefore more interesting, we assume that the tasks have dependencies (e.g. mutual exclusion).

The *Kernelized Monitor algorithm,* proposed by Mok [2], allocates the processor for non-interruptible time q and assumes that a critical section is executable within the time limit. The earliest policy is used for scheduling deadlines first.

The scheduling analysis done in this protocol requires the use of upper bounds on the times of execution of all the critical sections that appear in the tasks. In fact, the quantity must be calibrated on the longest executable critical section. Since these upper bounds can be too pessimistic, using the protocol kernelized monitor can lead to low processor utilization.

The *Priority Ceiling Protocol* is used to schedule a periodic set of tasks that have exclusive access to one or multiple common resources protected by traffic lights.

This protocol was created by Sha, Rajkmar, and Lehocky in 1990 to solve the problem of *priority inversion*. This arises when a high priority job has to wait for a higher priority job to be executed, typically due to other resources being used by running tasks.

If there are three tasks (T1, T2, and T3) with priority p1> p2> p3, all three use the resource R and the algorithm for scheduling the monotonic rate type.

Suppose that T1 and T3 need to access the resource to which the mutex S is associated.

If T3 starts processing and locks (S) before T1 starts, then T1 will be locked for an undefined time, that is, until T3 it will not do an unlock (S), freeing the resource S. In fact, T1 cannot continue execution without the resource S held by T3. In this case, T1 is penalized in favor of T3 in spite of the order of priorities p1> p3.

If, before T3 unlocks (S), T2 starts, then T3 will be suspended to allow T2 to be processed under the priorities p2> p3. In this case, T1 will have to wait for T2 to stop being processed. Indeed, T1 is blocked on T3, which in turn is blocked on T2 in spite of the order of priorities p1> p2.

The proposed algorithm is based on the following points:

- A task is allowed to enter the critical section only if its priority is higher than the task that is currently locking the resource.

- When it has finished using the critical section, it releases it, giving it the previous priority.

10.3 Review Questions and Answers

Try these review questions as a test of knowledge.

10.3.1 Review Questions

1. "A task is a set of events." Is this statement correct or incorrect?

2. What is scheduling ?

    a. Preventive: When a current task can be put on hold in order to finish an even more important task.

    b. Preventive: When a running task can be briefly paused in order to complete a more critical task.

    c.   Preemptive: When the currently executing process can be used to temporarily execute another task.

    d.   Preventive: When an ongoing task can be briefly paused to complete a less critical task.

3.   Which of the following task statements is correct?

    a.   Depending on the operating system, a task can be a process or a thread.

    b.   The job must be a program or a thread, depending on the operating system.

    c.   A task might be a process or a thread, depending on the version.

    d.   None of the preceding.

4.   Which of the following claims regarding events are true?

    a.   If the current task can't be paused until it's finished, it's non-preemptive. A schedule is a list of tasks that the processor has been allocated.

    b.   Non-preemptive is not whether a job in progress can be paused until it is completed. A schedule is a list of tasks that the processor has been allocated.

    c.   Non-preemptive is when the current task can't be halted until it's completed. A timetable is a set of responsibilities assigned to a specific event.

    d.   All of these are true.

5.   "A task is a set of instructions that is continually executed by the processor in the absence of other activities." Is this statement correct?

10.3.2 Answers

1. Answer: Incorrect, a task is a series of events.

2. Answer: B, preventive scheduling is when a running task can be briefly paused in order to complete a more critical task.

3. Answer: C, a task might be a process or a thread, depending on the version.

4. Answer: A, If the current task can't be paused until it's finished, it's non-preemptive. A schedule is a list of tasks that the processor has been allocated.

5. Answer: Incorrect, a task is a set of instructions that the processor executes in the absence of other operations until it is completed.

10.4 Summary

This chapter explained how scheduling works in real-time systems. Scheduling homogeneous processes arises when several processes with the same requests and time constraints must be efficiently served by the scheduling policy. For example, such a situation arises in a video server that must support the display of a fixed number of videos all characterized by the same frame rate, video resolution, data transmission frequency, etc.

In this situation, a simple but effective scheduling policy is round-robin. In fact, all processes are equally important; they have the same amount of work to do and crash when they have finished processing the current frame. The scheduling algorithm can be optimized by adding a timing mechanism to ensure that each process runs at the correct frequency. The simple precedent model rarely occurs in practice. A more realistic model provides for the presence of multiple processes competing for CPU use, each with its own workload and deadlines.

The next chapter focuses on modeling and discusses how model-based engineering helps in the distributed system. For the practical implementation of distributed systems, the model's guided engineering is an important concept.

## CHAPTER 11

Engineering Based on Models

Engineering-based models is an application development technique that prioritizes the creation of models or abstractions that are more closely related to specific domain notions than computational or algorithmic principles. This technique boosts productivity by optimizing system compatibility, simplifies the design process, and fosters individual and team communication and collaboration on the system.

Models allow technical and non-technical stakeholders to have the same vision and understanding, as well as promote and encourage interaction between them. Models also help with project planning by providing a clearer view of the system to be built and enabling for managing projects based on objective criteria.

11.1 Model-Driven Approach to Blockchain

In recent years, the notion of blockchain has acquired great traction in practice and research, as it offers a practical solution to the problems of anonymity and accountability in dispersed situations involving numerous parties that must share data and cooperate securely. However, the influence of business core network and configuration on successfully using blockchain technology remains largely unknown to date. This book offers a model-driven method that captures the features of current blockchain-driven business networks by combining an ontology with a layer model.

The levels help describe such networks in detail. The Blockchain Business Network Ontology (BBO) is also introduced, which formalizes the ideas and characteristics of the various components of a blockchain network. I demonstrate the usefulness of this work by assessing and applying it to a real-world blockchain use case.

To develop the blockchain business model, you need to have the approach of *model-driven engineering*.

© Joseph Thachil George 2022
J. T. George, *Introducing Blockchain Applications*, https://doi.org/10.1007/978-1-4842-7480-4_11

11.2 Model-Driven Development

By bringing together diverse viewpoints with varied degrees of abstraction, a model-based method aids in the understanding of a system. "A client is able to build on a model that includes a system's features and characteristics, which can then be used to completely rebuild the system in this context." Following a model-driven architecture or design helps in a variety of ways to comprehend and describe a system.[1]

- The links between the various parts, as well as their descriptions, contribute to a broad knowledge of the system, while also assisting in the development of scalable solutions, because a model is built on a well-defined nomenclature and taxonomy.

- To make the development of a system easier, an architectural frame may be used to mix and modify multiple models and explanatory levels.

- Automat may be used for a group of formalized metamodels, which can then be merged and converted into models with a greater degree of information.

- Technical standards are a necessary basis for expanding model-based effort acceptability and implementation.

11.2.1 The Blockchain Layer Model

Creating various models that specifically address diverse elements of a larger system aids in the development of a thorough knowledge of that system or phenomena. "Various levels of abstraction may be examined using these models, which can then be overlaid onto each other or whose information transmitted to other levels in order to comprehend the full scope of a concept."[1]

As a result, three fundamental layers (see Figure 11-1) have been defined to make it easier to describe blockchain-driven networks in a sound and comprehensive manner. These layers include everything from a business model perspective to a code-based viewpoint. All of these levels are essential because we anticipate blockchain technology to have a unique impact on each of them.

---

[1] Stefan Seebacher and Maria Maleshkova, Hawaii International Conference on System Sciences, 2018, "A Model-driven Approach for the Description of Blockchain Business Networks"

Because the layers are interrelated, the technological implementation has an impact on the network composition, which has an effect on the business model. Figure 11-1 is an example of layered blockchain.

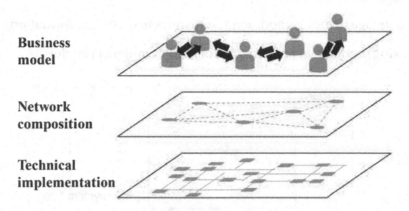

Figure 11-1. *Blockchain layers*

In order to create a model-driven method for defining blockchain transactions and blocks layers, you'll see how to build on these foundations with the help of models and metamodels.

11.2.2 Models and Metamodels

This section covers the fundamental ideas that underpin MDE, such as system, model, metamodel, as well as their relationships.

The *system* is defined in the context of MDE as "a general notion for denoting a software application, software platform, or other software artefact." [2] A system can also be built up of various subsystems, as illustrated in Figure 11-2, and it can interact with other systems. (Systems may interact with other systems.)

A model is an abstraction of phenomena in the real world: a metamodel is a further abstraction, which highlights properties of the model itself. A model conforms to its metamodel in the same way that a computer program conforms to the grammar of the programming language in which it is written.

[2] Rodrigues da Silva, Alberto. "Model-driven engineering: A survey supported by the unified conceptual model," Computer Languages Systems & Structures, 2015.

Domains where metamodels are used:

- A schema for semantic data that needs to be exchanged or stored

- A language that supports a particular method or process

- A language to express additional semantics to existing information

The following sections cover the details of models and metamodels.

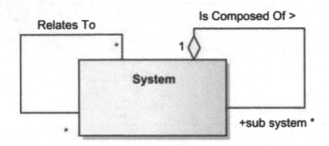

Figure 11-2. *System definition*

11.2.3 The Model

A *model* depicts a system that might or might not exist today or in the future. It's a term of reference considered valid as an example or prototype and worthy of imitation.

A model is worth considering since it includes the following details:

- A model can be a collection of assertions about the device/system which goes into the investigation.

- A model is the simplest version of a system that was formed with a specific goal in mind, and it should be capable of answering queries in place of the actual system.

- A model is a simplified edition of a system that was formed with a particular objective in mind, and it can reply to the queries for the real program.

A model, on the other hand, is a system in and of itself, with its own identity, complexity, constituents, linkages, and so on.

In particular, while considering a model of a model, you must keep in mind that one of them serves as a model of a model and, as a result, is a *system*. In summary, "model" is a system that helps describe and provide answers to the system under study without having to look at it directly, as shown in Figure 11-3.

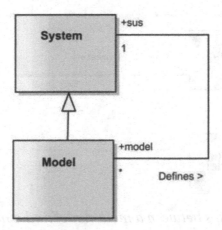

Figure 11-3. *Relationships between a model and a system*

There is also a relationship between the model and the system. With the help of models, you can design a system. By looking at models, you can understand how the system works. On the other hand, you can make a number of models based on the system architecture. That is the reason you can say that a model is a simplified edition of a system, and it is formed with a particular goal in the mind.[1]

11.2.4 The Metamodel

A *metamodel* is a type of model that specifies the architecture of a modeling language, based on prior research. However, the following facts must be understood from Figure 11-4.

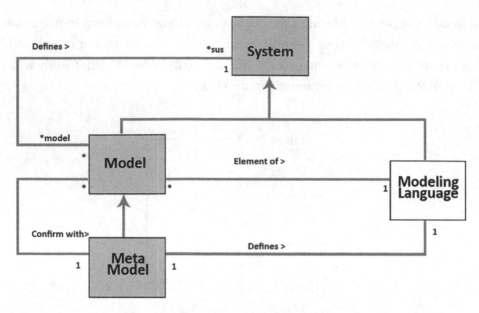

Figure 11-4. *Relationships between a metamodel and a model*

We can say that the modeling language will be a set of models, as defined by the relationship *Element Of* between *model* and *modeling language* (or a model is an element of a modeling language).

We can also say that this approach draws its rules from the distinction between the concept of a model and that of a metamodel.

A UML model is a representation that captures the important aspects of everything you want to model, from a certain point of view and under certain limitations. A model is structured in diagrams (UML diagrams), which represent the graphic means of expression. The model consists of three basic parts:

- **Classifiers:** They describe a set of objects. An object is an individual entity with a state and relationships with other objects.

- **Events (Events):** They describe a set of possible occurrences. An occurrence is something that happens and has consequences within the system.

- **Actions (Behaviors)**: They describe a set of possible executions. An execution represents the fulfillment of an algorithm in accordance with a set of rules.[3]

UML diagrams, on the other hand, contain graphic elements that represent elements of the model. For example, two associated classes defined within a package diagram are two types of classifiers and are represented by two rectangular symbols and a link representing the association symbol.

11.3 Building the Metamodel and Model

How to build the first metamodel is a well-known and recurrent metamodel problem. The official OMG specification describes the semantics of UML by breaking down the architecture in the package. Within each package, the elements of the model are defined in the following terms in a semiformal way:

- **Abstract-syntax:** Presented, through class diagrams expressed with the UML notation, the UML metamodel, its concepts (i.e. meta-classes), and its relationships and constraints. To these are added parts of text written in natural language (English).

- **Connotation:** Provided in natural language, it includes the description of elements that make up the UML metamodel and their relationships.

- **Formedness rules:** The rules and constraints to define models that are valid. These are expressed using both a formal language, OCL, and natural language.

---

[3] Minoli, . "Business Process Modeling", Enterprise Architecture A to Z Frameworks Business Process Modeling SOA and Infrastructure Technology, 2008.

The complexity of the UML metamodel is managed by organizing it into three packages: Foundation, Behavioral Elements, and Model Management. The first two are further decomposed into packages, each of which contains semantically related elements. Here is a brief description of each package:

- **Behavioral Elements:** This package specifies the structure needed to define the dynamic behaviors of a model. It consists of five subpackages.

- **Foundation:** This package represents the language infrastructure that specifies the structure static modeling. It is divided into three subpackages.

- **Model Management:** This package defines, among others, the model, package and subsystem necessary to organize different models and to group together elements that have features in common.

11.4 A Modeling Language's Category

According to professionals, there are some other ways you can define modeling languages. They say a modeling language may be divided into two types: specific and domain-specific. They are differentiated by a higher number of generic constructs, which facilitates their application in a variety of areas.

Because they provide comprehensive collection of structures and marking for defining and explaining software applications based on the object-oriented paradigm, or any type of system as defined by the system engineering discipline, UML and SysML are popular instances of specific and domain specific.[1]

DSLs, on the other hand, typically use a smaller set of structures or ideas that are more directly connected to the application area. Because a DSL is defined using domain concepts, it is typically easier to understand, grasp, validate, and interact with, facilitating collaboration between developers and domain specialists. Some argue that DSLs can improve productivity, dependability, reliability, and portability.[1]

Yet, there are also drawbacks to adopting a DSL, such as the expense of learning, creating, and sustaining a contemporary language, as well as the production tools needed to use it.

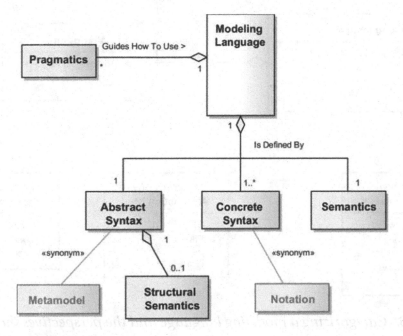

Figure 11-5. *Modeling language*

Others, argue that, because of the high quality and complexity of today's language workstations, tool support is no longer a significant obstacle.

Furthermore, findings suggest that software language engineers would not even evaluate their native languages, implying that additional study in the subject of software language processes, especially in the development of design, implementation, and assessment, is necessary.[1]

As illustrated in Figure 11-6, a modeling language may be classified by its software architecture attributes and organized by one or more views.

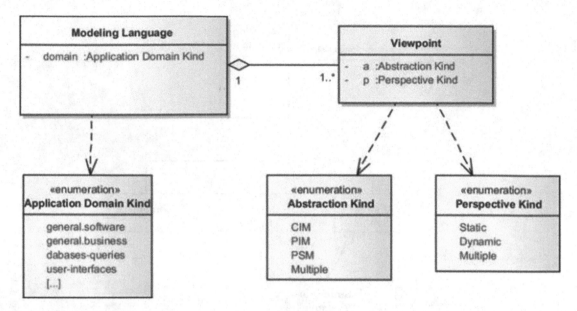

Figure 11-6. *Categorizing a modeling language and the perspectives that go with it*

11.5 Designing a Metamodel for CPSs

CPSs are complicated systems that monitor and regulate the physical environment while also assisting humans in their duties.

CPS are networked hybrid systems that combine software and hardware. As programmers, engineers, and scientists collaborate to build and implement such systems, they run into obstacles. Experts from many fields must comprehend the system in order to collaborate, regardless of their field.

We suggest a cyber-physical systems metamodel and an educational research method that programmers, engineers, and scientists can use, reuse, and modify for new applications of cyber-physical systems.

Data scientists and programmers utilize this metamodel to build a cyber-physical system that provides M1 system models that are understandable across fields. The metamodel includes both smart things and humans, which are often present in any cyber-physical system's design. It uses a composite architecture to enable the creation of cyber-physical systems with smart elements like leaf nodes.

11.6 CPS Metamodel Examples

Consider the following examples:

- **Transportation**: System for air traffic control and transportation management.

- **Health, medical:** Medical gadgets, health monitoring systems, telerobotic surgical-systems.

- **Manufacturing**: Automobiles, airplanes, factory automation systems, chemical process tracking, autonomous robotic spaces, and industry networks are all examples of industrial networks.

- **Environmental**: Farming, environmental, and geological systems are all examples of environmental science systems.

- **Aerospace**: Space exploration systems.

- **Buildings:** Assistive living and smart places in everyday life.

- **Public environment**: Intelligent water supply networks and emergency management.

- **Cyber-physical public systems**: These are CPSs that also consider human understanding, technological capabilities, and sociocultural factors.

The *meta-object facility* is introduced in the following section, backed by a base-metamodel for cyber-physical systems.

11.6.1 Meta-Object Facility

The meta-object facility is a standard for model-driven engineering of the Object Management Group. This comes from the UML language; Object Management Group needed a metamodeling architecture to define UML.[4]

It uses object-modeling methods to define any form of metadata. Even though it is usually associated with UML, it is independent from it.

---

[4]https://en.wikipedia.org/wiki/Meta-Object_Facility

To specify any type of metadata, MOF uses object modeling techniques. Even though it is sometimes confused with UML, it is not the same thing.

We use the stereotype mechanism of UML to create and expand intelligent objects on the CPS metamodel. M1-defined classes can be extended and reused utilizing the metamodel as a basis. A system is represented by these classes. The top-level design of an application on M1 is referred to as top-level design.

A *system-of-systems* (SoS) is a combination of a finite set of independent and operable constituent systems that are networked together for a length of time in order to achieve a higher purpose. An SoS integrates CSs.

System-of-Systems (SoS

Figure 11-7. *A categorization of a modeling language and the perspectives that go with it*

A *constituent system* includes a computer network (the cybersystem), a controlled item (the physical system), and perhaps human interaction.

An SoS could be:

- **Directed SoS:** An SoS having a centralized purpose and ownership of all CSs. A collection of control systems in an unmanned rocket is an example.

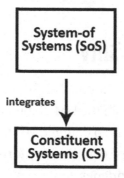

Figure 11-8. *An SoS integrates a CS*

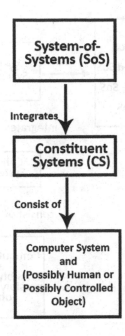

Figure 11-9. *An SoS*

- **Recognized SoS:** CSs are owned independently, but there are cooperative agreements among the owners to achieve a common goal.

- **Collaboration SoS:** Volunteer interactions among independent CSs with the objective of achieving a goal that benefits the individual CS.

- **Virtual SoS:** Core alignment and lack of a primary purpose.

Each CS has an interface based on which services are made available to other CSs, such as Reliable Interface (RUI), which serves as a CS's interface via which the CS's services are made available to other CSs.

RUIs are made up of the following components:

- Relied Upon Message Interface (RUMI)

- Relied Upon Physical Interface (RUPI)

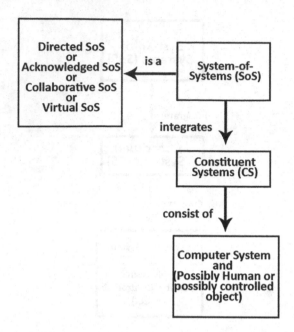

Figure 11-10. *SOS and CS*

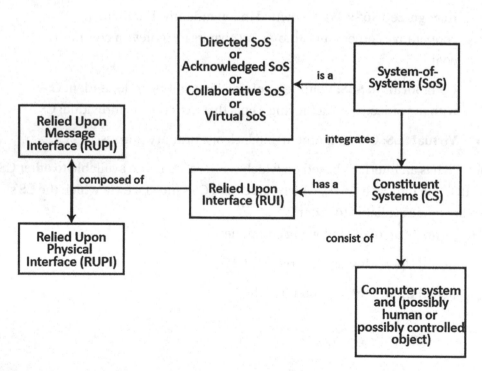

Figure 11-11. *RUMI and RUPI*

11.7 Review Questions

1. "Model-driven engineering is a software development approach that emphasizes the creation of models or abstractions that are closer to specific domain notions than computational or algebraic concepts." Is this statement correct or incorrect?

2. The modeling language is established by which of the following?

    a. By a collection of all possible models that correspond to the metamodel in issue, which is referred to as a metamodel.

    b. By a metamodel, which is a collection of models that adhere to the metamodel in question.

    c. By the metamodel, which is a collection of all feasible models that adhere to a certain metastate.

    d. None of the above.

3. Which of the following statements is correct for *event*?

    a. Virtual SoS is characterized by the absence of a core goal and central alignment.

    b. Virtual SoS has a lack of purpose and central alignment.

    c. Virtual SoS is characterized by a lack of focus and alignment.

    d. All of these.

4. "Metamodels include UML and the Common Warehouse metamodel." Is this statement correct or incorrect?

11.8 Review Answers

1. Answer: Correct, Model-driven engineering is a software development methodology that focuses on the construction of models or abstractions that are more closely related to specific domain concepts than computational or algebraic concepts.

2. Answer: A, A collection of all possible models that correspond to the metamodel in issue is referred to as a metamodel.

3. Answer: A, A virtual SoS is characterized by the absence of a core goal and central alignment.

4. Answer: Correct, UML and the Common Warehouse Metamodel are examples of metamodels.

11.9 Summary

Ever since humans started using computers, researchers have worked to raise the level of abstraction. Model-driven engineering (MDE) is the natural continuation of this trend, as well as a promising approach to address complexity of platforms and the inability of third-generation languages to alleviate this complexity and express dominance concepts effectively.

The Model-Driven Engineering (MDE) is at the top of the hierarchy and therefore the most abstract. It is recognized as a software engineering paradigm and considers models not only as supporting documentation, but also as a central focus of development in any engineering discipline and application domain. Model-Driven Development (MDD) is slightly lower in the hierarchy than MDE. This approach focuses on the disciplines of analysis, design, implementation, and requirements.

The concrete MDD approaches tend to define modeling languages to specify the system under study at different levels of abstraction. Model-Based Testing (MBT) is focused on the automation of the testing discipline. Testing models are used to represent the desired behavior of the system under study. Model-Driven Architecture (MDA) is an approach proposed by OMG and is mainly focused on the definition of models and their transformations.

To create an effective block chain application, systems must first be modeled. The previously-mentioned technique must be included when modeling systems. When you apply blockchain technology in the distributed system, as part of the modeling of distributed systems, you also need to model the blockchain layers in order to have a clear picture of the system architecture and systems of systems (SoS) functionality. All these models can be done with the help of the BLOCKLY 4SOS modeling technique.

As a part of model driven engineering, you need to consider BLOCKLY 4SOS to model SOS systems. The next chapter explains the BLOCKLY 4SOS.

CHAPTER 12

BLOCKLY 4SOS

BLOCKLY is a library that allows you to make block programming apps. Even if users do not really know a programming language, block programming allows them to construct scripts and programs using graphic blocks. In a drag-and-drop editor, BLOCKLY includes all you need to define and render blocks. Each block represents a single line of code that may be stacked and converted into code with ease. It can be used to let users personalize elements of the app and add actions to them.

12.1 SOS Modeling

While using this tool, it generates a standard SoS-block called ex-abundant block, to illustrate. The left-side toolbox contains all of the blocks required to build an SoS design. This conceptual model will assist the SoS designer. Furthermore, every exported block in BLOCKLY is connected to a perspective block, so all blocks connected to the communication point of view may be found under the Toolkit's Communication category.

Users must click and drag blocks from the flyout or toolbox to generate new blocks in BLOCKLY. An API for BLOCKLY was designed with the goal of improving usability and accuracy. The Field Dropdown() provides a list of appropriate blocks that may be linked to a certain block, making it easy for the users to build blocks.

After adding a Technique block, the tool displays how to add the other appropriate blocks: fault predicting, failure prevention, failure elimination, and failure tolerance. The Technique block is an abstraction block in profile, and the four blocks above inherit it.

A block can have three phases, as shown:

- A compressed view

- A partially compressed view

- An uncompressed view

211

© Joseph Thachil George 2022
J. T. George, *Introducing Blockchain Applications*, https://doi.org/10.1007/978-1-4842-7480-4_12

By decreasing the amount of blocks on the screen, a compressed display enables the user to see the current editing block (see Figure 12-1). The person can choose to just view the stated attributes since a partially-collapsed block only reveals the non-empty features of a block. Use Full View/Uncompressed View to examine all of a block's attributes. The user may flip between the three viewpoints by clicking on the block twice. See Figure 12-2.

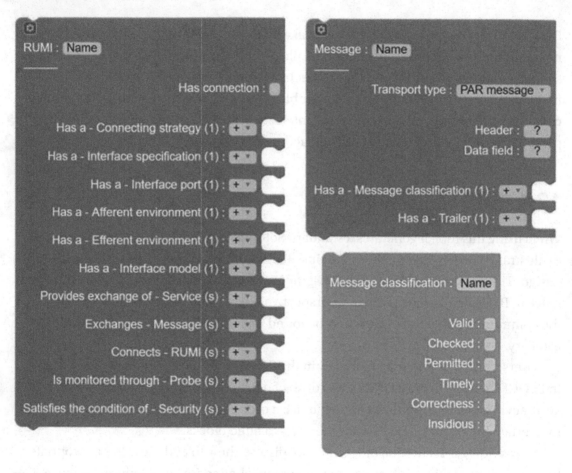

Figure 12-1. *SysML imported to BLOCKLY*

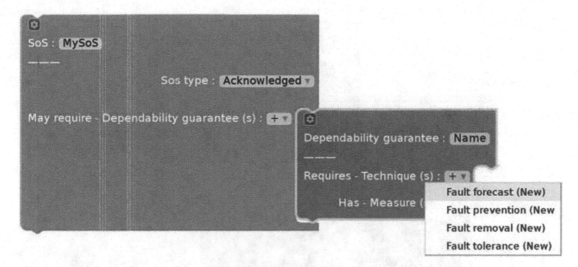

Figure 12-2. *Using a dropdown menu, the users can add blocks*

In addition, as illustrated in Figures 12-3 and 12-4, characteristics linked to selected building blocks can be shown for each block. This is accomplished by placing a mutator button on the upper-left side of each block.

The supporting facility uses a freely accessible open source plug-in called Type-Indicator 5 to create an intuitive modeling environment. This plugin highlights all the blocks that are compatible (in yellow) with the current block as it is being moved (block cs4).

The traceability of requirements must be examined and managed in an SoS project, therefore requirements management is critical. The needs may be broken down into categories based on points of view and building components, such as architecture, communication, and reliability.

As a result, full traceability is provided since each building block satisfies the collection of criteria that it fulfills, and each building block of requirements controls the collection of building blocks that maintains it. To make the design more obvious, BLOCKLY allows you to add comments to blocks.

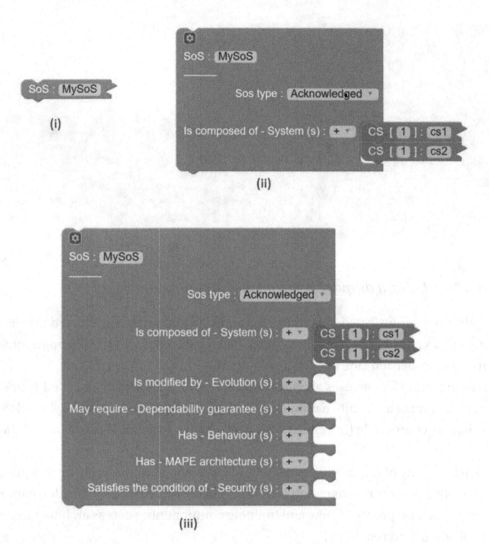

Figure 12-3. *A block can be viewed in three different ways: collapsed, partially collapsed, and uncollapsed*

An example of constraint usage is shown in Figure 12-4. Constraints can be utilized to find unusual twists that could be prone to an emerging stage in SoS. You can get these situations by using proper query in the models. When working with big models, it might be difficult to see the whole SoS, necessitating the use of specialized views.

Instead of using lines to display connection between blocks, BLOCKLY uses *collapse* methods to disguise the complexity of an SoS model. The model query is used to look for blocks that meet a set of requirements.

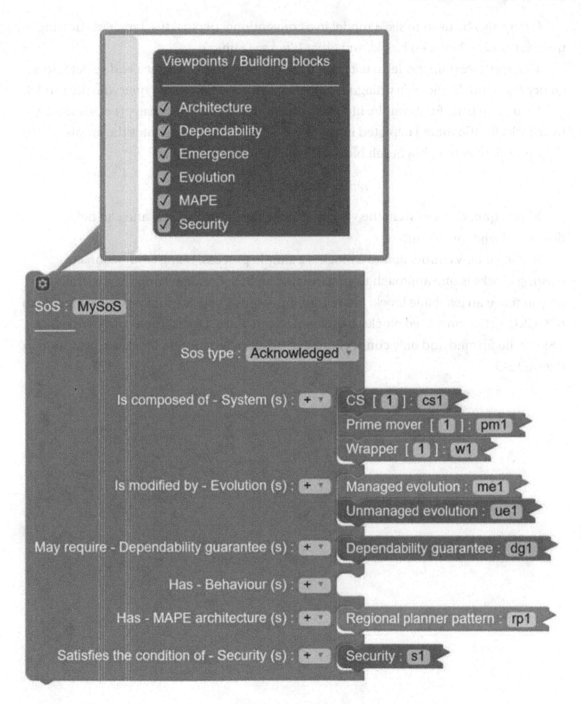

Figure 12-4. *A block's building-blocks could be activated or disabled*

It may also be used to see a model in a conventional perspective (such as showing the relationship between blocks and other blocks via lines).

To query a certain model, a user can right-click the working space and select Show Query Diagram. In the query diagram, the user can create filters for querying the model.[1]

Returning true, for example, indicates that no filtration is necessary (i.e., shows all the blocks for the model depicted in Figure 12-5). This query generates the graph in Figure 12-5, which highlights all blocks of type RUMI using the filter:[1]

$$return\ b.\ of\ type == RUMI$$

Model querying assists in the visualization of custom SoS views and can help discover design problems.

Adding a new connection to a block is a simple process. Using connections to existing blocks is one approach to constructing an SoS. Creating connections/links can let you reuse an available block, but it's not the same as copying and pasting a block into BLOCKLY. The connected blocks are referenced via links. For example, on a workspace, CSs can be formed and only connections can be joined to the SoS block, as illustrated in Figure 12-5.

---

[1] lnk.springer.com

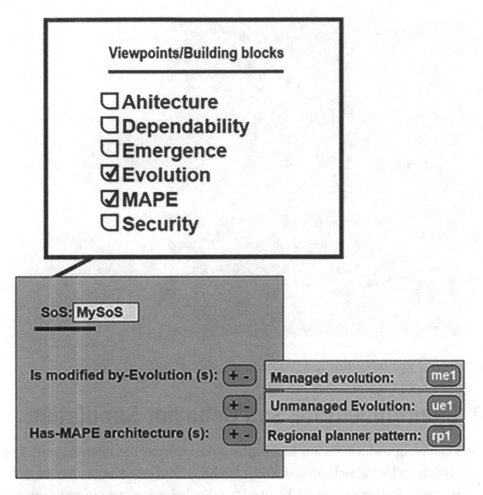

Figure 12-5. *Filtered view of SoS*

The modular SoS grouping enables the modularization of the design by allowing suitable blocks to be grouped together. For example, as illustrated in Figure 12-6, all CSs can be clustered together. The group block aids in the division of the model into useful groups.

Whenever a group's block is mentioned, the group name is also included to distinguish it from other blocks with similar titles.

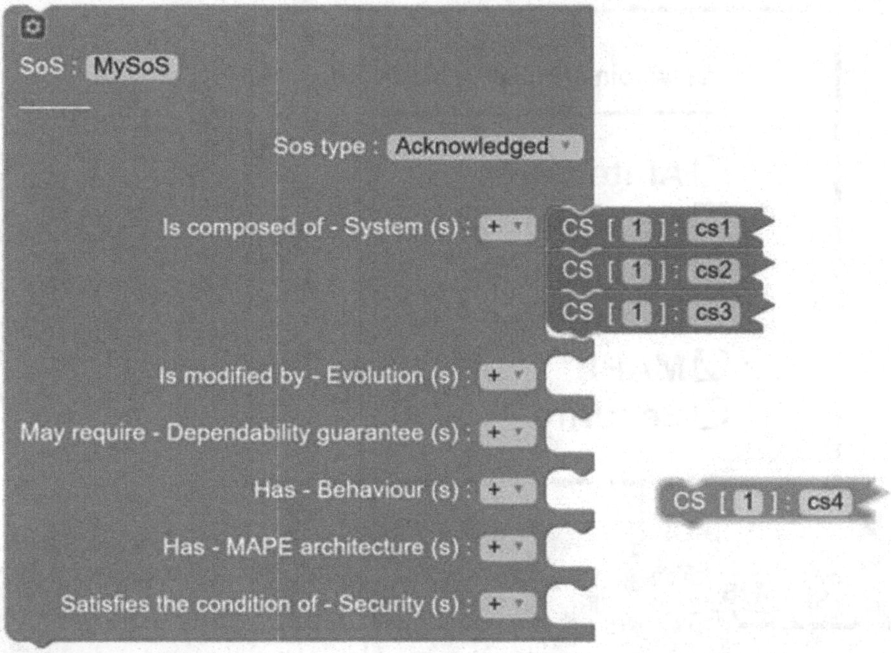

Figure 12-6. *Type Indicator cs4 plug-ins are shown with in yellow*

12.2 Environment for SoS Behavior Simulation

Behaviors can be introduced to any block after a static model has been created. The user can add a behavior by right-clicking the affected block and selecting Add Behavior. The Python programming language may be used to write behaviors, which represents the code that will be performed throughout the simulation (as seen in Figure 12-7).

The titles of the init, start, and run functions can be specified, and they are performed during startup, block startup, and simulation execution, respectively. A service block's run function has a specific understanding and is presented as a TCP-IP server.[1]

All the behavior code created for all the blocks is merged into a single file during code generation. XML and Code generation The model may be produced to XML and code for simulating after it has been imported by clicking the necessary buttons on the tool's top-right side.[1]

The following format is used to generate unique object names for all blocks:

`<blocktype> <blockname> <blockid>`

- **Components of a simulator**. The simulator is a collection of Python scripts that are used to run the designer's intended scenarios. The simulator's main components are the object initializer, directory, activity diagrams, GUI, program execution sequence diagram, log generation, and clock.

- **Initializer for objects**. The simulation uses the constructor of every block described in the model to initialize it. Individual inputs are treated as texts, numbers, or objects, whereas many inputs are treated as an array.

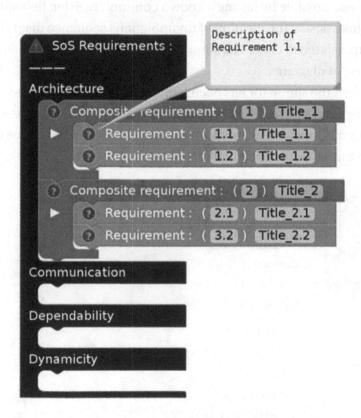

Figure 12-7. *Blocks linked to requirements management are an example of such blocks*

A member named "cardinality" may be found in some blocks such as CS or Wrapper or CPS. It specifies the number of items that will be simulated. This is accomplished by using Python's deep_copy() method on the original object. Every instance is given a unique ID ranging from 1 to n, where n is the model's cardinality.

For example, the following model generates an SoS called My_SoS with 200 CSs named cs_1. Every CS will have an instance ID property that ranges from 1 to 200.

One of the key components of the simulator is the log. It is a service that keeps track of the services provided by the various CSs in an SoS. CSs utilize it to do analysis for a certain service.

The registry is applied as a TCP-IP server in the simulator, allowing CSs to add, remove, and update their own relevant details.

The capacity to perform simulation on several linked computer systems sequence diagram sets is made possible by having a known common register. Related blocks for sequence diagrams assist in the creation of unambiguous sequence diagrams that may be immediately translated to code. The simulation replicates the sequence created by the user in the case of diagrams.

As a result, when the simulator has been launched and initialized, the code created from the sequence diagram (see Figure 12-8) is run instantly. To simulate a situation, a sequence diagram is joined to the model (see Figure 12-9); the sequence diagram is constructed with the support structure tool.

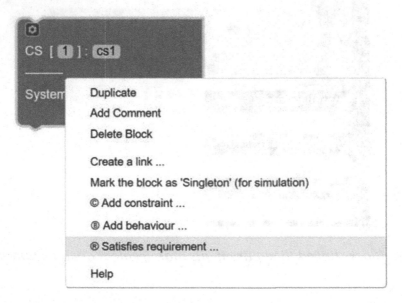

Figure 12-8. *Each block can fulfill certain criteria*

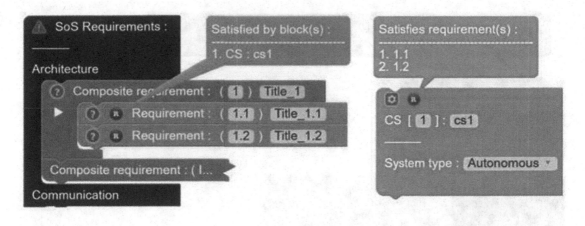

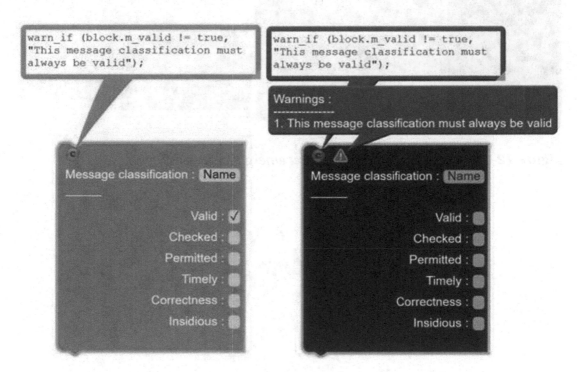

Figure 12-9. *An illustration of a constraint in which the validity of the member variable m is checked*

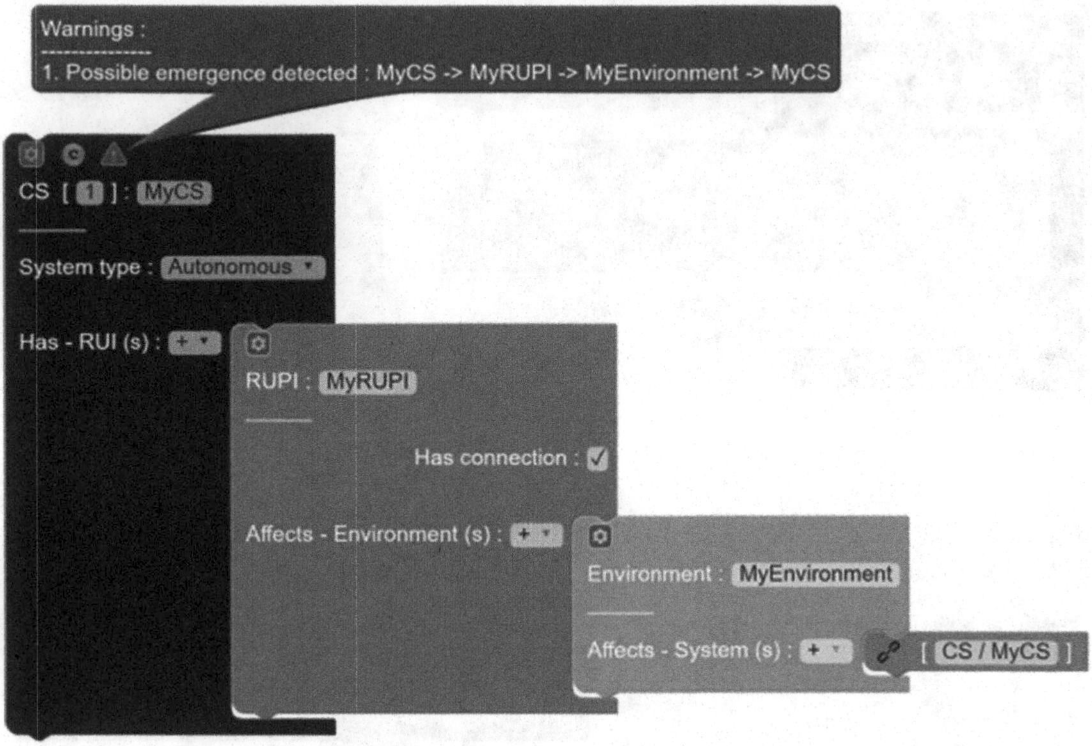

Warnings :
----
1. Possible emergence detected : MyCS -> MyRUPI -> MyEnvironment -> MyCS

CS [1] : MyCS

System type : Autonomous ▾

Has - RUI (s) : + ▾

RUPI : MyRUPI

Has connection : ☑

Affects - Environment (s) : + ▾

Environment : MyEnvironment

Affects - System (s) : + ▾   [CS / MyCS]

Figure 12-10. *Using constraints to detect emergence in a model*

Figure 12-11. *Result of the "return true" query*

12.3 Review Questions

1. "BLOCKLY is a library for creating applications with blocks. Users can utilize visual blocks to construct scripts and programs in block programming." Is this statement correct or incorrect?

2. Which of the following describes BLOCKLY 4SoS ?

   a. Each block represents a portion of code that can be layered and converted into a metamodel with ease.

   b. Each block represents a portion of code that could be stacked and converted into an algorithm with ease.

   c. Each block represents a coding chunk that can be readily stacked and translated.

   d. All the above.

3. Which of the following statements is correct for *simulator* components?

   a. A simulator is a collection of Python programs that are used to run the designer's intended scenarios.

   b. A simulator is a collection of programs designed to carry out the designer's planned scenarios.

   c. A simulator is a collection of Java applications that are used to run the scenarios that the designer has prepared.

   d. None of the above.

4. Which of the following statements is correct for *event* ?

   a. BLOCKLY comes with everything you need to create and render blocks in a drag-and-drop editor.

   b. BLOCKLY comes with everything you need to define and display blocks.

   c. BLOCKLY comes with everything you need to create and render blocks in an editor.

   d. All of these.

5. "Requirements management is a crucial component of the SoS architecture, since it allows for the viewing and monitoring of requirement traceability. The perspective and building blocks can be used to split requirements." Is this statement correct or incorrect?

12.4 Review Answers

1. Answer: Correct, BLOCKLY is a library for developing block-based apps. In block programming, users can use visual blocks to create scripts and programs.

2. Answer: C, Every block represents a coding chunk that could be readily stacked and translated.

3. Answer: B, A simulator is a collection of programs designed to carry out the designer's planned scenarios

4. Answer: A, BLOCKLY comes with everything you need to create and render blocks in a drag-and-drop editor.

5. Answer: Correct, because it enables for the viewing and monitoring of requirement traceability, requirements management is a critical component of the SoS design. To divide needs, the viewpoint and building blocks can be employed.

12.5 Summary

This chapter explained the BLOCKLY 4SOS tool. It is a system-of-systems modeling, validation, querying, and simulation tool.

The goal of the AMADEOS supporting facility is to make designing SoS with the AMADEOS ideas and the BLOCKLY tool simple and intuitive. This tool is very helpful when designing a distributed system (a cyber-physical system).

The next chapter outlines the first project of cyber-physical systems with the help of Kilobots.

CHAPTER 13

Cyber-Physical Systems Project

In this chapter, you learn how to develop a cyber-physical system based on an Italian game called Witch Calls Color.

This game has the following rules:

- One player is picked to be the witch.

- They call out a color, such as blue.

- The other children then run to touch an object of that color. (Clothes are not included, and only one person can touch an object.)

- If the witch catches a child who is not touching the color, they become the next witch. Then the original witch joins the other kids.

You are going to implement this project with the help of Kilobots. The movement of the witch and the color are implemented in Kilobots.

13.1 Using Kilobots

The *Kilobot* cluster is a cluster of 1,000 robots that may be used to create collective behavior that is automatic and has a long duration. Each robot has the basic functions of an autonomous swarm robot, but it is made up of a restricted number of pieces and assembled mostly by an automatic system.

Additionally, the system design allows a single individual to operate a huge Kilobot cooperative in an efficient and scalable manner, including programming it, turning it on, and refilling all the robots. The Kilobot swarm is used to investigate collective "virtual" intellect and to test innovative theories that link minimal personal qualities to cluster characteristics. See Figure 13-1.

225

© Joseph Thachil George 2022
J. T. George, *Introducing Blockchain Applications*, https://doi.org/10.1007/978-1-4842-7480-4_13

Using a mixed concept technique, you can obtain new algorithmic understanding about robustness, adaptability, personality, and an emerging in groups of limited individuals.

13.1.1 The Kilobots Movements

The following list shows the basic Kilobots movements:

- Upward motion

- Characteristics of rotating

- Keeping in touch with adjacent units

- Computing the difference between adjacent units.

- Having sufficient RAM to execute the Kilobots

The following extra parts were added to the Kilobot to expand its implementation:

- The capacity to estimate the amount of light in the environment

- Making the operations more flexible

Figure 13-1. *A Kilobot*

13.2 Project Requirements

13.2.1 Architecture

1. The Kilobots will operate in a space of at least 100x80cm.

2. The surface should be glossy and reflective for the infrared to work properly.

3. The SoS is composed of at least five Kilobots and a controller (one witch, two players, and two colors).

4. The SoS is composed of at least five Kilobots and a controller (one witch, two players, and two colors).

5. At the beginning of the program execution, there are assigned positions for the Kilobots.

6. Each Kilobot has an ID, color, and positions.

7. When the game starts, the player searches for the color and the witch searches for the player.

8. The witch and player Kilobots are waiting for the signal to each other to run.

9. The target color is chosen by the program.

10. During the game, all of the Kilobots are searching for each other.

11. During the game, the witch is trying to catch the players and the players are searching for the color. If the witch catches a player, that player will be the witch in the next round.

12. The round is finished when the Kilobots catch the color.

13. Each Kilobot has two independent motors.

14. Each Kilobot has an infrared transmitter and receiver.

15. The Kilobots can estimate relative distance from other bots from the environment.

16. The Kilobots will operate in one of at least three states: run, bootload, or sleep.

17. Through a message interface, each Kilobot can communicate with every other Kilobit.

13.2.2 Project Communication

1. The Kilobots can receive messages from the overhead controller.

2. The Kilobots are communicating when they are within 7.5cm distance of each other.

3. The connection between all the Kilobots is established at the beginning of each round.

4. There should be a unique Kilobot operating as a central communication coordinator.

13.2.3 Time

Each Kilobot will have a time-based internal clock. Kilobots can communicate over the network within 10 seconds of every message sent.

13.2.4 Dynamicity

A Kilobot moving out of the range of communication will start moving to find the other Kilobots in order to become a part of the network again.

13.2.5 Dependability

1. Availability: A charged battery is necessary for Kilobots.

2. Reliability: The Kilobots can start each game round only when they can communicate with all the others because they don't provide the necessary service.

3. Integrity: It is fundamental that the SoS doesn't have an improper state to function correctly.

13.3 Blockly4SoS Model

In this model, we have an SoS composed of five Kilobots and one overhead controller.

1.   The overhead controller has a RUMI (a Relied Upon Message Interface) that it uses to send information to the Kilobots about the state they must enter or sends the code that defines the behavior of Kilobots.

2.   The Kilobot with ID=0 is the central point of communication; it helps you define a better protocol of communication .

3.   Every Kilobot has a RUMI, which is the interface that they use to exchange messages, and a RUPI (Relied Upon Physical Interface), which is represented by the infrared sensor that catches information from the environment (for example, the distance from the other bots). The message channels are based on the infrared sensor at the hardware layer, but since that is used to directly communicate the data and exchange messages, those are RUMIs. Every characteristic of the Kilobots' SoS is related to a requirement.

13.4 Implementing the Project

In this project, you assign starting positions of Kilobots and specify them in the endstate.json file. At first, a Kilobot moves in a spiral way, trying to establish a connection with the other Kilobots in order to receive a signal.

In the first phase, every Kilobot sends an array of 10 bits, where all the bits are 0 except for the one at the array position equal to the Kilobot ID. When every Kilobot has an array, that means that every Kilobot is connected to all the other Kilobots one way and they are ready to communicate. The first phase is terminated.

In the second phase, all the Kilobots have formed a network and now act as an SoS. They select the witch and broadcast this information through the network of Kilobots. Every Kilobot resends the received message until the chosen witch receives it. Then the witch selects the target color to catch and broadcast this information.

In the next phase, the Kilobots try to catch the target. Every Kilobot evaluates the distance to the target Kilobot, identifying which of the neighbors have the field "distance to target" smaller than all the others. By adding the "distance to target" of the neighbor to the distance of Kilobot X to the neighbor's closest to the target, you can obtain an approximate distance to the target. This process starts from the Kilobots that are effectively communicating with the target, because they are the only ones able to obtain the real distance to the target. After that, this process will recursively happen up to the outermost node of the network.

So, every Kilobot in communication range can know the approximate distance to the target and the closest neighbor it needs to follow in order to reach the target. Kilobots can go out of range of communication. In such cases, they start moving in a spiral way until they find someone communicating with the target.

There is an emergent behavior—an unexpected and positive behavior—that when a Kilobot exits the range, it turns around 360 degrees and enters the range again.

13.5 Executing the Project

In this project, you assign the starting positions of the Kilobots and specify them in the `endstate.json` file. Now, we'll describe the simulation as per the settings you choose (most importantly, `randSeed = 2`).

In Figure 13-2, you can see the starting positions of the bots in this simulation. A circle around a bot means that it is transmitting; a line between two bots means they are communicating.

So, from Figure 13-2, you can see that at the start, only one bot (with ID =1) is transmitting. Initially, the goal of the bots is to create a network in which they are connected and can send and receive messages to any bot, so they start moving around, stopping only when they receive a message from a bot connected to the growing network, starting from bot 1. Bot 1 remains stopped.

After the bots create the network, they use this common channel to agree on the main game parameters and then start playing. During this phase, their job is either to run away from other bots or catch the one who has the chosen color. Also, this phase starts with only one bot transmitting; this is the target bot, or runner, which constantly sends its color and its distance from the target (which is 0, of course).

Bots that don't receive a message start moving around searching for anyone, the bots that actually get messages, and try to use the information about the distance from the target bot contained in those messages to catch the runner. See Figure 13-3.

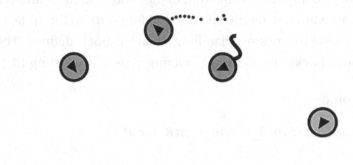

Figure 13-2. *Orbit bot*

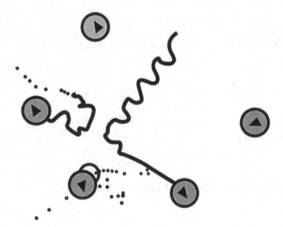

Figure 13-3. *Orbit bot*

13.6 Project Code

This is the main code for the project. It is developed in C language. To execute this code, you need a C language compiler. The rotation of the robot and movements (left and right and forward and backward) are defined in different functions in the code. Using void setup_message() function message handling of each robot is defined. The orbit_tooclose() function checks the adjacent robot movement (see Listing 13-1).

Listing 13-1. Orbit.c

```c
void smooth_set_motors(uint8_t ccw, uint8_t cw)
{
#ifdef KILOBOT
  uint8_t l = 0, r = 0;
  if (ccw && !OCR2A)
    l = 0xff;
  if (cw && !OCR2B)
    r = 0xff;
  if (l || r)
    {
      set_motors(l, r);
      delay(15);
    }
#endif

  set_motors(ccw, cw);
}

void set_motion(motion_t new_motion)
{
  switch(new_motion) {
  case STOP:
    smooth_set_motors(0,0);
    break;
  case FORWARD:
    smooth_set_motors(kilo_straight_left, kilo_straight_right);
    break;
```

```
  case LEFT:
    smooth_set_motors(kilo_turn_left, 0);
    break;
  case RIGHT:
    smooth_set_motors(0, kilo_turn_right);
    break;
  }
}

void orbit_normal()
{
  if (mydata->cur_distance < TOOCLOSE_DISTANCE) {
      mydata->orbit_state = ORBIT_TOOCLOSE;
    } else {
      if (mydata->cur_distance < DESIRED_DISTANCE)
          set_motion(LEFT);
      else
          set_motion(RIGHT);
    }
}

void orbit_tooclose() {
  if (mydata->cur_distance >= DESIRED_DISTANCE)
    mydata->orbit_state = ORBIT_NORMAL;
  else
    set_motion(FORWARD);
}

int EffectId;
int dist;
int id=10;

void loop() {
if(mydata->type==2)
{
set_color(RGB(0,1,0));
}
```

```
if(id<10)
{
  if(kilo_uid==id){
printf("id : %d   %d    %d   id:%d \n",kilo_uid,mydata->type,
mydata->typeEffect,id);
mydata->type=1;
set_color(RGB(1,0,0));

id=10;}
}

if(mydata->IdEffect<10){

switch(mydata->type)
{
case 1:{

if(mydata->typeEffect==2)
{
printf("this => %d    %d   %d\n",mydata->type,mydata->typeEffect,
mydata->IdEffect);

if(mydata->nowDist<40)
{
id=mydata->IdEffect;
set_color(RGB(0,1,0));
mydata->type=2;
set_motion(RIGHT);
}

else    if(mydata->beforIdEffect==mydata->IdEffect)
{
    if(mydata->nowDist>mydata->beforDist){
printf("befor :%d  now: %d   befordist:%d   nowdist:%d   move:%d\n",
mydata->beforIdEffect,mydata->IdEffect,mydata->beforDist,
mydata->nowDist,mydata->move);
```

```
        switch(mydata->move){
            case 0:

                set_motion(LEFT);mydata->move=1;

                break;

            case 1:set_motion(FORWARD);mydata->move=2;

                break;
            case 2:set_motion(RIGHT);mydata->move=0;

                break;
                }
}

}
mydata->beforIdEffect=mydata->IdEffect;
mydata->beforDist=mydata->nowDist;
mydata->IdEffect=10;

}
break;}
case 2:{

if(mydata->typeEffect==3)
{

if(mydata->nowDist<40)
{

set_color(RGB(0,0,0));

set_motion(FORWARD);

}
}

if(mydata->typeEffect==1)
{
```

```
    if(mydata->beforIdEffect==mydata->IdEffect)
{
    if(mydata->nowDist<mydata->beforDist){

        switch(mydata->move){
            case 0:
                set_motion(LEFT);mydata->move=1;

                break;

            case 1:set_motion(FORWARD);mydata->move=2;

                break;
            case 2:set_motion(RIGHT);mydata->move=0;

                break;
                }
}

}
mydata->beforIdEffect=mydata->IdEffect;
mydata->beforDist=mydata->nowDist;
mydata->IdEffect=10;

}

if(mydata->typeEffect==3)
{

    if(mydata->beforIdEffect==mydata->IdEffect)
{
    if(mydata->nowDist>mydata->beforDist){

        switch(mydata->move){
            case 0:

                set_motion(LEFT);mydata->move=1;

                break;

            case 1:set_motion(FORWARD);mydata->move=2;

                break;
```

```
            case 2:set_motion(RIGHT);mydata->move=0;

                break;
                }
}

}
mydata->beforIdEffect=mydata->IdEffect;
mydata->beforDist=mydata->nowDist;
mydata->IdEffect=10;

            }
break;}
case 3:{break;}

}

}
else   if(mydata->beforIdEffect<10){

        if(mydata->type<3){
            if(mydata->countmove>125){
                mydata->countmove=0;
                switch(mydata->move){
                case 0:
                set_motion(LEFT);mydata->move=1;

                break;
                case 1:set_motion(FORWARD);mydata->move=2;
                    mydata->countmove=100;
                    break;
                case 2:set_motion(RIGHT);mydata->move=0;

                    break;
                    }
                        }
mydata->countmove=mydata->countmove+1;
}
}

}
```

```
void message_rx(message_t *m, distance_measurement_t *d) {

mydata->nowDist = estimate_distance(d);
    mydata->dist = *d;

mydata->IdEffect= m->data[0];
mydata->typeEffect= m->data[1];

}

void setup_message(void)
{

switch(kilo_uid){
case 0:mydata->type=1; break;

case 1:mydata->type=2; break;
case 2:mydata->type=2; break;

case 3:mydata->type=3; break;
case 4:mydata->type=3; break;

}
  mydata->transmit_msg.type = NORMAL;
  mydata->transmit_msg.data[0] = kilo_uid & 0xff;
  mydata->transmit_msg.data[1]=mydata->type;

  mydata->transmit_msg.crc = message_crc(&mydata->transmit_msg);
}

message_t *message_tx()
{
  return &mydata->transmit_msg;
}

void setup()
{

  mydata->cur_distance = 0;
  mydata->new_message = 2;
mydata->beforDist=125;
```

```
mydata->state=-1;
mydata->IdEffect=10;
mydata->beforIdEffect=10;
mydata->move=0;
mydata->typeEffect=10;
  setup_message();

switch(kilo_uid){
case 0:set_color(RGB(1,0,0));
 mydata->new_message = 0;
break;

case 1:set_color(RGB(0,1,0));
 mydata->new_message = 1; break;
case 2:set_color(RGB(0,1,0));
 mydata->new_message = 2;break;

case 3:set_color(RGB(0,0,1));
 mydata->new_message = 3;break;
case 4:set_color(RGB(0,0,1));
 mydata->new_message = 4; break;

}
switch(kilo_uid){
case 0:mydata->type=1; break;

case 1:mydata->type=2; break;
case 2:mydata->type=2; break;

case 3:mydata->type=3; break;
case 4:mydata->type=3; break;

}

}

#ifdef SIMULATOR
```

```
static char botinfo_buffer[10000];
char *cb_botinfo(void)
{
  char *p = botinfo_buffer;
  p += sprintf (p, "ID: %d beforIdeffect:%d
ideffect:%d  beforDist:%d  nowDist:%d    type:%d\n",
 kilo_uid,mydata->beforIdEffect,mydata->IdEffect,
mydata->beforDist,mydata->nowDist,mydata->type);

  if (mydata->orbit_state == ORBIT_NORMAL)
    p += sprintf (p, "State: ORBIT_NORMAL\n");
  if (mydata->orbit_state == ORBIT_TOOCLOSE)
    p += sprintf (p, "State: ORBIT_TOOCLOSE\n");

  return botinfo_buffer;
}
#endif

int main() {
    kilo_init();
    kilo_message_rx = message_rx;

    SET_CALLBACK(botinfo, cb_botinfo);

      kilo_message_tx = message_tx;

    kilo_start(setup, loop);

    return 0;
}
*********************************************************
```

In this next project, we assigned starting positions to the Kilobots and specified them in the endstate.json file, as shown in Listing 13-2.

Listing 13-2. *endstate.json*

```
{
  "bot_states": [
    {
      "ID": 0,
      "direction": 0.24680567903004347,
      "state": {},
      "x_position": -223.0,
      "y_position": -156.0
    },
    {
      "ID": 1,
      "direction": 5.8484504331042393,
      "state": {},
      "x_position": -258.0,
      "y_position": 185.0
    },
    {
      "ID": 2,
      "direction": 4.8963292787052639,
      "state": {},
      "x_position": 56.320128808496456,
      "y_position": -190.86350829767215
    },
    {
      "ID": 3,
      "direction": 4.3219605347985022,
      "state": {},
      "x_position": 32.498282727499863,
      "y_position": -215.63645771384685
    },
    {
      "ID": 4,
      "direction": 5.5296756682271786,
      "state": {},
```

```
        "x_position": 248.0,
        "y_position": -44.0
    }
  ],
  "ticks": 224
}
```

In this project, the basic structure of Kilobots is defined and specified in the kilombo.json file, as shown in Listing 13-3.

Listing 13-3. *kilombo.json*

```
{
    "botName" : "Orbit bot",
    "randSeed" : 1,
    "nBots" : 5,
    "timeStep" : 0.0416666,
    "__note" : "0.04166 is 24 FPS which matches the movie frame rate",
    "__timeStep" : 0.03225,
    "simulationTime" : 0,
    "commsRadius" : 100,
    "showComms" : 0,
    "showCommsRadius" : 0,
    "distributePercent" : 0.8,
    "displayWidth"  : 800,
    "displayHeight" : 700,
    "displayWidthPercent" : 80,
    "displayHeightPercent" : 80,
    "displayScale"  : 1,
    "showHist" : 1,
    "histLength": 4000,
    "storeHistory": 1,
    "imageName" : "./movie4/f%04d.bmp",
    "saveVideo" :  0,
    "saveVideoN" : 1,
    "stepsPerFrame" : 1,
    "finalImage" : null,
```

```
    "stateFileName" : "simstates.json",
    "stateFileSteps" : 0,
    "colorscheme" : "bright",
    "speed": 7,
    "turnRate" : 22,
    "GUI"   : 1 ,
    "msgSuccessRate" : 0.8,
    "distanceNoise" : 2
}
```

In this next project, the basic structure of orbit is defined and specified in the
orbit.h file, as shown in Listing 13-4.

Listing 13-4. *orbit.h*

```
{
    "botName" : "Orbit bot",
    "randSeed" : 1,
    "nBots" : 5,
    "timeStep" : 0.0416666,
    "__note" : "0.04166 is 24 FPS which matches the movie frame rate",
    "__timeStep" : 0.03225,
    "simulationTime" : 0,
    "commsRadius" : 100,
    "showComms" : 0,
    "showCommsRadius" : 0,
    "distributePercent" : 0.8,
    "displayWidth"  : 800,
    "displayHeight" : 700,
    "displayWidthPercent" : 80,
    "displayHeightPercent" : 80,
    "displayScale"  : 1,
    "showHist" : 1,
    "histLength": 4000,
    "storeHistory": 1,
    "imageName" : "./movie4/f%04d.bmp",
    "saveVideo" :  0,
```

```
    "saveVideoN" : 1,
    "stepsPerFrame" : 1,
    "finalImage" : null,
    "stateFileName" : "simstates.json",
    "stateFileSteps" : 0,
    "colorscheme" : "bright",
    "speed": 7,
    "turnRate" : 22,
    "GUI"  : 1 ,
    "msgSuccessRate" : 0.8,
    "distanceNoise" : 2
}
```

If you upload the following GitHub file to https://blockly4sos.resiltech.com/latest/demos/amadeos/i.html, you will get the Blockly4Sos diagram for this project. Figure 13-4 shows the output.

https://github.com/JosephThachilGeorge/Blockly4SoS

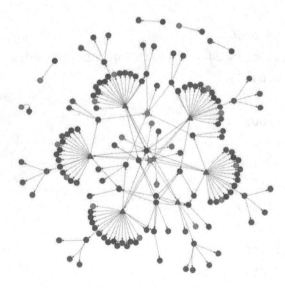

Figure 13-4. *BlocklySoS output*

13.7 Summary

This chapter discussed how to create a cyber-physical system based on the Italian game, Witch Calls Color. This project illustrates the features of cyber-physical systems and the communication used by distributed systems. This project is modeled with the help of the BlocklySoS modeling diagram. The next chapter will dive into a more complex project, which will help you better understand the distributed systems architecture.

CHAPTER 14

Using a MATLAB Smart Farm Project

This project illustrates how to effectively control mutual exclusive access to a shared resource. To implement exclusivity in this manner, the project is created in MATLAB using the Simulink framework. The name of the project is *Smart Farm*. In this project, a fleet of autonomous robots performs a series of farming tasks, including preparing the soil, watering the plants, and producing the harvested plants.

14.1 Description of the Smart Farm Project

The project addresses a case study of distributed, mutual exclusive access to a shared resource. The context is a *smart farm*, where a fleet of autonomous robots prepares the soil, waters the plants, harvests plant production, and so on.

Each robot moves cyclically between the fields and the main farm buildings and stores. The geography of the farm is such that there are two main production fields (named North and South), reachable from the main farm premises by a rural road that passes over a small bridge on a river (see Figure 14-1). Only one robot at a time can use the bridge, which means that robots need to negotiate exclusive access to the bridge by means of V2V communication, with no centralized control center.

© Joseph Thachil George 2022
J. T. George, *Introducing Blockchain Applications*, https://doi.org/10.1007/978-1-4842-7480-4_14

Figure 14-1. *Bridge on a river*

Each robot can be seen as cycling through different modes of operation, represented in Figure 14-2. When a robot needs to move to a field or to the farm building, it enters Ask4Bridge mode, in which it asks for access to the bridge, communicating this request to the other robots, which are in the Ask4Bridge or Bridge modes.

The main objective of the project is to define the distributed communication protocol that allows exclusive access to the bridge, in order to avoid collisions over the bridge.

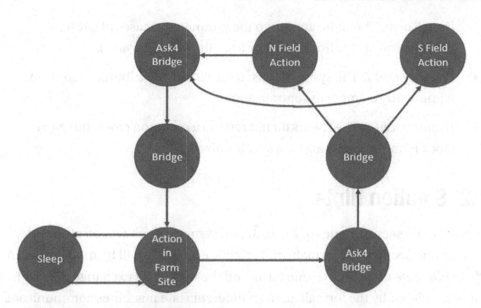

Figure 14-2. *Modes of operation*

14.1.1 Project Requirements

The system must meet the following requirements:

- *Requirement 1*: The system is composed of a non-predetermined number of identical robots communicating with each other via a wireless connection.

- *Requirement 2*: Each robot follows the cyclic modes of operation behavior described in Figure 14-2.

- *Requirement 3*: No two robots can access the bridge at the same time (mutual exclusion, safety).

- *Requirement 4*: A robot that is not granted bridge access waits until the bridge is cleared, and only then issues a new access request.

- *Requirement 5*: If a robot issues a bridge access request, sooner or later, it is granted access (*liveness*).

- *Requirement 6*: If access to the bridge is granted to a robot coming from the North field, and there are at least two other robots R1 and R2 coming—R1 also from the North, and R2 from the farm or from South—then the next access cannot be granted to R1, coming again from North. The same applies to the symmetrical cases of a robot crossing the bridge from South or from the farm (*fairness*).

- *Requirement 7*: The system is based on a totally distributed algorithm, without any element of centralization.

- *Requirement 8*: The robots do not refer to a common clock, but each clock is autonomous and not synchronized.

14.1.2 Solution Hints

The robots can be seen as nodes of a distributed system, which will be modeled using the given specification formalism. Typically each node will be modeled as an *extended finite state machine* of some form, and the nodes will exchange data using the mechanisms offered by the formalism to let different state machines communicate.

The nodes (robots) are identified with a number, and their identifier can be used to send point-to-point communications when necessary.

As a suggestion, you can organize the solution based on a 2PC (two-phase commit protocol) algorithm (standard or linear), in which you need to define a coordinator, sending its proposal to the others.

A robot R1 asking for access to the bridge is acting as the coordinator at each run. Hence, it broadcasts the access request to the other robots. A robot receiving this request from R1, when working in any mode other than `Ask4Bridge` or `Bridge`, simply replies `agree`. A robot in `Bridge` mode will reply instead with `abort`, since it currently occupies the bridge. A robot R2 receiving this request from R1, when in mode `Ask4Bridge`, replies `abort` if its identifier is lower than that of R1; otherwise, it replies `agree`. But in this case, R2 has also to `abort` the algorithm run that it had launched when it entered `Ask4Bridge` mode.

A robot leaving the `Bridge` mode broadcasts the information that the bridge is free to the other nodes, so that the ones in `Ask4Bridge` mode can retry their requests.

Note that a node should be able to start its own 2PC run *and* listening to messages incoming from other robots engaged in other 2PC (two-phase commit protocol) runs at the same time. This requires the use of some concurrent threads, or *statechart* regions.

In the first phase, you should focus on the 2PC scheme by considering a fixed set of three or four robots and accurately studying their interactions, ignoring the liveness and fairness requirements and considering only three operating modes (`Ask4Bridge`, `Field Action`, and `Bridge`).

In the second phase, you extend the model to consider the other operating modes, possibly a larger number of robots and/or the liveness/fairness requirements.

Note that, in general, the tools (in order to be able to simulate or formally verify the model) need to instantiate a fixed number of objects (nodes) by physically copying and pasting.

14.2 Implementing the Project

The project is designed with three robots that move cyclically between the fields and the main agricultural buildings and stores. The geography of the farm is such that there are two main production fields (named North and South). The movements of robots satisfy the three basic requirements of concurrency control in distributed system using mutual exclusion, as mentioned earlier.

In addition to that, the system is based on a totally distributed algorithm, without any element of centralization. The robots do not refer to a common clock, but each clock is autonomous and not synchronized.

The project is implemented in MATLAB and the robots are designed with the help of the Simulink tool. The following MATLAB dependencies are needed for implementation:

- Simulink

- Stateflow

- Robotics System Toolbox

- Navigation Toolbox

The next section covers the built-in features that are available in Simulink and used in this project.

14.2.1 Environment Models

The built-in Robotics Visualizer in MATLAB enables you to simulate and prototype algorithms in a 2D mobile robotics environment. The multi-robot ecosystem also enables for the development and prototype of algorithms in a 2D multi-robot mobile robotic environment. These functions are accessible through the MATLAB and Simulink interfaces.

14.2.2 Sensor Models

In this project, the Lidar Sensor simulates 2D line-of-sight sensors for visualization and algorithm prototyping. This feature is available in MATLAB and the Simulink interface (see Figure 14-3).

Figure 14-3. The sensor

14.2.3 Multi-Robot Lidar Sensor

In addition to the features listed previously, the Multi-Robot Lidar Sensor was utilized to mimic two-dimensional line-of-sight detectors for the multi-robot environment. This sensor will test for a line-of sight for an occupancy map as well as other for robots using a finite radius in the environment. This feature is available in the MATLAB and Simulink interface.

14.3 The System Architecture

This project implements the two-phase commit protocol technology for the movement of the robots.

Only one process can run the crucial section (CS) at a time under the system architecture. Mutual exclusions cannot be implemented in a distributed network using shared variables or a local kernel. The only way to create distributed mutual exclusion is using message forwarding. Unforeseen communication latency and partial information of the system status are dealt with via distributed system algorithms (see Figure 14-4).

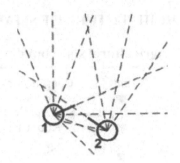

Figure 14-4. *Multi-sensor*

To avoid collisions between the robots that are crossing the bridge, the architecture is designed in a such a way that, when a robot needs to move to a field or to the farm building, it enters the Ask4Bridge mode. There, it asks for access to the bridge, communicating this request to the robots that are in Ask4Bridge mode. The distributed communication protocol (two-phase commit protocol) allows exclusive access, to avoid collisions over the bridge.

A transaction is defined as a set of actions in the aforementioned architecture. Depending on the application criteria, each transaction is given a deadline. The operations are considered to be firm and genuine and have the same severity level. A transaction with a past-due date will be canceled right away.

When a transaction is ready to "commit," the two-phase commit protocol kicks in. A solitary coordinating machine initiates it (in this case, Robot 1). Robots 2 and 3 are the other players, and they will wait for orders from the supervisor (Robot 1).

This technique ensures that transactions are atomic: either the whole transaction is reflected in the system's final state, or none of this is. The transaction will be terminated if even a single individual is unable to submit. To put it another way, each employee has "veto" power over a transaction. The two-phase commit protocol's fundamental flow is depicted in Figure 14-5.

SYSTEM ARCHITECTURE OF SMART FARM

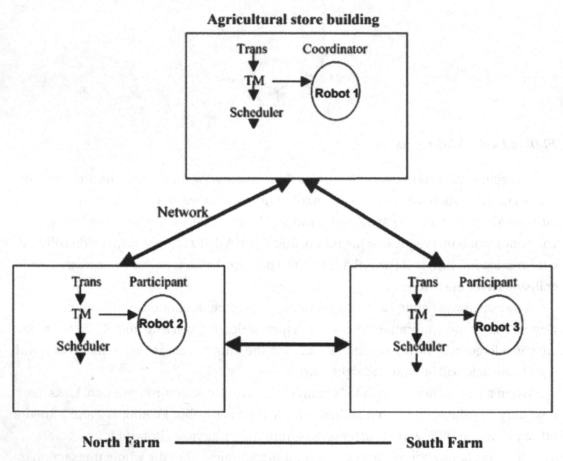

Figure 14-5. *System architecture of the smart farm*

14.4 System Modeling

All the modeling is done with the help of MATLAB. Using the Simulink tool, I have developed a State flow model for the movement of the robots. To move the robots, the program uses the Robotics System Toolbox and the Navigation Toolbox. (To perform this task, note that the free plug-in is available in MATLAB.)

14.4.1 Robot Visualizer and Lidar Sensor

The Robot Visualizer is used to develop the robot architecture. Additionally, using the Lidar Sensor for each robot, the movement of the robots can be verified. The Lidar Sensor may also mimic two-dimensional line-of-sight sensors, as shown in Figure 14-6.

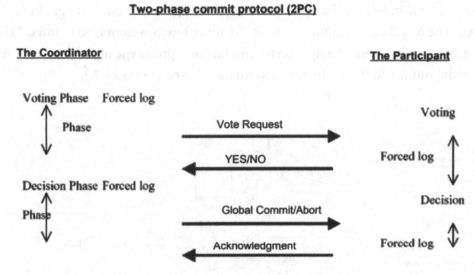

Figure 14-6. *Two-phase commit protocol(2PC)*

14.4.2 Obstacle Avoidance Logic and *2*PC Protocol Concept

To prevent robots from colliding while moving from one state to another, the project uses the 2PC protocol concept for transition. To implement this concept, the project includes a different mode of movement for robots (based on vote). If one robot wants to move to a different state, it asks for Ask4Bridge mode. Then the coordinator determines whether any other robots have requested the same mode. If not, it allows further movement. To prevent robots from colliding while they're moving, the project also uses obstacle avoidance logic, which is available in MATLAB.

14.4.3 Architecture of North and South Farm and Storehouse

There is a feature in MATLAB called the *multi-robot environment* that's used to construct different fields, such as the North and South Farm and the Store. In this platform, you could build "n" number of robots and track their movement.

This is a built-in feature that's available in the Navigation Toolbox plugin in MATLAB. The MATLAB definition of the multi-robot environment is as follows: "The Multi-Robot Environment enables you to simulate and prototype algorithms in a two-dimensional multi-robot mobile robotics situation." (See Figure 14-7.)

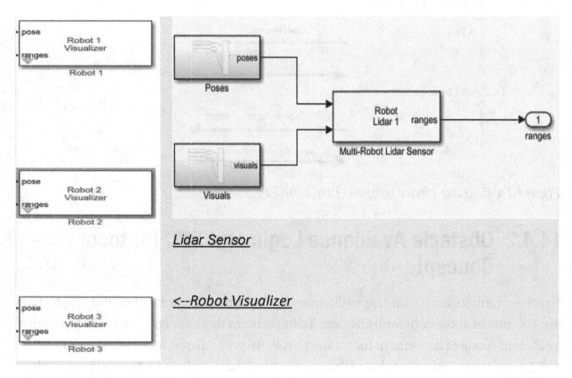

Figure 14-7. Robot Visualizer and Lidar Sensor

14.5 Implementing the Two-Phase Commit Protocol

When a transaction is ready to "commit," the 2PC protocol kicks in. A single supervisor system initiates it (Robot 1, in the initial stage).

The 2PC protocol has two phases, as shown here (assume in the initial stage, that Robot 1 is the coordinator and Robots 2 and 3 are participants).

- **Phase 1:** The supervisor, Robot 1, asks each individual if they have finished their tasks for the transaction and are prepared to commit. Each member gives a yes or no answer.

- **Phase 2:** All of the answers are counted by the organizer. If all of the workers said yes, the transaction will be completed. It will abort if this does not happen. The supervisor sends a message to each employee with the final commits choice and gets a response.

This technique assures that actions are atomic: either the whole action is reflected in the system's final state, or none of this is. If even a single party is unable to commit, the transaction will be canceled. To put it another way, each party has *veto power* over a transaction.

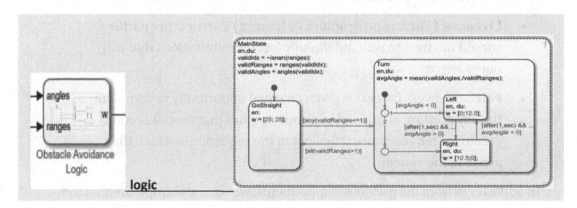

Figure 14-8. *Obstacle avoidance logic*

It also assures the long-term viability of transactions. Before answering "yes" in Step 1, each party double-checks that all of a transaction's writes have been durably written to storage. This allows the supervisor to make a final decision regarding a transaction without being concerned about a participant's failure if they voted "yes" (see Figure 14-8).

14.5.1 Requirements

This project satisfies three basic requirements of concurrency control in distributed systems when using mutual exclusion:

- Mutual exclusion and safety

- Liveness

- Fairness

Enabling several processes to access a common resource or data source is done in a mutually exclusive way:

- There are no common variables in a distributed system that may be utilized to construct mutual exclusion and synchronization primitives.

- The only way to share information is through data transfer.

This three basic requirements are met as follows:

- **Mutual exclusion, safety:** Only one process can run the crucial portion at any given time.

- **Liveness:** (There is no deadlock or hunger.) Two or more parties should not have to wait indefinitely for communications that will never arrive.

- **Fairness:** Every process is given an equal opportunity to complete the key portion. In principle, fairness implies that crucial section execution requests are carried out in the sequence in which they arrive in the system.

In addition to from the previous requirements, we have also implemented the following requirements:

- The system is composed of a non-predetermined number of identical robots communicating with each other via a wireless connection with the help of a Lidar Sensor and obstacle avoidance logic.

- Each robot follows the cyclic modes of operation behavior with the help of the Robot Visualizer tool.

- A robot that is not granted bridge access waits until the bridge is cleared, and only then issues a new access request, with the help of 2PC protocol concept.

The system is based on a totally distributed algorithm, without any element of centralization, with the help of the 2PC protocol concept.

14.5.2 Problems Encountered

While implementing this project, the following problems appeared:

- There is a lack of scalability due to the hindering characteristics of the two-phase commit protocol.

  The two-phase commit protocol's biggest issue is that it is a hindering protocol. Some parties cannot complete their operations if the supervisor fails permanently. It will stall until a commit or rollback is received after a player has submitted an agreement message to the supervisor.

- Once a participant has acknowledged that it is ready to commit, it must be able to commit the transaction afterward, even if it crashed in between. This requires checkpointing to persistence storage.

- The very worst situation occurs when the supervisor is also a participant and votes on the protocol's conclusion. Then perhaps a crash to the supervisor wipes out both it and a member, ensuring that the protocol will stay blocked, despite the fact that only one loss occurred. 2PC is still a common consensus protocol due to its low communication complexity. However, in the event of a failure, the difficulty can rise to O if every node volunteers to be the recovery node $O(n2)O(n2)O(n2)$.

Nevertheless, the fact that 2PC might block due to a supervisor failing is a serious issue that severely reduces availability. If a transaction may be turned back at any moment, the protocol can recover as nodes time out, but if commit choices must be treated as permanent, a single failure can bring the entire system to a halt. Furthermore, a three-phase commit protocol has been developed that eliminates the blocking issues of 2PC at the cost of an additional message delay (see Figure 14-9).

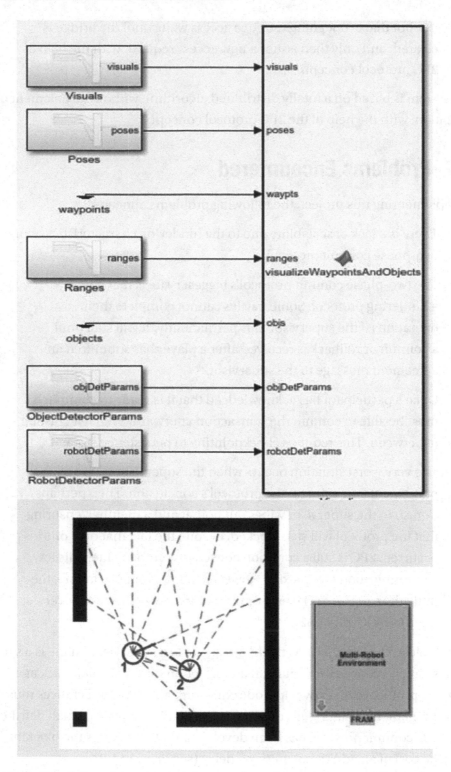

Figure 14-9. *Model architecture of the north and south farm and storehouse*

14.6 Summary

In distributed computer systems, the committing protocols provide global atomicity. This ensures that transactions across a computer network do not end up on all nodes in the network, or on none at all if all nodes fail.

Distributed computing is a method of collaborating on a project using networked, standalone computers. A central computer splits the task and delivers it to the client computer to finish, according to this paradigm. This approach can withstand single client failures, thanks to commit mechanisms.

The drawback of the *two-phase commit protocol* is that if the coordinator fails, all client resources are potentially frozen indefinitely. A timeout transition is used in committed three-phase protocols to compensate for this shortcoming. A timeout transition allows resources to be released at a predetermined time if the coordinating computer fails.

I've covered an essential protocol that may be utilized in the design of distributed systems in this chapter. With two phases—the commit request phase and the commit phase—two-phase commit methods assure atomicity. Computer coordination sends a request to every other client computer on the network during the commit request phase, then waits for a response message from each client. Step 2 is done if all messages are received; if there is a client error and not all messages are received, Step 1 is performed. All clients are notified of the disruption.

Using MATLAB this way is a perfect example of a distributed system. The robots' movement is designed with the help of MATLAB tools. Two-phase commit protocol was used for the transaction of messages in the distributed system. This project is a case study of distributed mutual exclusive access to a shared resource. The setting was a smart farm, where a fleet of autonomous robots conducts activities such as soil preparation, plant watering, harvesting plant production, and so on.

The next chapter covers an example of an advanced project with more features of a distributed system. The project is called *Platoon*.

CHAPTER 15

The Platoon Project

This chapter explains how to develop a cyber-physical system based on a game called *Platoon*.

Platoon was a video game released in 1987-1988 by Ocean Software, first for 8-bit home computers and then for 16-bit ones and for the Nintendo Entertainment System. Inspired by the war movie *Platoon*, it is composed of levels with different gameplay mechanics, both in third and first person. In 1988, Sunsoft also developed an arcade conversion, known as *Vs. Platoon,* based on the NES and Nintendo Vs. Series system licensed from Nintendo. According to Wikipedia, the game features a few stages.[1]

The game consists of four levels:[1]

- *Jungle and village:* "Through a labyrinth of horizontal scrolling environments connected by perpendicular passages, with two-dimensional movement and third-person lateral view". The path is haunted by traps and the Viet Cong. The player controls one soldier at a time, but can replace the soldier at any time with one of the others, for example to avoid putting those already wounded at risk. They can jump and crouch, shoot and throw grenades, both with limited ammo. In the last part, the huts of the village are explored, which become temporarily transparent, in search of objects necessary to continue.

- *Guerrillas:* The game becomes a first person shooter with a minimap taking up half the screen. When you meet the guerrillas, who also emerge from the water that floods the tunnels, the movement stops and you go to check the viewfinder. When you enter a room, the viewfinder becomes a pointer to examine objects; in this way there are elements necessary to continue—supplies and traps.

---

[1] https://it.wikipedia.org/wiki/Platoon_(videogioco_1987)

© Joseph Thachil George 2022
J. T. George, *Introducing Blockchain Applications*, https://doi.org/10.1007/978-1-4842-7480-4_15

- *Bunker:* This is a fixed screen viewfinder shooter; the image is dark and only the flashes of gunfire are noticeable by the enemies, unless the player temporarily lights the scene with a flare. Ammunition and flares are limited.

- *Barnes Jungle and Bunker:* A maze of fixed 2.5D third-person screens, to cross from the bottom to the top of the screen, avoiding obstacles and shooting enemies with the help of a compass. Ammo and total time are limited. The final boss is Barnes, to be hit with grenades.

Each of the five platoon members can take four hits before dying. There is also an overall morale gauge, which decreases when innocent civilians are injured or hit, and is recharged by gathering food and medicine. You are defeated if morale drops to zero, as well as if all team members die.

In this chapter, you learn how to implement this game with the help of Kilobots movements.

15.1 The Game Environment

1. AE-1: The Kilobots will operate on a whiteboard.

2. AE-2: An obstacle will be located in the middle of the whiteboard.

15.1.1 SoS Organization

1. ASoS-1: The SoS is composed of N Kilobots.

2. ASoS-2: The SoS is also composed of a controller that loads the program in the Kilobots memory.

3. ASoS-3: The SoS platoons among the Kilobots composing the SoS.

4. ASoS-4: When the SoS starts, the Kilobots are positioned in a straight line, at a distance of D cm.

5. ASoS-5: When the SoS operates, the distance between Kilobots is maintained at approximately D cm.

6. ASoS-6: The leader is decided before execution.

7. ASoS-7: All the Kilobots know the leader's ID.

15.1.2 CS-Level

1. CCS-1: Each Kilobot has a RUMI to exchange messages.

2. Each Kilobot has a RUMI to communicate with the controller.

3. The controller has a RUMI to communicate with the Kilobots.

4. Each Kilobot has a RUMI to estimate distances.

15.1.3 SOS-Level

1. CSoS-1: Each Kilobot will use its RUMI to exchange information about direction, when it is joining the platoon, and when it is leaving the platoon.

2. CSoS-2: When the SoS starts, each Kilobot notifies the adjacent follower it is the leader by transmitting a message.

3. CSoS-3: Each Kilobot has a RUPI to estimate distance between the sender and the receiver using signal power.

15.1.4 Viewpoint Emergence

1. E-1: The interaction of multiple Kilobots leads to a unique platoon.

15.1.5 Viewpoint Dynamicity

1. D-1: The platoon allows any Kilobot to become a member.

2. D-2: The platoon is composed of at least two Kilobots.

3. D-3: The introduction of a Kilobot into the platoon is allowed only at its tail.

4. D-4: The platoon allows only the last Kilobot to leave.

15.1.6 Viewpoint Time

1.   T-1: The Kilobot will measure time according to a local clock T-2.
     Timely-related events are triggered by message exchange.

2.   T-3: When a Kilobot starts, it will prepare motors for Mms.

15.2 The Cyber-Physical Systems

Kilobots will assist you in putting your concept into action. Kilobots were used to execute platoon mobility. The Kilobot swarm is a ten-thousand-robot (1024) swarm that may be used to develop and test collective behavior in high-growth swarms.

Every robot has the fundamental capabilities of an independent swarm robot (configurable controller, rudimentary movement, and local communication), but they are constructed with low-cost parts and built mainly by an automatic system.

Furthermore, the system's architecture enables a single operator to simply and flexibly control a large Kilobot collective, including "hands-off" coding, switching on, and charging all robots. This project utilizes the Kilobot swarm to examine collective "artificial" intelligence (e.g., sync, collectively transport, and identity) and to test novel ideas that relate minimum individual capabilities to swarm behaviors.

This project hopes to gain new algorithmic insights into robustness, scalability, self-organization, and emerging collectives of restricted individuals utilizing a mixed theory-experiment approach.

15.3 Kilobot Source Code

Listing 15-1. Platoon source code

```
#include <kilombo.h>
#include "platoon.h"
#include <math.h>

#ifdef SIMULATOR
#include <stdio.h> // for printf
#include <stdlib.h>
```

```
#else
#include <avr/io.h>   // for microcontroller register defs
#endif

#define RED RGB(3,0,0)
#define GREEN RGB(0,3,0)
#define BLUE RGB(0,0,3)
#define WHITE RGB(3,3,3)
#define STRAIGHT 1
#define LEFT 2
#define JOIN 3
#define QUIT 4
#define OK 5
#define LEAVE 6
#define SPEED_DOWN 7
#define TURN_LEFT_DELAY 126
#define GO_STRAIGHT_DELAY 700
#define JOIN_DELAY 150
#define FOLLOW_DELAY 220
#define STANDARD_DISTANCE 80
#define NORMAL_SPEED 70
#define CAN_LEAVE 2
#define CAN_JOIN 3
#define LEAVE_TIME 2500
#define END_TIME 20000

REGISTER_USERDATA(USERDATA)

void message_rx(message_t *m, distance_measurement_t *d) {
    mydata->new_message = 1;
    mydata->received_msg=*m;
    mydata->dist = *d;
}

void setup_message(uint8_t data) {
    mydata->transmit_msg.type = NORMAL;
    mydata->transmit_msg.data[0] = kilo_uid & 0xff; //low byte of ID,
    currently not really used for anything
```

```
        mydata->transmit_msg.data[1] = data;
        mydata->transmit_msg.crc = message_crc(&mydata->transmit_msg);
}

message_t *message_tx() {
  return &mydata->transmit_msg;
}

void setupUserData(){
    mydata->cur_distance = 0;
      mydata->new_message = 0;
      mydata->turning = 0;
    mydata->joining = 0;
    mydata->following = 0;
      mydata->follower_id = kilo_uid+1;
}

void setup() {
      setupUserData();
      if (kilo_uid == 0)
            set_color(WHITE); // color of the leader bot
      else if(kilo_uid == CAN_JOIN)
      {
            mydata->my_leader = 255;
            set_color(BLUE); //color of the joining bot
      }
      else
      {
            set_color(RED); // color of the moving bots
            mydata->my_leader = kilo_uid-1;
      }

}
```

```
// LEADER CODE
/*******************************************************************/

int checkDistance() {
    if (mydata->new_message && mydata->received_msg.data[0] == mydata->
    follower_id) {
        if (estimate_distance(&mydata->dist) > STANDARD_DISTANCE+3)
            return SPEED_DOWN;
    }
    return -1;
}

void speedCorrection(int distance){
    if (distance == SPEED_DOWN)
      set_motors(0,0);
    else
      set_motors(kilo_turn_left, kilo_turn_right);
}

void leader() {
    mydata->myClock = kilo_ticks%(GO_STRAIGHT_DELAY+TURN_LEFT_DELAY);
    if (mydata->myClock < GO_STRAIGHT_DELAY) {
        speedCorrection(checkDistance());
        setup_message(STRAIGHT);
    } else {
        setup_message(LEFT);
        set_motors(kilo_turn_left, 0);
    }
}

/*******************************************************************/
// FOLLOWER CODE
/*******************************************************************/

int handleMessage() {
    if (mydata->new_message && mydata->received_msg.data[0] ==
    mydata->my_leader) {
        return mydata->received_msg.data[1];
    }
```

```
        return 0;
}

int handleOther() {
    if(mydata->new_message && mydata->received_msg.data[0] != mydata->
    my_leader) {
        return mydata->received_msg.data[1];
    }
    return 0;
}

int goStraight() {
    return (kilo_ticks - mydata->message_timestamp < 346);
}

int goLeft() {
    int timestamp_isok = (kilo_ticks - mydata->message_timestamp >= 346);
    int passed_delay = kilo_ticks - mydata->message_timestamp < 346 +TURN_
    LEFT_DELAY;
    return (timestamp_isok && passed_delay);
}

int handleTurnLeft() {
        if (goStraight()) {
            setup_message(STRAIGHT);
            set_motors(kilo_turn_left,kilo_turn_right);
            return 1;
        } else if (goLeft()){
            setup_message(LEFT);
            set_motors(kilo_turn_left, 0);
            return 1;
        } else {
            setup_message(STRAIGHT);
            set_motors(kilo_turn_left, kilo_turn_right);
            return 0;
        }
}
```

```
void leave() {
    setup_message(LEAVE);
    mydata->my_leader = 255;
    set_color(GREEN);
    set_motors(kilo_turn_left,kilo_turn_right);
}

void join() {
    set_motors(kilo_turn_left,kilo_turn_right);
    setup_message(JOIN);
    if(mydata->new_message && mydata->received_msg.data[1] == OK)
    {
        mydata->my_leader = mydata->received_msg.data[0];
        mydata->joining = 1;
    }
}

void prepareToFollow() {
    mydata->follow_timestamp = kilo_ticks;
    mydata->joining = 0;
    mydata->following = 1;
}

void followPlatoon() {
    if(kilo_ticks< mydata->follow_timestamp + FOLLOW_DELAY) {
        set_motors(kilo_turn_left,kilo_turn_right);
            set_color(RED);
    }
    else mydata->following = 0;
}

int checkJoin(){
    if(mydata->following){
        followPlatoon();
        return 1;
    }
```

```
    if(mydata->joining){
            prepareToFollow();
        return 1;
    }
    if(kilo_ticks == LEAVE_TIME && kilo_uid == CAN_LEAVE) {
        leave();
        return 1;
    }
    if(kilo_ticks >= LEAVE_TIME + JOIN_DELAY && kilo_uid == CAN_JOIN &&
    mydata->my_leader == 255) {
        join();
        return 1;
    }
    if(handleOther() == JOIN) {
      setup_message(OK);
      return 1;
    }
    return 0;
}

void follower() {
    if(checkJoin()) return;
    int message = handleMessage();
    if (mydata->turning == 0 && message == LEFT) {
            mydata->message_timestamp = kilo_ticks;
            mydata->turning = 1;
    }
    if (mydata->turning == 0 && message == STRAIGHT) {
            speedCorrection(checkDistance());
            setup_message(STRAIGHT);
    } else if (mydata->turning == 1) {
            mydata->turning = handleTurnLeft();
    }

}
```

```
/****************************************************************/
// COMMON CODE
/****************************************************************/
void loop() {

    if(kilo_ticks >= END_TIME) {
        set_color(RGB(0,0,0));
        set_motors(0,0);
    }
    else
    {
      if(kilo_ticks< 32) spinup_motors();
        if (kilo_uid == 0) leader();
        else follower();
    }
}

void initMessageFunctions(){
    kilo_message_rx = message_rx;
    kilo_message_tx = message_tx;
}

int main() {
    kilo_init();
    initMessageFunctions();
    kilo_start(setup, loop);
    return 0;
}
```

Listing 15-2. endstate.json

```json
{
  "bot_states": [
    {
      "ID": 0,
      "direction": 9.3774271885570943,
      "state": {},
      "x_position": 263.28312031961627,
```

```
      "y_position": -153.00242098913
    },
    {
      "ID": 1,
      "direction": 9.2974330575267956,
      "state": {},
      "x_position": 272.14245496760822,
      "y_position": -78.255749422064071
    },
    {
      "ID": 2,
      "direction": 4.7057699363876493,
      "state": {},
      "x_position": -324.34376414595039,
      "y_position": -186.66926101606919
    },
    {
      "ID": 3,
      "direction": 2.785910791660513,
      "state": {},
      "x_position": 266.71626481529483,
      "y_position": -17.907987160522111
    }
  ],
  "ticks": 4830
}
```

Listing 15-3. kilombo json

```
{
    "botName" : "Join Tail",
    "randSeed" : 1,
    "nBots" : 4,
    "formation": "rline",
    "timeStep" : 0.0416666,
    "__note" : "0.04166 is 24 FPS which matches the movie frame rate",
```

```
    "__timeStep" : 0.03225,
    "simulationTime" : 0,
    "commsRadius" : 100,
    "showComms" : 1,
    "showCommsRadius" : 0,
    "distributePercent" : 0.8,
    "displayWidth"  : 640,
    "displayHeight" : 424,
    "displayWidthPercent" : 80,
    "displayHeightPercent" : 80,
    "displayScale"  : 1,
    "showHist" : 1,
    "histLength": 4000,
    "storeHistory": 1,
    "imageName" : "./movie4/f%04d.bmp",
    "saveVideo"  :  0,
    "saveVideoN" : 1,
    "stepsPerFrame" : 1,
    "finalImage" : null,
    "stateFileName" : "simstates.json",
    "stateFileSteps" : 0,
    "colorscheme" : "bright",
    "speed": 7,
    "turnRate" : 22,
    "GUI"   : 1 ,
    "msgSuccessRate" : 0.8,
    "distanceNoise" : 2
}
```

Listing 15-4. start-positions.json

```
{
  "bot_states": [
      {
      "ID": 0,
      "direction": 1.57,
```

```
      "state": {},
      "x_position": 100.0,
      "y_position": 0.0
    },
    {
      "ID": 1,
      "direction": 1.57,
      "state": {},
      "x_position": 20.0,
      "y_position": 0.0
    },
    {
      "ID": 2,
      "direction": 1.57,
      "state": {},
      "x_position": -60.0,
      "y_position": 0.0
    },
    {
      "ID": 3,
      "direction": 1.57,
      "state": {},
      "x_position": -210.0,
      "y_position": 0.0
    }
  ],
  "ticks": 7292
}
```

Listing 15-5. platoon.h

```
#ifndef M_PI
#define M_PI 3.141592653589793238462643383279502884197169399375105820974944
#endif

// declare motion variable type
typedef enum {
```

```
    STOP,
    FORWARD,
    LEFT,
    RIGHT
} motion_t;

// declare state variable type
typedef enum {
    ORBIT_TOOCLOSE,
    ORBIT_NORMAL,
} orbit_state_t;

// declare variables

typedef struct {
    uint8_t cur_distance;
    uint8_t new_message;
    distance_measurement_t dist;
    message_t received_msg;
    message_t transmit_msg;
    uint8_t my_leader;
  uint8_t joining;
  uint8_t following;
    int message_timestamp;
    int turning;
    int myClock;
    int turn_timestamp;
    int follower_id;
  int follow_timestamp;
} USERDATA;
```

Listing 15-6. kilombo.json

```
{
    "botName" : "Join Tail",
    "randSeed" : 1,
    "nBots" : 4,
    "formation": "rline",
```

```
    "timeStep" : 0.0416666,
    "__note" : "0.04166 is 24 FPS which matches the movie frame rate",
    "__timeStep" : 0.03225,
    "simulationTime" : 0,
    "commsRadius" : 100,
    "showComms" : 1,
    "showCommsRadius" : 0,
    "distributePercent" : 0.8,
    "displayWidth"  : 640,
    "displayHeight" : 424,
    "displayWidthPercent" : 80,
    "displayHeightPercent" : 80,
    "displayScale"  : 1,
    "showHist" : 1,
    "histLength": 4000,
    "storeHistory": 1,
    "imageName" : "./movie4/f%04d.bmp",
    "saveVideo" :  0,
    "saveVideoN" : 1,
    "stepsPerFrame" : 1,
    "finalImage" : null,
    "stateFileName" : "simstates.json",
    "stateFileSteps" : 0,
    "colorscheme" : "bright",
    "speed": 7,
    "turnRate" : 22,
    "GUI"  : 1 ,
    "msgSuccessRate" : 0.8,
    "distanceNoise" : 2
}
```

Kilobots can perform cooperative transport, which means they can move a huge object by working collectively. Kilobot collectives may also use S-DASH to shape diverse shapes and repair them if they get distorted. They may also vary their size depending on the type.

They imitate insects in one program by launching from a "home" site, which is a static Kilobot, and spreading across the region looking for "food," which is another static Kilobot. When a Kilobot discovered the "food," it returned to its "home" location to drop it off.

Another program led a group of robots to follow a lead robot in a single file. The robots were careful not to drive too far ahead of the others so that they did not fall behind. They also coordinated their activity, such as flashing their lights, with the help of their sensor. A user can conduct scalable tasks using an infrared controller and infrared receivers. This means they don't have to visit each robot individually to do simple chores like charging or programming.

15.4 Kilobots Movement

Here is the general movement of the Kilobots:

1. Progress is made.

2. Robots rotate.

3. Robots keep in touch with adjacent units.

4. Calculate the distance between the adjacent units.

5. Verify that there is sufficient RAM to execute S-DASH.

The following extra parts were added to the Kilobot to expand its applications:

- Ability to measure the amount of light in the environment.

- Ability to allow for scalable operations.

15.5 Cyber-Physical Modeling

You can find this model in the GitHub repository. Look for the final-model.xml file in https://github.com/JosephThachilGeorge/Platoon-Project.

Since the XML file is large, this section explains a few parts of the code.

To add a block modeling diagram, follow these instructions:

1. Drag the block/workspace with the mouse.

2. Minimize/maximize/partially minimize a block by double-clicking it.

3. Drag and drop new blocks from the Toolbox from the left side.

4. Add related blocks to this block by clicking the (+) dropdown.

5. Right-click the block/workspace to see a menu.

6. Close this comment by clicking the button.

As you can see in the beginning of the project, the SOS organization has various requirements. These requirements are shown in the XML file. These are the requirements for the Cyber System of Systems (CSoS):

```
----------------------------------------
1. CSoS-1.4
                    </requirement>
                    <data>CSoS-1.4</data>
                    <statement name="cs:CS">
                      <block type="__link" id="136">
                        <field name="link_to">CS / Kilobot</field>
                        <data>CS : 3 : 1</data>
                      </block>
                    </statement>
                  </block>
                </statement>
                <next>
                  <block type="execute$s" id="120">
                    <field name="function"> joinPlatoon</field>
                    <field name="#CS">+</field>
                    <requirement pinned="false" h="100" w="200">
                    Satisfies requirement(s) :
```

----

1. CSoS-1.4
2. CSoS-1.6

```
                    </requirement>
                    <data>CSoS-1.4,CSoS-1.6</data>
                    <statement name="cs:CS">
                      <block type="__link" id="129">
                        <field name="link_to">CS / Kilobot</field>
                        <data>CS : 3 : 1</data>
                      </block>
                    </statement>
                  </block>
                </next>
              </block>
            </statement>
            <statement name="on_failure:sequence">
            <block type="execute$s" id="127">
                <field name="function">doNothing</field>
                <field name="#CS">+</field>
                <statement name="cs:CS">
                  <block type="__link" id="128">
                    <field name="link_to">CS / Kilobot</field>
                    <data>CS : 3 : 1</data>
                  </block>
                </statement>
              </block>
            </statement>
          </block>
        </statement>
      </block>
    </statement>
```

```
            <next>
              <block type="If$s" id="525">
                <field name="name">Send OK</field>
                <field name="on_condition"> == JOIN</field>
                <field name="#CS">+</field>
                <field name="#state_variable">+</field>
                <field name="#sequence">+</field>
                <field name="#sequence">+</field>
                <statement name="cs:CS">
                  <block type="__link" id="526">
                    <field name="link_to">CS / Kilobot</field>
                    <data>CS : 3 : 1</data>
                  </block>
                </statement>
                <statement name="check_on:state_variable">
                  <block type="__link" id="527">
                    <field name="link_to">State variable / received_msg
                    </field>
                    <data>state_variable : 112 : 1</data>
                  </block>
                </statement>
                <statement name="on_success:sequence">
                  <block type="While$s" id="326">
                    <field name="name">turn_check</field>
                    <field name="condition">==1</field>
                    <field name="#CS">+</field>
                    <field name="#state_variable">+</field>
                    <field name="#sequence">+</field>
                    <requirement pinned="false" h="100" w="200">Satisfies
                    requirement(s) :
```

----

1. CSoS-1.5

```
</requirement>
<data>CSoS-1.5</data>
<statement name="cs:CS">
  <block type="__link" id="327">
    <field name="link_to">CS / Kilobot</field>
    <data>CS : 3 : 1</data>
  </block>
</statement>
<statement name="check_on:state_variable">
  <block type="__link" id="328">
    <field name="link_to">State variable / is_turning
    </field>
    <data>state_variable : 321 : 1</data>
  </block>
</statement>
<next>
  <block type="execute$s" id="528">
    <field name="function"> sendOk</field>
    <field name="#CS">+</field>
    <requirement pinned="false" h="100"
    w="200">Satisfies requirement(s) :
```

----

1. CSoS-1.5

```
</requirement>
<statement name="cs:CS">
  <block type="__link" id="529">
    <field name="link_to">CS / Kilobot</field>
    <data>CS : 3 : 1</data>
  </block>
```

```
                    </statement>
                  </block>
                </next>
              </block>
            </statement>
            <statement name="on_failure:sequence">
              <block type="execute$s" id="530">
                <field name="function"> doNothing</field>
                <field name="#CS">+</field>
                <statement name="cs:CS">
                  <block type="__link" id="531">
                    <field name="link_to">CS / Controller</field>
                    <data>CS : 2 : 1</data>
                  </block>
                </statement>
              </block>
            </statement>
          </block>
        </next>
      </block>
    </next>
  </block>
 /next>
  </block>
</next>
  </block>
</statement>
```

```
                    <statement name="on_failure:sequence">
                       <block type="execute$s" id="188">
                         <field name="function">doNothing</field>
                         <field name="#CS">+</field>
                         <statement name="cs:CS">
                           <block type="__link" id="189">
                             <field name="link_to">CS / Kilobot</field>
                             <data>CS : 3 : 1</data>
                           </block>
                         </statement>
                       </block>
                     </statement>
                   </block>
                 </next>
               </block>
             </statement>
           </block>
         </statement>
       </block>
     </next>
   </block>
 </statement>
</block>
<block type="requirements" id="8" x="2211" y="57">
  <statement name="Architecture_requirements">
    <block type="simple_requirement" id="12">
      <field name="req_id">AE-1</field>
      <field name="title">Whiteboard width x height</field>
      <requirement pinned="false" h="100" w="200">Satisfied by block(s) :
```

The message transfer is done with the help of RUPI (Relied Upon Physical Interface) and RUMI (Relied Upon Message Interface). The message transfer from one Kilobot to another is designed in this session.

----

1. RUMI : Message Exchange
```
        </requirement>
        <data>63</data>
        <next>
          <block type="simple_requirement" id="34">
            <field name="req_id">CCS-3</field>
            <field name="title">Controller RUMI</field>
            <requirement pinned="false" h="100" w="200">Satisfied by block(s) :
```
----
1. RUMI : Kilobot program load
```
            </requirement>
            <data>65</data>
            <next>
              <block type="simple_requirement" id="36">
                <field name="req_id">CCS-4</field>
                <field name="title">RUPI kilobot</field>
                <requirement pinned="false" h="100" w="200">Satisfied by
                block(s) :
```
----
1. RUPI : Calculate Distance
```
                </requirement>
                <data>61</data>
                <next>
                  <block type="simple_requirement" id="38">
                    <field name="req_id">CSoS-1</field>
                    <field name="title">kbot-kbot RUMI utilization</field>
                    <requirement pinned="false" h="100" w="200">Satisfied
                    by block(s) :
```
----
1. RUMI : Message Exchange
```
                </requirement>
                <data>63</data>
                <next>
                  <block type="simple_requirement" id="40">
                    <field name="req_id">CSoS-2</field>
```

```
            <field name="title">Leader notification</field>
            <requirement pinned="false" h="100" w="200">
            Satisfied by block(s) :
```

It also uses an Automated Surface Observing System (ASOS), which observes the nearby cyber-physical system components. It has a security and internal clock system, a controller, and dynamicity. An example is shown here:

```
1. ASoS-3
    </requirement>
    <data>ASoS-3</data>
    <statement name="is_composed_of:system">
      <block type="CS$s" id="2">
        <field name="cardinality">1</field>
        <field name="name">Controller</field>
        <field name="system_type">autonomous</field>
        <field name="#boundary">+</field>
        <field name="#state_space">+</field>
        <field name="#HMI">+</field>
        <field name="#CPS">+</field>
        <field name="#service">+</field>
        <field name="#role_player">+</field>
        <field name="#physical_system">+</field>
        <field name="#RUI">+</field>
        <field name="#dependability_guarantee">+</field>
        <field name="#fault_containment_region">+</field>
        <field name="#MAPE_algorithm">+</field>
        <field name="#security">+</field>
        <field name="#clock">+</field>
        <field name="#system_resource">+</field>
        <field name="#architectural_style">+</field>
        <field name="#subsystem">+</field>
        <field name="#state_variable">+</field>
        <field name="#interface">+</field>
```

```
        <field name="#dynamicity">+</field>
        <requirement pinned="false" h="100" w="200">Satisfies requirement(s) :
--------------------------------------
1. ASoS-2
        </requirement>
        <data>ASoS-2</data>
        <statement name="has:RUI">
          <block type="RUMI$s" id="65" collapsed="true">
            <field name="name">Kilobot program load</field>
            <field name="has_connection">FALSE</field>
            <field name="#connecting_strategy">+</field>
            <field name="#interface_specification">+</field>
            <field name="#interface_port">+</field>
            <field name="#afferent_environment">+</field>
            <field name="#efferent_environment">+</field>
            <field name="#interface_model">+</field>
            <field name="#service">+</field>
            <field name="#message">+</field>
            <field name="#RUMI">+</field>
            <field name="#probe">+</field>
            <field name="#security">+</field>
            <requirement pinned="false" h="100" w="200">Satisfies
requirement(s) :
--------------------------------------
```

Another part of the XML file is T1, T2, T3, and T4, which are transport messages. They help illustrate how messages transfer between CCS-1, CSoS-1, T-2 or TI or T3 or T4.

- T-1: The Kilobots measure time according to a local clock.

- T-2: Time-related events are triggered by message exchange.

- T-3: When a Kilobot starts, it will prepare motors for Mms.

These requirements are designed with the help of the following code:

3. T-2

```
</requirement>
<data>CCS-1,CSoS-1,T-2</data>
<statement name="exchanges:message">
  <block type="message$s" id="157" collapsed="true">
    <field name="name">JOIN</field>
    <field name="transport_type">PAR_message</field>
    <field name="header"> ? </field>
    <field name="data_field"> ? </field>
    <field name="#message_classification">+</field>
    <field name="#trailer">+</field>
    <next>
      <block type="message$s" id="158" collapsed="true">
        <field name="name">LEAVE</field>
        <field name="transport_type">PAR_message</field>
        <field name="header"> ? </field>
        <field name="data_field"> ? </field>
        <field name="#message_classification">+</field>
        <field name="#trailer">+</field>
        <next>
          <block type="message$s" id="159"
          collapsed="true">
            <field name="name">DIRECTION</field>
            <field name="transport_type">PAR_message
            </field>
            <field name="header"> ? </field>
            <field name="data_field"> ? </field>
            <field name="#message_classification">+
            </field>
            <field name="#trailer">+</field>
            <next>
              <block type="message$s" id="160"
              collapsed="true">
                <field name="name">Leader Notify</field>
```

```
                              <field name="transport_type">PAR_
                              message</field>
                              <field name="header">  ?  </field>
                              <field name="data_field">  ?  </field>
                              <field name="#message_
                              classification">+</field>
                              <field name="#trailer">+</field>
                              <requirement pinned="false" h="100"
                              w="200">Satisfies requirement(s) :
```

----

1. CSoS-2

```
                              </requirement>
                              <data>CSoS-2</data>
                              <next>
                                <block type="message$s" id="226"
                                collapsed="true">
                                  <field name="name">LOAD_PRGRM</field>
                                  <field name="transport_type">PAR_
                                  message</field>
                                  <field name="header">  ?  </field>
                                  <field name="data_field">  ?
                                  </field>
                                  <field name="#message_
                                  classification">+</field>
                                  <field name="#trailer">+</field>
                                </block>
                              </next>
                            </block>
                          </next>
                        </block>
                      </next>
                    </block>
                  </next>
                </block>
              </statement>
```

```
        <statement name="connects:RUMI">
          <block type="__link" id="156">
            <field name="link_to">RUMI / Message Exchange</field>
            <data>RUMI : 63 : 0</data>
            <next>
              <block type="__link" id="235">
                <field name="link_to">RUMI / Kilobot program
                load</field>
                <data>RUMI : 65 : 0</data>
              </block>
            </next>
          </block>
        </statement>
      </block>
    </next>
  </block>
</statement>
<statement name="may_require:dependability_guarantee">
  <block type="dependability_guarantee$s" id="77" collapsed="true">
    <field name="name">Starting Position = Straight line</field>
    <field name="#technique">+</field>
    <field name="#measure">+</field>
    <requirement pinned="false" h="100" w="200">Satisfies
    requirement(s) :
-------------------------------------

1. T-3

    </requirement>
    <next>
      <block type="dependability_guarantee$s" id="147"
      collapsed="true">
        <field name="name">Starting Distance = 8 cm</field>
        <field name="#technique">+</field>
        <field name="#measure">+</field>
        <next>
```

```
                        <block type="dependability_guarantee$s" id="148"
                        collapsed="true">
                          <field name="name">Running Distance between
                          7 cm and 9 cm</field>
                          <field name="#technique">+</field>
                          <field name="#measure">+</field>
                        </block>
                    </next>
                  </block>
                </next>
              </block>
            </next>
          </block>
        </statement>
        <statement name="has:state_variable">
          <block type="state_variable$s" id="66" collapsed="true">
            <field name="name">kilo_uid</field>
            <field name="value"> ? </field>
            <field name="#state">+</field>
            <next>
              <block type="state_variable$s" id="67">
                <field name="name">leader_uid</field>
                <field name="value"></field>
                <field name="#state">+</field>
                <requirement pinned="false" h="100" w="200">Satisfies
                requirement(s) :
-------------------------------------
1. T-1
                </requirement>
                <data>T-1</data>
                <next>
                  <block type="state_variable$s" id="112">
                    <field name="name">received_msg</field>
                    <field name="value"> ? </field>
                    <field name="#state">+</field>
```

```
<next>
  <block type="state_variable$s" id="321">
    <field name="name">is_turning</field>
    <field name="value">  ?  </field>
    <field name="#state">+</field>
    <statement name="describes_a:state">
      <block type="state$s" id="323">
        <field name="name">kilobot turning
        </field>
      </block>
    </statement>
  </block>
</next>
          </block>
        </next>
      </block>
    </next>
  </block>
</statement>
<statement name="has:dynamicity">
  <block type="__link" id="249">
    <field name="link_to">Dynamic service / JoinLeave</field>
    <data>dynamic_service : 238 : 0</data>
  </block>
</statement>
          </block>
        </next>
      </block>
    </statement>
  </block>
<block type="sequence_diagram$s" id="227" x="87" y="96">
  <field name="name">Platoon</field>
  <field name="#sub_sequence">+</field>
```

```
    <statement name="has:sub_sequence">
      <block type="sub_sequence$s" id="230">
        <field name="name">Start</field>
        <field name="#sequence">+</field>
        <statement name="has:sequence">
          <block type="execute$s" id="247">
            <field name="function">Send Program</field>
            <field name="#CS">+</field>
            <statement name="cs:CS">
              <block type="__link" id="251">
                <field name="link_to">CS / Controller</field>
                <data>CS : 2 : 1</data>
                <next>
                  <block type="__link" id="319">
                    <field name="link_to">CS / Kilobot</field>
                    <data>CS : 3 : 1</data>
                  </block>
                </next>
              </block>
            </statement>
            <next>
              <block type="execute$s" id="252">
                <field name="function">Init State Variables</field>
                <field name="#CS">+</field>
                <statement name="cs:CS">
                  <block type="__link" id="254">
                    <field name="link_to">CS / Kilobot</field>
                    <data>CS : 3 : 1</data>
                  </block>
                </statement>
                <next>
                  <block type="execute$s" id="253">
                    <field name="function">spinup_motors</field>
                    <field name="#CS">+</field>
                    <statement name="cs:CS">
```

```
          <block type="__link" id="256">
              <field name="link_to">CS / Kilobot</field>
              <data>CS : 3 : 1</data>
              </block>
            </statement>
          </block>
        </next>
      </block>
    </next>
  </block>
</statement>
<next>
  <block type="sub_sequence$s" id="138">
    <field name="name">Main</field>
    <field name="#sequence">+</field>
    <statement name="has:sequence">
      <block type="While$s" id="139">
        <field name="name">MainLoop</field>
        <field name="condition"> < 20000</field>
        <field name="#CS">+</field>
        <field name="#state_variable">+</field>
        <field name="#sequence">+</field>
        <requirement pinned="false" h="100" w="200">Satisfies
        requirement(s) :
-------------------------------------

1. T-4

        </requirement>
        <data>T-4</data>
        <statement name="cs:CS">
          <block type="__link" id="140">
            <field name="link_to">CS / Kilobot</field>
            <data>CS : 3 : 1</data>
          </block>
        </statement>
        <statement name="check_on:state_variable">
```

```
    <block type="__link" id="141">
      <field name="link_to">State variable / kilo_ticks</field>
      <data>state_variable : 250 : 1</data>
    </block>
  </statement>
  <statement name="has:sequence">
    <block type="If$s" id="142">
      <field name="name">LeaderPrgrm</field>
      <field name="on_condition">  == 0</field>
      <field name="#CS">+</field>
      <field name="#state_variable">+</field>
      <field name="#sequence">+</field>
      <field name="#sequence">+</field>
      <statement name="cs:CS">
        <block type="__link" id="143">
          <field name="link_to">CS / Kilobot</field>
          <data>CS : 3 : 1</data>
        </block>
      </statement>
      <statement name="check_on:state_variable">
        <block type="__link" id="144">
          <field name="link_to">State variable / kilo_uid
          </field>
          <data>state_variable : 66 : 1</data>
        </block>
      </statement>
      <statement name="on_success:sequence">
        <block type="sub_sequence$s" id="231" collapsed="true">
          <field name="name">Go Straight Leader</field>
          <field name="#sequence">+</field>
          <statement name="has:sequence">
            <block type="While$s" id="237">
              <field name="name">StraightDelay</field>
              <field name="condition">kilo_ticks mod 826 <
              700</field>
```

```
<field name="#CS">+</field>
<field name="#state_variable">+</field>
<field name="#sequence">+</field>
<statement name="cs:CS">
  <block type="__link" id="239">
    <field name="link_to">CS / Kilobot</field>
    <data>CS : 3 : 1</data>
  </block>
</statement>
<statement name="check_on:state_variable">
  <block type="__link" id="246">
    <field name="link_to">State variable
/ kilo_ticks</field>
    <data>state_variable : 250 : 1</data>
  </block>
</statement>
<statement name="has:sequence">
  <block type="execute$s" id="343">
    <field name="function">goStraight</field>
    <field name="#CS">+</field>
    <statement name="cs:CS">
      <block type="__link" id="346">
        <field name="link_to">CS / Kilobot
        </field>
        <data>CS : 3 : 1</data>
      </block>
    </statement>
    <next>
      <block type="execute$s" id="348">
        <field name="function">sendStraight
        </field>
        <field name="#CS">+</field>
        <statement name="cs:CS">
          <block type="__link" id="349">
            <field name="link_to">CS / Kilobot
            </field>
```

```
                        <data>CS : 3 : 1</data>
                    </block>
                  </statement>
                </block>
              </next>
            </block>
          </statement>
        </block>
      </statement>
      <next>
        <block type="sub_sequence$s" id="232"
        collapsed="true">
          <field name="name">Turn Left Leader</field>
          <field name="#sequence">+</field>
          <statement name="has:sequence">
            <block type="While$s" id="240">
              <field name="name">TurnDelay</field>
              <field name="condition">kilo_ticks mod 826
              >=700</field>
              <field name="#CS">+</field>
              <field name="#state_variable">+</field>
              <field name="#sequence">+</field>
              <statement name="cs:CS">
                <block type="__link" id="241">
                  <field name="link_to">CS / Kilobot
                  </field>
                  <data>CS : 3 : 1</data>
                </block>
              </statement>
              <statement name="check_on:state_variable">
                <block type="__link" id="245">
                  <field name="link_to">State variable /
                  kilo_ticks</field>
                  <data>state_variable : 250 : 1</data>
                </block>
```

```
        </statement>
        <statement name="has:sequence">
          <block type="execute$s" id="344">
            <field name="function">turnLeft</field>
            <field name="#CS">+</field>
            <statement name="cs:CS">
              <block type="__link" id="345">
                <field name="link_to">CS /
                Kilobot</field>
                <data>CS : 3 : 1</data>
              </block>
            </statement>
            <next>
              <block type="execute$s" id="350">
                <field name="function">sendLeft
                </field>
                <field name="#CS">+</field>
                <statement name="cs:CS">
                  <block type="__link" id="351">
                    <field name="link_to">CS /
                    Kilobot</field>
                    <data>CS : 3 : 1</data>
                  </block>
                </statement>
              </block>
            </next>
          </block>
        </statement>
      </block>
    </statement>
  </block>
</next>
</block>
</statement>
<statement name="on_failure:sequence">
```

```
<block type="execute$s" id="183" collapsed="true">
  <field name="function">doNothing</field>
  <field name="#CS">+</field>
  <statement name="cs:CS">
    <block type="__link" id="184">
      <field name="link_to">CS / Kilobot</field>
      <data>CS : 3 : 1</data>
    </block>
  </statement>
</block>
</statement>
<next>
  <block type="If$s" id="185">
    <field name="name">FollowerPrgrm</field>
    <field name="on_condition"> != 0</field>
    <field name="#CS">+</field>
    <field name="#state_variable">+</field>
    <field name="#sequence">+</field>
    <field name="#sequence">+</field>
    <statement name="cs:CS">
      <block type="__link" id="186">
        <field name="link_to">CS / Kilobot</field>
        <data>CS : 3 : 1</data>
      </block>
    </statement>
    <statement name="check_on:state_variable">
      <block type="__link" id="187">
        <field name="link_to">State variable / kilo_
        uid</field>
        <data>state_variable : 66 : 1</data>
      </block>
    </statement>
    <statement name="on_success:sequence">
      <block type="If$s" id="145" collapsed="true">
        <field name="name">Go Straight Follower</field>
```

```
<field name="on_condition"> == STRAIGHT &&
sender == LEADER</field>
<field name="#CS">+</field>
<field name="#state_variable">+</field>
<field name="#sequence">+</field>
<field name="#sequence">+</field>
<statement name="cs:CS">
  <block type="__link" id="146">
    <field name="link_to">CS / Kilobot</field>
    <data>CS : 3 : 1</data>
  </block>
</statement>
<statement name="check_on:state_variable">
  <block type="__link" id="150">
    <field name="link_to">State variable /
    received_msg</field>
    <data>state_variable : 112 : 1</data>
  </block>
</statement>
<statement name="on_success:sequence">
  <block type="execute$s" id="522">
    <field name="function"> goStraight</field>
    <field name="#CS">+</field>
    <requirement pinned="false" h="100"
    w="200">Satisfies requirement(s) :
```

The environment for this project is represented by AE-1 and AE-2. In AE-1, the Kilobots operate on a whiteboard and in AE-2, an obstacle is located in the middle of the whiteboard. The AE-1 and AE-2 environments are shown here:

```
1. AE-1
   </requirement>
   <data>AE-1</data>
   <statement name="has:entity">
```

```
        <block type="__link" id="192">
          <field name="link_to">CS / Controller</field>
          <data>CS : 2 : 0</data>
          <next>
            <block type="__link" id="193">
              <field name="link_to">CS / Kilobot</field>
              <data>CS : 3 : 0</data>
              <next>
                <block type="thing$s" id="194" collapsed="true">
                  <field name="name">Obstacle</field>
                  <field name="#dynamicity">+</field>
                  <requirement pinned="false" h="100" w="200">Satisfies
                  requirement(s) :
-------------------------------------
1. AE-2
                  </requirement>
                  <data>AE-2</data>
                </block>
              </next>
            </block>
          </next>
        </block>
      </statement>
      <statement name="has:state_variable">
        <block type="state_variable$s" id="195">
          <field name="name">width</field>
          <field name="value">1000</field>
          <field name="#state">+</field>
          <next>
            <block type="state_variable$s" id="196">
              <field name="name">height</field>
              <field name="value">1000</field>
              <field name="#state">+</field>
              <next>
                <block type="state_variable$s" id="197">
```

```
        <field name="name">obstacle width</field>
        <field name="value">700</field>
        <field name="#state">+</field>
        <next>
          <block type="state_variable$s" id="198">
            <field name="name">obstacle height</field>
            <field name="value">700</field>
            <field name="#state">+</field>
          </block>
        </next>
      </block>
    </next>
  </block>
  </next>
  </block>
  </statement>
</block>
<block type="SoS$s" id="1" x="1059" y="-98">
  <field name="name">Kilobot platooning</field>
  <field name="sos_type">acknowledged</field>
  <field name="#system">+</field>
  <field name="#evolution">+</field>
  <field name="#dependability_guarantee">+</field>
  <field name="#behaviour">+</field>
  <field name="#security">+</field>
  <comment pinned="false" h="159" w="767">This is an example System-of-
  Systems (SoS) block named "example_block", on the work-space.
```

The next ones are about dynamicity and these are named DI, D2, D3, and D4.

- D-1: The platoon will allow any Kilobot to become a member.

- D-2: The platoon is composed of at least two Kilobots.

- D-3: The introduction of a Kilobot in the platoon is allowed only at its tail.

- D-4: The platoon allows only the last Kilobot to leave.

These requirements are implemented with the following code:

```
--------------------------------------
1. D-4
2. D-5
        </requirement>
        <data>D-4,D-5</data>
        <statement name="can_access:state_variable">
          <block type="__link" id="243">
            <field name="link_to">State variable / leader_uid</field>
            <data>state_variable : 67 : 0</data>
            <next>
              <block type="__link" id="149">
                <field name="link_to">State variable / kilo_uid</field>
                <data>state_variable : 66 : 0</data>
              </block>
            </next>
          </block>
        </statement>
        <next>
          <block type="service$s" id="244" collapsed="true">
            <field name="name">Join</field>
            <field name="#state_variable">+</field>
            <requirement pinned="false" h="100" w="200">Satisfies
            requirement(s) :
--------------------------------------
1. D-1
2. D-3
        </requirement>
        <data>D-1,D-3</data>
        <statement name="can_access:state_variable">
          <block type="__link" id="248">
```

```
          <field name="link_to">State variable / kilo_uid</field>
          <data>state_variable : 66 : 0</data>
        </block>
      </statement>
    </block>
  </next>
</block>
    </statement>
  </block>
<block type="emergent_phenomenon$s" id="228" collapsed="true" x="748"
y="1454">
  <field name="name">Platooning</field>
  <field name="#behaviour">+</field>
  <statement name="causes:behaviour">
    <block type="expected_and_beneficial_behaviour$i" id="229">
      <field name="name">Unique Platoon</field>
      <requirement pinned="false" h="100" w="200">Satisfies requirement(s) :
------------------------------------

2. D-2

      </requirement>
      <data>ASoS-1,D-2</data>
      <statement name="has:RUI">
        <block type="RUPI$s" id="61">
          <field name="name">Calculate Distance</field>
          <field name="has_connection">FALSE</field>
          <field name="#connecting_strategy">+</field>
          <field name="#interface_specification">+</field>
          <field name="#interface_port">+</field>
          <field name="#afferent_environment">+</field>
          <field name="#efferent_environment">+</field>
          <field name="#interface_model">+</field>
          <field name="#thing">+</field>
          <field name="#environment">+</field>
          <field name="#RUPI">+</field>
          <field name="#probe">+</field>
```

```
                    <field name="#security">+</field>
                    <requirement pinned="false" h="100" w="200">Satisfies
                    requirement(s) :
```

The SOS level is designed as follows. CSoS-1: Each Kilobot will use its RUMI to exchange information about direction, when it is joining the platoon, and when it is leaving the platoon. CSoS-2: When the SoS starts, each Kilobot notifies its adjacent follower that it is the leader by transmitting a message. CSoS-3: Each Kilobot has a RUPI to estimate the distance between the sender and receiver using signal power.

The following code explains the CSoS systems:

----

1. CSoS-2

```
                         </requirement>
                         <data>CSoS-2</data>
                         <next>
                           <block type="message$s" id="226"
                           collapsed="true">
                             <field name="name">LOAD_PRGRM</field>
                             <field name="transport_type">PAR_
                             message</field>
                             <field name="header">  ?  </field>
                             <field name="data_field">  ?  </field>
                             <field name="#message_
                             classification">+</field>
                             <field name="#trailer">+</field>
                           </block>
                         </next>
                       </block>
                     </next>
                   </block>
                 </next>
               </block>
```

```
          </statement>
          <statement name="connects:RUMI">
            <block type="__link" id="156">
              <field name="link_to">RUMI / Message Exchange</field>
              <data>RUMI : 63 : 0</data>
              <next>
                <block type="__link" id="235">
                  <field name="link_to">RUMI / Kilobot program
                  load</field>
                  <data>RUMI : 65 : 0</data>
                </block>
              </next>
            </block>
          </statement>
        </block>
      </next>
    </block>
  </statement>
  <statement name="may_require:dependability_guarantee">
    <block type="dependability_guarantee$s" id="77"
    collapsed="true">
      <field name="name">Starting Position = Straight line</field>
      <field name="#technique">+</field>
      <field name="#measure">+</field>
      <requirement pinned="false" h="100" w="200">Satisfies
      requirement(s) :
----------------------------------------
----------------------------------------
1. CSoS-1.2
                                </requirement>
                                <data>CSoS-1.2</data>
                                <statement name="cs:CS">
                                  <block type="__link" id="155">
                                    <field name="link_to">CS /
                                    Kilobot</field>
```

```
                         <data>CS : 3 : 1</data>
                    </block>
                  </statement>
                </block>
              </next>
            </block>
          </statement>
          <statement name="on_failure:sequence">
            <block type="execute$s" id="164">
              <field name="function">doNothing</field>
              <field name="#CS">+</field>
              <statement name="cs:CS">
                <block type="__link" id="165">
                  <field name="link_to">CS / Kilobot</field>
                  <data>CS : 3 : 1</data>
                </block>
              </statement>
            </block>
          </statement>
          <next>
            <block type="If$s" id="166" collapsed="true">
              <field name="name">Turn Left Follower</field>
              <field name="on_condition"> == LEFT &&
              sender == LEADER</field>
              <field name="#CS">+</field>
              <field name="#state_variable">+</field>
              <field name="#sequence">+</field>
              <field name="#sequence">+</field>
              <statement name="cs:CS">
                <block type="__link" id="168">
                  <field name="link_to">CS / Kilobot</field>
                  <data>CS : 3 : 1</data>
                </block>
              </statement>
              <statement name="check_on:state_variable">
```

```
<block type="__link" id="169">
  <field name="link_to">State variable /
  received_msg</field>
  <data>state_variable : 112 : 1</data>
</block>
</statement>
<statement name="on_success:sequence">
  <block type="execute$s" id="170">
    <field name="function">turnLeft</field>
    <field name="#CS">+</field>
    <requirement pinned="false" h="100"
    w="200">Satisfies requirement(s) :
```
----
1. CSoS-1.1
```
    </requirement>
    <data>CSoS-1.1</data>
    <statement name="cs:CS">
      <block type="__link" id="171">
        <field name="link_to">CS /
        Kilobot</field>
        <data>CS : 3 : 1</data>
      </block>
    </statement>
    <next>
    <block type="execute$s" id="172">
      <field name="function">sendLeft
      </field>
      <field name="#CS">+</field>
      <requirement pinned="false" h="100"
      w="200">Satisfies requirement(s) :
```
----
1. CSoS-1.1
```
      </requirement>
      <data>CSoS-1.1</data>
      <statement name="cs:CS">
        <block type="__link" id="173">
```

```
                              <field name="link_to">CS /
                              Kilobot</field>
                              <data>CS : 3 : 1</data>
                          </block>
                        </statement>
                      </block>
                    </next>
                  </block>
              </statement>
              <statement name="on_failure:sequence">
                <block type="execute$s" id="174">
                  <field name="function">doNothing</field>
                  <field name="#CS">+</field>
                  <statement name="cs:CS">
                    <block type="__link" id="175">
                      <field name="link_to">CS /
                      Kilobot</field>
                      <data>CS : 3 : 1</data>
                    </block>
                  </statement>
                </block>
              </statement>
              <next>
                <block type="If$s" id="176" collapsed="true">
                  <field name="name">kilo_ticks check
                  </field>
                  <field name="on_condition"> > 2000
                  </field>
                  <field name="#CS">+</field>
                  <field name="#state_variable">+</field>
                  <field name="#sequence">+</field>
                  <field name="#sequence">+</field>
                  <statement name="cs:CS">
                    <block type="__link" id="178">
                      <field name="link_to">CS /
                      Kilobot</field>
```

```
      <data>CS : 3 : 1</data>
    </block>
  </statement>
  <statement name="check_on:state_
  variable">
    <block type="__link" id="177">
      <field name="link_to">State
      variable / kilo_ticks</field>
      <data>state_variable : 250 : 1</data>
    </block>
  </statement>
  <statement name="on_success:sequence">
    <block type="sub_sequence$s" id="233"
    collapsed="true">
      <field name="name">Leave</field>
      <field name="#sequence">+</field>
      <statement name="has:sequence">
        <block type="If$s" id="114">
          <field name="name">canLeave
          </field>
          <field name="on_condition">==
          LAST_IN_PLATOON</field>
          <field name="#CS">+</field>
          <field name="#state_
          variable">+</field>
          <field name="#sequence">+</field>
          <field name="#sequence">+</field>
          <statement name="cs:CS">
            <block type="__link" id="115">
              <field name="link_to">CS /
              Kilobot</field>
              <data>CS : 3 : 1</data>
            </block>
          </statement>
          <statement name="check_
          on:state_variable">
```

```
                              <block type="__link" id="116">
                                <field name="link_to">State
                                variable / kilo_uid</field>
                                <data>state_variable : 66 :
                                1</data>
                              </block>
                          </statement>
                          <statement name="on_
                          success:sequence">
                              <block type="execute$s"
                              id="352">
                                <field name="function">
                                sendLeave</field>
                                <field name="#CS">+</field>
                                <requirement pinned="false"
                                h="100" w="200">Satisfies
                                requirement(s) :
```

1. CSoS-1.3

```
                              </requirement>
                              <data>CSoS-1.3</data>
                              <statement name="cs:CS">
                                <block type="__link"
                                id="353">
                                    <field name="link_to">
                                    CS / Kilobot</field>
                                    <data>CS : 3 : 1</data>
                                </block>
                              </statement>
                              <next>
                                <block type="execute$s"
                                id="354">
                                    <field name="function">
                                    goAway</field>
                                    <field name="#CS">+
                                    </field>
```

```
                                   <requirement
                                   pinned="false" h="100"
                                   w="200">Satisfies
                                   requirement(s) :
------------------------------------

1. CSoS-1.3
                                   </requirement>
                                   <data>CSoS-1.3</data>
                                   <statement name="cs:CS">
                                     <block type="__link"
                                     id="355">
                                       <field name="link_
                                       to">CS / Kilobot
                                       </field>
                                       <data>CS : 3 : 1
                                       </data>
                                     </block>
                                   </statement>
                                 </block>
                               </next>
                             </block>
                           </statement>
                           <statement name="on_
                           failure:sequence">
                             <block type="execute$s"
                             id="179" collapsed="true">
                               <field name="function">
                               doNothing</field>
                               <field name="#CS">+</field>
                               <statement name="cs:CS">
                                 <block type="__link"
                                 id="180">
                                   <field name="link_to">
                                   CS / Kilobot</field>
                                   <data>CS : 3 : 1</data>
                                 </block>
```

```
                          </statement>
                        </block>
                      </statement>
                    </block>
                  </statement>
                </block>
              </statement>
              <statement name="on_failure:sequence">
                <block type="execute$s" id="181">
                  <field name="function">doNothing
                  </field>
                  <field name="#CS">+</field>
                  <statement name="cs:CS">
                    <block type="__link" id="182">
                      <field name="link_to">CS /
                      Kilobot</field>
                      <data>CS : 3 : 1</data>
                    </block>
                  </statement>
                </block>
              </statement>
              <next>
                <block type="sub_sequence$s" id="234"
                collapsed="true">
                  <field name="name">Join</field>
                  <field name="#sequence">+</field>
                  <statement name="has:sequence">
                    <block type="sub_sequence$s"
                    id="123">
                      <field name="name">
                      checkSequence</field>
                      <field name="#sequence">+</field>
                      <statement name="has:sequence">
                        <block type="If$s" id="124">
                          <field name="name">
                          idCheck</field>
```

```
<field name="on_
condition">  == 255</field>
<field name="#CS">+</field>
<field name="#state_
variable">+</field>
<field name="#sequence">+
</field>
<field name="#sequence">+
</field>
<statement name="cs:CS">
  <block type="__link"
  id="126">
    <field name="link_to">
    CS / Kilobot</field>
    <data>CS : 3 : 1</data>
  </block>
</statement>
<statement name="check_
on:state_variable">
  <block type="__link"
  id="125">
    <field name="link_to">
    State variable /
    leader_uid</field>
    <data>state_variable :
    67 : 1</data>
  </block>
</statement>
<statement name="on_
success:sequence">
  <block type="While$s"
  id="117">
    <field name="name">
    sendingJoin</field>
    <field name="condition">
    != OK</field>
```

```
<field name="#CS">+
</field>
<field name="#state_
variable">+</field>
<field name=
"#sequence">+</field>
<statement name="cs:CS">
  <block type="__link"
  id="119">
    <field name="link_
    to">CS / Kilobot
    </field>
    <data>CS : 3 : 1
    </data>
  </block>
</statement>
<statement name="check_
on:state_variable">
  <block type="__link"
  id="118">
    <field name="link_
    to">State variable /
    received_msg</field>
    <data>state_
    variable : 112 :
    1</data>
  </block>
</statement>
<statement name=
"has:sequence">
  <block type=
  "execute$s" id="135">
    <field name=
    "function">sendJoin
    </field>
    <field name=
    "#CS">+</field>
```

```
<requirement pinned=
"false" h="100"
w="200">Satisfies
```

This xml code is listed in this GitHub repository :

https://github.com/JosephThachilGeorge/Platoon-Project/blob/main/final-model.xml

Note that to run this code you can use any model simulator that accepts xml files.

Once you execute, you will get models shown in Figures 15-1a and 15-1b.

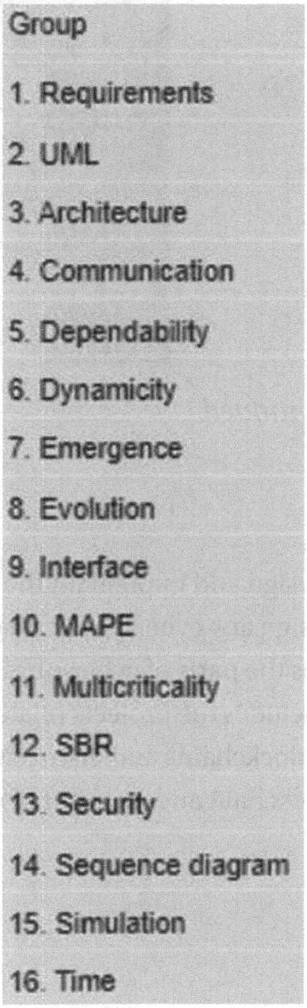

Group

1. Requirements

2. UML

3. Architecture

4. Communication

5. Dependability

6. Dynamicity

7. Emergence

8. Evolution

9. Interface

10. MAPE

11. Multicriticality

12. SBR

13. Security

14. Sequence diagram

15. Simulation

16. Time

Figure 15-1a. *The models*

Figure 15-1b. *The models, continued*

15.6 Summary

The project platoon helps you design and implement the cyber-physical system. The same concept can be used to design any cyber-physical system in the real world. The Kilobot movement illustrates the parts of cyber-physical systems and their characteristics. This chapter concludes the projects related to cyber-physical systems. So far, you've seen how to develop blockchains and distributed systems. In the next chapter, you learn about the future of blockchain and distributed cyber-physical systems.

## CHAPTER 16

Blockchain Technology and Distributed System Future Scope and B-Coin Project

Blockchain systems have attracted various industry stakeholders, including those in finance, healthcare, utilities, real estate, and government, since it solves many security problems in distributed systems. Public blockchains will play a significant role in cyber-security and Internet of Things (IoT) security as the commercial, government, and military sectors become more comfortable with it. At the same time, security and privacy problems in public blockchains will need to be addressed before they can be incorporated into existing core cloud and IoT devices.[1]

The development of blockchain systems will bring new concerns linked to the Internet of Smart Things, including trust, security, and privacy. Academia and business are collaborating to create blockchain platforms to address these urgent cloud and IoT security issues.[1]

We now know that blockchain platforms address issues such as cloud-based data proofing, information sharing, cloud storage, smart vehicles, IoT mass transit security, attack surface analysis, double spending prevention, trustless platform security, failure consensus protocols, statistics, and performance measures in cloud and IoT systems.

---

[1] *Blockchain for Distributed Systems Security*, Wiley, 2019

© Joseph Thachil George 2022
J. T. George, *Introducing Blockchain Applications*, https://doi.org/10.1007/978-1-4842-7480-4_16

Military and commercial organizations have also used cloud technology to enable data storage, on-demand computation, and dynamic provisioning. Cloud services' ecosystems are diverse and dynamic. They necessitate interoperability since they incorporate multiple hardware and software components from several suppliers.

16.1 Blockchain and IoT Security

Vehicles, infrastructures, home monitors, smart healthcare imaging, and wearable electronics have all embraced the Internet of Things (IoT) as the principal way to optimize interconnectedness between the cyber and physical worlds. In the IoT context, security is still a major problem. Despite considerable advancements in security in the area of information technology in recent years, security at the application level remains an open research issue.

16.1.1 Blockchain Implementations and Use Cases in IoT

The distributed ledger technology that underpins cryptocurrency, particularly Bitcoin, is known as blockchain. It's already being used in a number of industries, notably in retail to move items through supply chains more easily and securely, and in medicine to preserve the integrity of contracts, clinical studies, and the medications themselves.

The quality of the products is constantly checked by incorporating blockchain into these and other industries. A blockchain-focused research center has also been formed to encourage the development and commercialization of the technology and its potential to transform the IoT ecosystem.

16.1.2 Challenges with Integrating Blockchain Into IoT

The IoT blockchain is gaining traction, but it is not without its challenges. To begin, the blockchain's central idea is the chain of activities that have been completed. The chain is created by storing a reference to earlier operations, which are referred to in Bitcoin as *blocks*. Creating blocks, on the other hand, is a computationally expensive task that necessitates several processors and a significant amount of time. Because it's tough to make a single block, manipulating it would be far more complex—you'd have to fake the preceding block and then follow the chain you made to modify it.

16.2 Safety Recommendations

If properly managed, blockchain can significantly reduce costs and improve efficiency in IoT systems. However, technological adoption in IoT-enabled workplaces is far from ideal. Only 10% of blockchain ledgers in operation, for instance, are expected to integrate embedded technologies by 2020. Additionally, most IoT systems have a long way to go before they are computationally capable of handling the load.

IoT users, both people and companies, should seek multi-layered security with end-to-end security that spans from the gateway to the endpoint and is capable of preventing potential network attacks and compromises, in addition to timely software upgrades to avoid downtime. This includes the following:

- **Changing the default credentials**. IoT botnets have been found to use manufacturer default credentials to connect to linked devices. To decrease the danger of a device breach, it is advised that users enable secure passwords and use unique and complicated passwords.

- **Strengthening the router's security**. A network is made susceptible by a weak router. Using security management solutions to protect routers helps users keep track of all devices connected while protecting privacy and productivity.

- **Configuring security devices**. The device's default settings must be evaluated and modified to meet the needs of the user. To improve security, it's a good idea to personalize features and turn off those that aren't needed. Keep an eye on the network traffic. Actively monitoring for unusual behavior on the Internet can assist consumers in avoiding harmful efforts. Real-time scanning provided by security solutions may also be used to identify malware automatically and effectively.

- **Implementing additional security measures**. For extra protection, users should activate firewalls and use the Wi-Fi Protected Access II security protocol. Web reputations and application control-based technologies also give greater network visibility.

16.3 Blockchain Security and Privacy

Security and privacy threats can be exploited on blockchain networks. Several chapters characterize attack surfaces, identify vulnerabilities in consensus protocols, discuss privacy and security threats to blockchain without and with required authorization, diagnose problems to defend against duplicate spending, and isolate effective defenses adopted by blockchain technology or proposed by researchers to mitigate the risks.

Through cryptography, there is blockchain-based document ownership of all existing currencies inside a cryptocurrency ecosystem at any one time. A transaction is stored in a "block" on the blockchain once it has been confirmed and cryptographically verified by other network members or nodes.

The timing of the transaction, prior transactions, and transaction details are all stored in a block. Events are kept chronologically and cannot be altered after they have been entered as a block. Since the birth of Bitcoin and the initial use of blockchain technology, this technology has stimulated the development of additional cryptocurrencies and applications.

Data is not validated and controlled by a single organization, as in traditional systems, due to decentralization. Rather, every node or computer connected to the network verifies the authenticity of transactions. Cryptography secures and verifies transactions and data in the blockchain technology.

Data breaches have grown more prevalent as the use of technology has increased. Personal data and information are stored, abused, and misused, posing a danger to privacy. Numerous people are advocating for blockchain technology to be widely used because it can increase user privacy, data security, and data ownership.

16.4 The Future Scope

Despite the fact that there are numerous blockchain systems on the market and that substantial research and development is being done on specific blockchain aspects, additional study in the following categories is required.

16.4.1 Blockchain Architecture: Private, Public, or Hybrid-Public Blockchain Design

Transactions are conducted in a decentralized manner. Commercial businesses, on the other hand, are wary of incorporating a public blockchain into their corporate solutions, due to worries about privacy, performance, and reaction time. To solve these problems, more R&D in the public blockchain system is required.

Meanwhile, corporate players are moving closer to private/approved consensus mechanisms. Depending on the type of governance, this architecture might range from a single member to a consortium that controls the blockchain platform. The architecture, protocol, or method by which transactions are verified on these blockchain platforms has administrative components.

16.4.2 Inducement

In Bitcoin, there is a monetary incentive to join the blockchain platform; however, there are no monetary incentives in use cases like provenance and identity management. To achieve maximum involvement, the incentive structure must be included in the protocol.

To guarantee that blockchain protocols function to maximize advantages for the use case, mechanisms for incentive design may be generated from use cases. While trust management of the public blockchain may prevent manipulations or fraud, it is critical that the architecture incorporate incentive mechanisms with anti-fraud or anti-justice qualities. The processes involved in motivating participation need the development of theoretical models.

16.4.3 Data Privacy

Because blockchain transactions are public, data analysis techniques may be used to analyze the vast quantities of data included inside them. The identities of participants and the precise transactions they have done might be revealed as a result of this research. Stealth addresses, homomorphic cryptography, and zero-knowledge proof are among the approaches used to solve privacy problems in public blockchain systems. A mix of approaches is necessary to obtain the appropriate level of anonymity.

16.5 Having Realistic Expectations of Blockchain

Blockchain technology has been gaining attention for some time, and it can perhaps be said that despite being a complex technology, it has become a "mainstream" theme. Blockchain technology issues have been addressed by large newspapers, radios, and television shows that normally rarely focus on such innovative technologies. In many cases, blockchain technology is proposed as "the solution" to problems and needs that have never been truly satisfied by traditional technology. The expectations, not only of companies but of consumers, on blockchain technology have greatly increased. On the one hand, this situation favors debate and growth, but on the other hand it creates a dangerous situation because some of the "beneficial effects" "that today are attributed to blockchain technology are the result of misunderstandings. It is important to emphasize that blockchain technology cannot solve all our problems. The following sections discuss some of these issues.

16.6 Food Certification

In the agri-food sector, blockchain technology has growing consensus, precisely because it can provide guarantees of reliability on often complex and fragmented supply chains, not only due to the size of the companies but because of the culture of the organizations or countries in which they are located. Blockchain technology guarantees the certainty, the immutability, and the transparency of the data that accompanies production.

We must not think that blockchain is, in itself, a guarantee of quality, which can "by itself" guarantee not only the certification but the quality of the product. Blockchain technology certifies the data and guarantees its identity and transparency for all actors. But if the original data does not correctly represent the product that goes into production, if that data is "wrong" to begin with, blockchain technology does not correct it. On the contrary, blockchain ensures that that "wrong" data is kept intact throughout the supply chain. As they say, "garbage in, garbage out".

The transparency of blockchain is a possible corrective, because everyone can see that the data and everyone can (if they are able to do so) ascertain its value and propose a correction. Blockchain technology guarantees the process of managing that data for all participants.

16.7 Smart Contracts and Notaries

Smart contracts can cause some confusion when compared to the discipline of the traditional contract. However, by briefly reviewing the essential requirements of the contract governed by civil code, it is easy to identify numerous similarities that could constitute the legal basis for assimilating smart contracts into the discipline of the traditional contract.[2]

It is possible to state that the space of operation of this principle coincides with the space of operation of private autonomy; as an agreement, the contract is by definition a bilateral act. However, there are possible unilateral acts that can be classified in the contractual legal regime. In this case, they are non-intrusive unilateral acts of the legal sphere, as they "leave intact the power of the subject involved to totally self-determine with respect to the situation created."[3] Examples of these types of contracts are power of attorney, wills, and waivers.

16.7.1 Applying Blockchain Technology to Smart Contracts

At this junction, a quick description of how blockchain technology pertains to a smart contract and how a contract might physically assume a directly technical shape, as opposed to natural language, is required.

Preliminarily, it's important to note that the parties' involvement is plainly required at the outset. The parties will decide the contract's conditions by mutual agreement. The core of the structure may be considered to be made up of three major elements: the account (also known as the parties' identity), the assets you have (assets), and the contract.

We use the term "account" to refer to an address that may be used to identify a person, entity, or group of individuals who will proceed to interact with the ledger in question, the so-called "ledger" of which we spoke previously in the chapter. Instead,

---

[2] Security and Privacy on Blockchain RUI ZHANG and RUI XUE, State Key Laboratory of Information Security, Institute of Information Engineering, Chinese Academy of Sciences, China and School of Cyber Security, University of Chinese Academy of Sciences, China.

[3] V. Roppo, "Il contratto", in Trattato di diritto privato, a cura di G. Iudica e P. Zatti, Milano, 2011, p. 28.

products, often known as "assets," contain both tangible and intangible items, as well as invoices and units of value transferred.

Assets can be defined more broadly as a collection of values traded and held by one or more parties that have access to the cryptographic key that permits a contract to be settled. The contract, defined as a logical series of activities that mediates the transfer of cash and data between the parties, is the final prerequisite (accounts).

These accounts change their status by sending updates to the master register, which include approved transactions. Before being collected and sequenced into a block, transactions are transmitted and validated for their integrity and for data integrity.

The account holder on the network digitally signs all transactions on the ledger. This gives the ledger three key characteristics that distinguish it from traditional network traffic:

- Authentication as part of harmful activity cannot be misrepresented as utilizing an account that isn't a part of the transaction if it isn't.

- The transaction's integrity, because the receipt of the transaction cannot be altered once it has occurred.

- Non-malleability, because any modifications to the transaction will invalidate the issuer's signature and render the transaction void.

Before being added to the chain, each provision is negotiated and accepted by both parties. Once the clause has been accepted, it is placed into the first block and converted from plain language to an encrypted language that the system can understand.

The parties' real actions are to input, using their cryptographic keys, both the clauses intended to perform the contract and the actions that the system will carry out automatically in the case of a breach. The contract will advance if the system records the fulfillment of the fact referred to in the clause; if, on the other hand, the clause's content is broken, the contract will use technologies that make the remedies given by the parties individually or by law.

It will not be feasible to utilize the "backup" method if you find yourself in a scenario where one party claims to have a contract with certain provisions and the other claims to have the same contract, but with different clauses. The blockchain, like other everyday technology such as mobile phones and computers, has a data storage mechanism.

No doubt, smart contracts based on blockchain technology can bring enormous benefits to companies, organizations, and public administrations. The prospects are unquestionable and sectors such as insurance, logistics, and procurement are already reaping important benefits from it. Here too there remains a point of utmost attention in the transition phase from the real, physical, and digital world, in the certainty of providing correct information by subjects, persons, or companies.

How to manage this passage the scenario is still open to debate. The function of the notary can play an important role in providing guarantees about secure data. Again, the blockchain does not ascertain the "truth" or quality of the information. The blockchain guarantees its incorruptibility, protects the data from possible violations, and transparently exposes changes to all the actors involved. In this way, blockchain speeds up any identification of "errors," but it is not an "intelligent system" that can guarantee quality.

16.7.2 Developing Blockchain in the Market

Blockchain technology is a recent phenomenon that has experienced an important series of accelerations and that has created many expectations. At the same time, developing and implementing blockchain is not an easy task and no single company can make it happen. For everyone—producers and companies and user organizations—blockchain is an ecosystem phenomenon, of a collaborative type.

If, on the one hand, the level of attention that accompanies blockchain is very high, on the other hand, the number of concrete cases, of projects actually in production in companies and organizations, is still quite low.

16.7.3 The Geopolitics of the Blockchain

Blockchain has the characteristics of a revolution, and it also has disruptive characteristics, which can be destabilizing. For this and other reasons, there are very different ways of approaching the blockchain technology. There are countries or geographical areas that have embraced it (such as Dubai, Estonia, and Singapore), and there are countries that are taking a very careful and pragmatic approach, for example with an intense study of new regulations appropriate to management of such an innovative phenomenon (such as Switzerland, Austria, and Malta).

Then there is Europe, which is looking for its own dimension and is doing so with a series of initiatives, including the European Blockchain Partnership. There are also countries that are looking at blockchain with skepticism.

16.7.4 Books, Whitepapers, and Blockchains

With blockchain, an intense activity of publication, study, and in-depth analysis began with a rich publication of books and whitepapers. In the blockchain books section, you will find books specifically related to blockchain. In the books and whitepapers section, you will find information about the potential of Industry 4.0 and digital transformation, including selected texts related to the issues of digital transformation in companies.

16.8 Bitcoin (B-Coin) Sample Project

This project illustrates a cryptocurrency implemented in Python on top of blockchain technology. It is a simple blockchain cryptocurrency and should be used only for educational purposes. This blockchain network has no central authority. The information in it is open for everyone to see. Recall the main properties of blockchain technology:

- Decentralization

- Transparency

- Immutability

In this simple implementation of blockchain, B-Coin is built on top of the blockchain implementation. You can find more information in the original paper, found in the original Bitcoin repository at `https://github.com/bitcoin`.

Here are the project's requirements:

- Python 3.1 or 3.2

- Flask or Django

- Requests

- Postman

16.8.1 The Project Code

The following task is done using the code found in `bitcoin.py`. It has a class called `blockchain`. Note that this class creates blocks with five fields—`index`, `timestamp`, proof, `previous_hash`, and `transactions`. Additionally, we have a proof of work for mining the block. The goal is to have four leading zeros in the resultant hash. (See Listing 16-1.)

It has the following functions and methods:

```
# add transactions
# adding the node
# replacing the chain with the longest chain
```

In addition to these methods, it has the POST and GET methods for managing blocks in the chain.

Listing 16-1. bitcoin.py

```
***********
# Creating a block chain
class Blockchain:
    def __init__(self):
        # our whole chain
        self.chain=[]
        # list of transactions
        self.transactions = []
        # genesis block
        self.create_block(proof= 1 , previous_hash='0')
        # nodes in the network should be unique
        self.nodes = set()
    """
    This class is for method is for creating block with five fields
    index, timestamp, proof, previous_hash,transactions
    """
    def create_block(self, proof, previous_hash):
        block={'index' : len(self.chain) + 1,
                'timestamp' : str(datetime.datetime.now()),
                'proof' : proof,
                'previous_hash' : previous_hash,
                'transactions' : self.transactions}
        # empty the transactions after all are added to the block
        self.transactions = []
        self.chain.append(block)
        return block
```

```
    # Getting the old block
    def get_previous_block(self):
        return self.chain[-1]

# We have a proof of work for mining the block.

# The goal is to have four leading zeros in the resultant hash.

    def proof_of_work(self,previous_proof):
        new_proof = 1
        check_proof = False

        # create a hash and look if new_proof**2 - previous_proof**2 has
            leading 4 0s else increment the proof and check
        while check_proof is False:
            hash_operation = hashlib.sha256(str(new_proof**2 - previous_
            proof**2).encode()).hexdigest()
            if hash_operation[:4]=='0000':
                check_proof =  True
            else:
                new_proof +=1
        return new_proof

# Hashing
# json. dumps() accepts a json object as input and returns a string.
# The hex() function returns a string after converting the string to bytes.
    def hash(self,block):
        encoded_block = json.dumps(block, sort_keys = True).encode()
        return hashlib.sha256(encoded_block).hexdigest()

    # Checking if a block is valid or not
    def is_chain_valid(self, block):
        previous_block = self.chain[0]
        block_index=1
        while block_index < len(self.chain):
            block = self.chain[block_index]

            # Check if the previous hash in the current block differs from
                the preceding block's original hash.
```

```
            if block['previous_hash'] != self.hash(previous_block):
                return False

            # Check if the resultant hash of the proof**2 - previous_
              proof**2 does not have 4 leading 0s
            previous_proof = previous_block['proof']
            proof = block['proof']
            hash_operation = hashlib.sha256(str(proof**2 - previous_
            proof**2).encode()).hexdigest()
            if hash_operation[:4] !='0000':
                return False

            # update the block and increase the index
            previous_block=block
            block_index +=1
        return True

# add transactions
# We'll send it to Postman in json format as a sample request.
def add_transaction(self, sender, receiver, amount):
    self.transactions.append({'sender' : sender,
                              'receiver' : receiver,
                              'amount' : amount})
    previous_block = self.get_previous_block()
    # return the index of the current block (+1 for genesis block)
    return previous_block['index'] + 1

# adding the node
def add_node(self,address):
    # parsed_url = urlparse('http://127.0.0.1:1000/')
    # parsed_url.netloc - '127.0.0.1:1000'
    parsed_url = urlparse(address)
    self.nodes.add(parsed_url.netloc)

# replacing the chain with the longest chain
def replace_chain(self):
    # taking all of our nodes
    network = self.nodes
```

```
            longest_chain = None
            # max_length is set to the current length
            max_length = len(self.chain)
            # go through all of the nodes and see all of their chains
            for node in network:
                response = requests.get(f'http://{node}/get_chain')
                # if chain is valid
                if response.status_code == 200:
                    # get its length and the chain
                    length = response.json()['length']
                    chain = response.json()['chain']
                    # if it has the length greater than the current length
                      update the max_length and the longest chain
                    if length > max_length and self.is_chain_valid(chain):
                        max_length = length
                        longest_chain = chain
            # if longest_chain is set chain the chain to the longest_chain
            if longest_chain:
                self.chain = longest_chain
                return True
            return False

# Creating a web app
app = Flask(__name__)

# Creating a port 1000 address for the node.
# uuid4() generates a globally unique identifier at random (UUID -
generated using synchronization methods that ensure no two processes can
obtain the same UUID)
node_address = str(uuid4()).replace('-', '')

# Putting together a blockchain
blockchain=Blockchain()

# Mining a block
@app.route('/mine_block', methods = ['GET'])
def mine_block():
    """
```

We'll use the previous block's proof to compute the new proof and build the current block using that proof and the prior hash.
```
    """
    previous_block = blockchain.get_previous_block()
    previous_proof = previous_block['proof']
    proof = blockchain.proof_of_work(previous_proof)
    previous_hash = blockchain.hash(previous_block)
    # We may award the bcoin if we mine a block. The miner who receives the
        block can be chosen.
    blockchain.add_transaction(sender = node_address, receiver =
    'Bharathi', amount = 1)
    block = blockchain.create_block(proof, previous_hash)

    # Return the response
    response = {'message' : 'You just mined a block, congrats!',
                'index' : block['index'],
                'timestamp' : block['timestamp'],
                'proof' : block['proof'],
                'previous_hash' : block['previous_hash'],
                'transactions' : block['transactions']}
    # With an application/json mimetype, return a JSON representation of
        the supplied parameters (Multipurpose Internet Mail Extensions or
        MIME type).
    return jsonify(response), 200

# Getting the blockchain
@app.route('/get_chain', methods = ['GET'])
def get_chain():
    # Return the response
    response = {'chain' : blockchain.chain,
                'length' : len(blockchain.chain)}
    return jsonify(response), 200

# Checking if the Blockchain is valid
@app.route('/is_valid', methods = ['GET'])
def is_valid():
    is_valid = blockchain.is_chain_valid(blockchain.chain)
```

```
    if is_valid:
        response = {'message': 'Everything is fine. The Blockchain is
        correct..'}
    else:
        response = {'message': 'Weve got an issue. The Blockchain isnt
        trustworthy..'}
    return jsonify(response), 200

# Adding a new transaction to the blockchain
@app.route('/add_transaction', methods = ['POST'])
def add_transaction():
    # We're sending the transactions to Postman in json format, thus we'll
      get them back in json format.
    json = request.get_json()
    # checking if it contains all of the keys
    transaction_keys = ['sender', 'receiver', 'amount']
    if not all(key in json for key in transaction_keys):
        return 'Some elements of the transactions are missing', 400
    # We will add the transaction and return the answer as added if it has
      all of the components.
    index = blockchain.add_transaction(json['sender'],json['receiver'],json
    ['amount'])
    response = {'message' : fThis transaction will be added to the Block
    {index}'}
    return jsonify(response), 201

# Our blockchain is becoming more decentralized.

#Connecting new nodes
@app.route('/connect_node', methods = ['POST'])
def connect_node():
    # connecting all of the other nodes manually
    json = request.get_json()
    nodes = json.get('nodes')
```

```
    # return none if node field is null
    if nodes is None:
        return 'No node', 400
# We'll manually add the nodes. This is repeated for each node.
# Because our nodes are a set, it will only include unique values if done
separately for each node.
    for node in nodes:
        blockchain.add_node(node)
    # show the nodes and mark the answer as all connected
    response = {'message' : 'All of the nodes are now linked together. The
    node has now been added to the Bitcoin blockchain.',
                'total_nodes' : list(blockchain.nodes)}
    # http 201 created
    return jsonify(response), 201

# Replacing the chain by the longest chain
@app.route('/replace_chain', methods = ['GET'])
def replace_chain():
    # If any chain is longer, the longest chain will be displayed instead,
      otherwise the same chain will be displayed.
    is_chain_replaced = blockchain.replace_chain()
    if is_chain_replaced:
        response = {'message': 'Because the nodes are different, the
        longest chain is used to replace the chain..',
                    'new_chain' : blockchain.chain}
    else:
        response = {'message': 'Everything is fine. The chain is the most
        extensive.', 'new_chain' : blockchain.chain}
    return jsonify(response), 200

# Running the app on the port
app.run(host = '0.0.0.0', port = 1001)
```

****

The next Python files are bcoin-node-1001.py, bcoin-node-1002.py, and bcoin-node-1003.py. These files represent each node (Bitcoins 1001, 1002, and 1003).

- bcoin-node-1001.py: Has a class called Blockchain which manages nodes in the blockchain (or bitcoin node-1001). Additionally, it has functions for creating blocks, functions for adding transactions, and functions for validating blocks. In addition to this, the main block has GET and POST methods (see Listing 16-2).

- bcoin-node-1002.py: Has a class called Blockchain which manages nodes in the blockchain (or bitcoin node-1002). Additionally, it has functions for creating blocks, functions for adding transactions, and functions for validating blocks. In addition to this , the main block has GET and POST methods (see Listing 16-3).

- bcoin-node-1003.py: Has a class called Blockchain which manages nodes in the blockchain (or bitcoin node-1003). Additionally, it has functions for creating blocks, functions for adding transactions, and functions for validating blocks. In addition to this, the main block has GET and POST methods (see Listing 16-4).

The following code listings show Python codes for three different Bitcoins.

Listing 16-2. bcoin-node-1001.py

```python
# This is the Python class for Blockchain
class Blockchain:
    def __init__(self):
        self.chain=[]
        self.transactions = []
        self.create_block(proof= 1 , previous_hash='0')
        self.nodes = set()
#Function for creating block
    def create_block(self, proof, previous_hash):
        block={'index' : len(self.chain) + 1,
                'timestamp' : str(datetime.datetime.now()),
                'proof' : proof,
                'previous_hash' : previous_hash,
                'transactions' : self.transactions}
```

```
        self.transactions = []
        self.chain.append(block)
        return block

    def get_previous_block(self):
        return self.chain[-1]

    def proof_of_work(self,previous_proof):
        new_proof = 1
        check_proof = False

        while check_proof is False:
            hash_operation = hashlib.sha256(str(new_proof**2 -
            previous_proof**2).encode()).hexdigest()
            if hash_operation[:4]=='0000':
                check_proof =  True
            else:
                new_proof +=1
        return new_proof

    def hash(self,block):
        encoded_block = json.dumps(block, sort_keys = True).encode()
        return hashlib.sha256(encoded_block).hexdigest()

    def is_chain_valid(self, block):
        previous_block = self.chain[0]
        block_index=1
        while block_index < len(self.chain):
            block = self.chain[block_index]

            if block['previous_hash'] != self.hash(previous_block):
                return False

            previous_proof = previous_block['proof']
            proof = block['proof']
            hash_operation = hashlib.sha256(str(proof**2 -
            previous_proof**2).encode()).hexdigest()
            if hash_operation[:4] !='0000':
                return False
```

```
                previous_block=block
                block_index +=1
            return True

#Function for adding transaction

    def add_transaction(self, sender, receiver, amount):
        self.transactions.append({'sender' : sender,
                        'receiver' : receiver,
                        'amount' : amount})
        previous_block = self.get_previous_block()
        return previous_block['index'] + 1

    def add_node(self,address):
        parsed_url = urlparse(address)
        self.nodes.add(parsed_url.netloc)

    def replace_chain(self):
        network = self.nodes
        longest_chain = None
        max_length = len(self.chain)
        for node in network:
            response = requests.get(f'http://{node}/get_chain')
            if response.status_code == 200:
                length = response.json()['length']
                chain = response.json()['chain']
                if length > max_length and self.is_chain_valid(chain):
                    max_length = length
                    longest_chain = chain
        if longest_chain:
            self.chain = longest_chain
            return True
        return False

app = Flask(__name__)

node_address = str(uuid4()).replace('-', '')

blockchain=Blockchain()
```

```
@app.route('/mine_block', methods = ['GET'])
def mine_block():
    previous_block = blockchain.get_previous_block()
    previous_proof = previous_block['proof']
    proof = blockchain.proof_of_work(previous_proof)
    previous_hash = blockchain.hash(previous_block)
    blockchain.add_transaction(sender = node_address, receiver =
    'Bharathi', amount = 1)
    block = blockchain.create_block(proof, previous_hash)

    response = {'message' : 'Congrats, you just mined a block!',
                'index' : block['index'],
                'timestamp' : block['timestamp'],
                'proof' : block['proof'],
                'previous_hash' : block['previous_hash'],
                'transactions' : block['transactions']}
    return jsonify(response), 200

#Get method for blockchain
@app.route('/get_chain', methods = ['GET'])
def get_chain():
    response = {'chain' : blockchain.chain,
                'length' : len(blockchain.chain)}
    return jsonify(response), 200

 #Validate method for blockchain

@app.route('/is_valid', methods = ['GET'])
def is_valid():
    is_valid = blockchain.is_chain_valid(blockchain.chain)
    if is_valid:
        response = {'message': 'Everything is fine. The Blockchain is
        correct.'}
    else:
        response = {'message': 'Weve got an issue. The Blockchain isnt
        trustworthy..'}
    return jsonify(response), 200
```

```
#POST method for blockchain

@app.route('/add_transaction', methods = ['POST'])
def add_transaction():
    json = request.get_json()
    transaction_keys = ['sender', 'receiver', 'amount']
    if not all(key in json for key in transaction_keys):
        return 'Some transactional components are missing.', 400
    index = blockchain.add_transaction(json['sender'],json['receiver'],json
    ['amount'])
    response = {'message' : This transaction will be added to the Block
    {index}'}
    return jsonify(response), 201

 #Connect to the node

@app.route('/connect_node', methods = ['POST'])
def connect_node():
    json = request.get_json()
    nodes = json.get('nodes')
    if nodes is None:
        return 'No node', 400
    for node in nodes:
        blockchain.add_node(node)
    response = {'message' : 'All of the nodes are now linked together. The
    node has now been added to the Bitcoin blockchain',
                'total_nodes' : list(blockchain.nodes)}
    return jsonify(response), 201

 #method for changing mode

@app.route('/replace_chain', methods = ['GET'])
def replace_chain():
    is_chain_replaced = blockchain.replace_chain()
    if is_chain_replaced:
        response = {'message': 'Because the nodes are different, the
        longest chain is used to replace the chain..',
```

```
                        'new_chain' : blockchain.chain}
    else:
        response = {'message': 'Everything is fine. The Blockchain is correct.
        The chain is the longest one','new_chain' : blockchain.chain}
    return jsonify(response), 200

app.run(host = '0.0.0.0', port = 1001)

*********************************************************
```

Listing 16-3. bcoin-node-1002.py

```
class Blockchain:
    def __init__(self):
        self.chain=[]
        self.transactions = []
        self.create_block(proof= 1 , previous_hash='0')
        self.nodes = set()

    def create_block(self, proof, previous_hash):
        block={'index' : len(self.chain) + 1,
                'timestamp' : str(datetime.datetime.now()),
                'proof' : proof,
                'previous_hash' : previous_hash,
                'transactions' : self.transactions}
        self.transactions = []
        self.chain.append(block)
        return block

    def get_previous_block(self):
        return self.chain[-1]

    def proof_of_work(self,previous_proof):
        new_proof = 1
        check_proof = False
```

```
        while check_proof is False:
            hash_operation = hashlib.sha256(str(new_proof**2 - previous_
            proof**2).encode()).hexdigest()
            if hash_operation[:4]=='0000':
                check_proof =  True
            else:
                new_proof +=1
        return new_proof

    def hash(self,block):
        encoded_block = json.dumps(block, sort_keys = True).encode()
        return hashlib.sha256(encoded_block).hexdigest()

    def is_chain_valid(self, block):
        previous_block = self.chain[0]
        block_index=1
        while block_index < len(self.chain):
            block = self.chain[block_index]

            if block['previous_hash'] != self.hash(previous_block):
                return False

            previous_proof = previous_block['proof']
            proof = block['proof']
            hash_operation = hashlib.sha256(str(proof**2 -
            previous_proof**2).encode()).hexdigest()
            if hash_operation[:4] !='0000':
                return False

            previous_block=block
            block_index +=1
        return True

    def add_transaction(self, sender, receiver, amount):
        self.transactions.append({'sender' : sender,
                        'receiver' : receiver,
                        'amount' : amount})
        previous_block = self.get_previous_block()
        return previous_block['index'] + 1
```

```
def add_node(self,address):
    parsed_url = urlparse(address)
    self.nodes.add(parsed_url.netloc)

def replace_chain(self):
    network = self.nodes
    longest_chain = None
    max_length = len(self.chain)
    for node in network:
        response = requests.get(f'http://{node}/get_chain')
        if response.status_code == 200:
            length = response.json()['length']
            chain = response.json()['chain']
            if length > max_length and self.is_chain_valid(chain):
                max_length = length
                longest_chain = chain
    if longest_chain:
        self.chain = longest_chain
        return True
    return False

app = Flask(__name__)

node_address = str(uuid4()).replace('-', '')

blockchain=Blockchain()

@app.route('/mine_block', methods = ['GET'])
def mine_block():
    previous_block = blockchain.get_previous_block()
    previous_proof = previous_block['proof']
    proof = blockchain.proof_of_work(previous_proof)
    previous_hash = blockchain.hash(previous_block)
    blockchain.add_transaction(sender = node_address, receiver = 'Meghna',
    amount = 1)
    block = blockchain.create_block(proof, previous_hash)
```

```
    response = {'message' : 'Youve just mined a block, so congrats!',
                'index' : block['index'],
                'timestamp' : block['timestamp'],
                'proof' : block['proof'],
                'previous_hash' : block['previous_hash'],
                'transactions' : block['transactions']}
    return jsonify(response), 200

@app.route('/get_chain', methods = ['GET'])
def get_chain():
    response = {'chain' : blockchain.chain,
                'length' : len(blockchain.chain)}
    return jsonify(response), 200

@app.route('/is_valid', methods = ['GET'])
def is_valid():
    is_valid = blockchain.is_chain_valid(blockchain.chain)
    if is_valid:
        response = {'message': 'Everything is fine. The Blockchain is
        correct..'}
    else:
        response = {'message': 'We ve got an issue. The Blockchain isnt
        trustworthy..'}
    return jsonify(response), 200

@app.route('/add_transaction', methods = ['POST'])
def add_transaction():
    json = request.get_json()
    transaction_keys = ['sender', 'receiver', 'amount']
    if not all(key in json for key in transaction_keys):
        return 'Some transactional components are missing.', 400
    index = blockchain.add_transaction(json['sender'],json['receiver'],json
    ['amount'])
    response = {'message' : f'This transaction will be added to the Block
    {index}'}
    return jsonify(response), 201
```

```
@app.route('/connect_node', methods = ['POST'])
def connect_node():
    json = request.get_json()
    nodes = json.get('nodes')
    if nodes is None:
        return 'No node', 400
    for node in nodes:
        blockchain.add_node(node)
    response = {'message' : 'All of the nodes are now linked together. The
node has now been added to the Bitcoin blockchain.',
              'total_nodes' : list(blockchain.nodes)}
    return jsonify(response), 201

@app.route('/replace_chain', methods = ['GET'])
def replace_chain():
    is_chain_replaced = blockchain.replace_chain()
    if is_chain_replaced:
        response = {'message': 'Because the nodes are different, the
        longest chain is used to replace the chain..',
                    'new_chain' : blockchain.chain}
    else:
        response = {'message': 'Everything seems to be fine. It is the most
        extensive chain.',
                    'new_chain' : blockchain.chain}
    return jsonify(response), 200

app.run(host = '0.0.0.0', port = 1002)
```

Listing 16-4. bcoin-node-1003.py

```
class Blockchain:
    def __init__(self):
        self.chain=[]
        self.transactions = []
        self.create_block(proof= 1 , previous_hash='0')
        self.nodes = set()
```

```
def create_block(self, proof, previous_hash):
    block={'index' : len(self.chain) + 1,
           'timestamp' : str(datetime.datetime.now()),
           'proof' : proof,
           'previous_hash' : previous_hash,
           'transactions' : self.transactions}
    self.transactions = []
    self.chain.append(block)
    return block

def get_previous_block(self):
    return self.chain[-1]

def proof_of_work(self,previous_proof):
    new_proof = 1
    check_proof = False

    while check_proof is False:
        hash_operation = hashlib.sha256(str(new_proof**2 - previous_
        proof**2).encode()).hexdigest()
        if hash_operation[:4]=='0000':
            check_proof =  True
        else:
            new_proof +=1
    return new_proof

def hash(self,block):
    encoded_block = json.dumps(block, sort_keys = True).encode()
    return hashlib.sha256(encoded_block).hexdigest()

def is_chain_valid(self, block):
    previous_block = self.chain[0]
    block_index=1
    while block_index < len(self.chain):
        block = self.chain[block_index]

        if block['previous_hash'] != self.hash(previous_block):
            return False
```

```
        previous_proof = previous_block['proof']
        proof = block['proof']
        hash_operation = hashlib.sha256(str(proof**2 - previous_
        proof**2).encode()).hexdigest()
        if hash_operation[:4] !='0000':
            return False

        previous_block=block
        block_index +=1
    return True

def add_transaction(self, sender, receiver, amount):
    self.transactions.append({'sender' : sender,
                        'receiver' : receiver,
                        'amount' : amount})
    previous_block = self.get_previous_block()
    return previous_block['index'] + 1

def add_node(self,address):
    parsed_url = urlparse(address)
    self.nodes.add(parsed_url.netloc)

def replace_chain(self):
    network = self.nodes
    longest_chain = None
    max_length = len(self.chain)
    for node in network:
        response = requests.get(f'http://{node}/get_chain')
        if response.status_code == 200:
            length = response.json()['length']
            chain = response.json()['chain']
            if length > max_length and self.is_chain_valid(chain):
                max_length = length
                longest_chain = chain
    if longest_chain:
        self.chain = longest_chain
        return True
    return False
```

```
app = Flask(__name__)

node_address = str(uuid4()).replace('-', '')

blockchain=Blockchain()

@app.route('/mine_block', methods = ['GET'])
def mine_block():
    previous_block = blockchain.get_previous_block()
    previous_proof = previous_block['proof']
    proof = blockchain.proof_of_work(previous_proof)
    previous_hash = blockchain.hash(previous_block)
    blockchain.add_transaction(sender = node_address, receiver = 'Meghna',
    amount = 1)
    block = blockchain.create_block(proof, previous_hash)

    response = {'message' : 'You just mined a block, congrats!!',
                'index' : block['index'],
                'timestamp' : block['timestamp'],
                'proof' : block['proof'],
                'previous_hash' : block['previous_hash'],
                'transactions' : block['transactions']}
    return jsonify(response), 200

@app.route('/get_chain', methods = ['GET'])
def get_chain():
    response = {'chain' : blockchain.chain,
                'length' : len(blockchain.chain)}
    return jsonify(response), 200

@app.route('/is_valid', methods = ['GET'])
def is_valid():
    is_valid = blockchain.is_chain_valid(blockchain.chain)
    if is_valid:
        response = {'message': 'Everything is fine. The Blockchain is
        correct.'}
```

```
    else:
        response = {'message': 'We ve got an issue. The Blockchain isnt
        trustworthy..'}
    return jsonify(response), 200

@app.route('/add_transaction', methods = ['POST'])
def add_transaction():
    json = request.get_json()
    transaction_keys = ['sender', 'receiver', 'amount']
    if not all(key in json for key in transaction_keys):
        return 'Some elements of the transactions are missing', 400
    index = blockchain.add_transaction(json['sender'],json['receiver'],json
    ['amount'])
    response = {'message' : f'This transaction will be added to the Block
    {index}'}
    return jsonify(response), 201

@app.route('/connect_node', methods = ['POST'])
def connect_node():
    json = request.get_json()
    nodes = json.get('nodes')
    if nodes is None:
        return 'No node', 400
    for node in nodes:
        blockchain.add_node(node)
    response = {'message' : 'All of the nodes are now linked together. The
    node has now been added to the Bcoin blockchain.',
                'total_nodes' : list(blockchain.nodes)}
    return jsonify(response), 201

@app.route('/replace_chain', methods = ['GET'])
def replace_chain():
    is_chain_replaced = blockchain.replace_chain()
    if is_chain_replaced:
        response = {'message': 'Because the nodes are different, the
        longest chain is used to replace the chain..',
                    'new_chain' : blockchain.chain}
```

```
    else:
        response = {'message': 'Everything is fine. The chain is the most
        extensive.',
                        'new_chain' : blockchain.chain}
    return jsonify(response), 200

app.run(host = '0.0.0.0', port = 1003)
```
****

Example node addresses (nodes.json in Listing 16-5) and transaction formats are
shown in the .json files (transaction.json in Listing 16-6).

Listing 16-5. nodes.json

```
{
    "nodes" : ["http://127.0.0.1:1001",
               "http://127.0.0.1:1002",
               "http://127.0.0.1:1003"]
}
```

****

To add a transaction, copy the contents from transaction.json and POST it in the
JSON format to http://127.0.0.1:1001/add_transaction in Postman, as shown in
Listing 16-6.

Listing 16-6. transaction.json

```
-

                                {
                                        "sender": "",
                                        "receiver": "",
                                        "amount": 10
                                }
```

****

16.8.2 Changing the Blockchain into Cryptocurrency

To change the blockchain into cryptocurrency, follow these steps. First you have to add a transaction:

self.transactions = [] transaction to be created before

self.create_block Function

Then ; add_transaction(self, sender, receiver, amount)

Now you create a consensus:

self.nodes = set()   **this is for init method**

add_node(self, address)   **add node method for adding a new node**

replace_chain(self)   **replace chain with long one**

Now you have to decentralize the blockchain and apply consensus and transaction to it. In this sample coin, there are three nodes. They utilize the following addresses and ports listed (Flask):

- Node 1: http://127.0.0.1:1001/

- Node 2: http://127.0.0.1:1002/

- Node 3: http://127.0.0.1:1003/

To decentralize the Bitcoin network, mine blocks, send transactions, and apply consensus, copies of the code (bitcoin.py) have been created:

- Node 1: bitcoin_node_1_1001.py

- Node 2: bitcoin_node_2_1002.py

- Node 3: bitcoin_node_3_1003.py

Once the application is running on Flask, Postman requests are used to query the blockchain, create transactions, and apply a consensus. In this case, port 1001 was utilized (Node 1).

16.8.3 GET

Get chain: `http://127.0.0.1:1001/get_chain`

   Mine block: `http://127.0.0.1:1001/mine_block`

   Replace chain: `http://127.0.0.1:1001/replace_chain`

16.8.4 POST

Add transaction: `http://127.0.0.1:1001/add_transaction`

   Connect node: `http://127.0.0.1:1001/connect_node`

   Source code: `https://github.com/JosephThachilGeorge/Bitcoin`

   By looking at this project, you have come to know the concept of Bitcoin and how to mine it. So the question is, who are the miners?

16.9 Functions of the Nodes

The Bitcoin network is formed of nodes, that is, computers in communication with each other, thanks to Bitcoin's open source software.

Nodes can have different functions: some nodes validate the regularity of transactions and other nodes propagate transactions to other nodes. The nodes of interest in this article are called "miners" and they create the chain of blocks, called blockchain, where all transactions are forever recorded.

Now let's see what miners do. Mining nodes are owned by private citizens or companies that invest huge resources to solve a mathematical problem that can only be solved by trial and error. Anyone can mine Bitcoin money; let's see what you need to have:

- For mining, you need specialized equipment; often, video cards for video games would suffice. However, there are now powerful processors (ASICS) developed to calculate the SHA-256 equation of Bitcoin to enhance the odds of winning.

- The second condition is to generate or purchase a large amount of electricity to power computers and associated cooling equipment; in fact, mining these machines heats up the surroundings and you must maintain an ideal temperature to maintain the machine's physical integrity.

- • The next stage is to plan out how many hours will be needed to run the mining farm. Personnel working at Bitcoin mines are also responsible for the upkeep and replacement of machines, which, when used to their full computing capability, rapidly fail.

All of this while competing with other miners.

Once the operations begin, your calculators do nothing but compute the same equation (SHA-256) over and over again, taking data from the Bitcoin network as input, and then trying to add a new number to the equation to see whether the output matches the protocol's requirements. The result is a hexadecimal number of this type:

0000000000000000000041a4e1c92831e9291407e6d79072f0d140c3ff44d11e0

On first try, the mining machine inserts the number 1 into the SHA-256 equation and checks the output to see how many zeros are in front of the number. It recalculates SHA-256 using the same set of transactions on the second try and adds the number 2. On the third attempt it adds the number 3, and so on, until it obtains a number that starts with zeros. The outcome is completely random. These are huge numbers; in reality, every 10 minutes or so, one of the computers across the world discovers the exact number of zeros required by the protocol at that time.

When a miner discovers a viable solution, the entire computer network is vulnerable to transaction blockage. Because the conclusion is mathematically repeatable and verifiable, all miners can check it quickly and simply. The transactions included inside the mined block are 100% legitimate and may be added to the block chain.

The miner is a node or a user who has installed Bitcoin on their computer, but in addition to validating and propagating transactions, the miner also bears the responsibility of expending energy to solve the mathematical challenge that underpins the authorization to write in blockchain.

These specific nodes make accessible energy resources in order to earn the prize while also ensuring that the system is protected against double spending in the absence of a centralized coordinator.

16.9.1 Create a New Candidate Block by Combining Valid Transactions

The nearest nodes instantly check if you have the funds to spend once you send your transaction. The transaction is queued to be executed by the miners if this verification passes. The transaction is collected by a miner, who then combines it with other transactions in the ether to form a candidate block of transactions to be added to the blockchain. The miner's job at this stage is to calculate the number that begins with 0.

16.9.2 Computing Power on the Defensive Wall (Hash Rate)

Because the amount of hash power (computing power) brought into the system is fully committed to ensuring that there are no fraudulent transactions, even miners who do not win the Bitcoins in the last block have contributed to Bitcoin's security. This protective wall defends against double spending as well as intruders attempting to tamper with the blockchain's facts.

Each miner can theoretically have a distinct set of transactions, and the first miner to discover a solution using the transactions they select gets to add their candidate block to the blockchain. When the network has agreed on which is the last valid block, the race starts to find the next block.

When the system's processing capacity is good enough that valid blocks are discovered in fewer than 10 minutes, the mathematical puzzle's complexity is increased by increasing the number of zeros in front of the solution to be found. While the system facilitates the solution by requiring miners to find a number with fewer zeros in front if the system's computing power is insufficient and requires that new blocks are only found every 15 minutes, the system facilitates the solution by requiring miners to find a number with fewer zeros in front if the system's computing power is insufficient.

This technique adapts to the difficulty dependent on the system's computational capacity. As a result, as computer power declines, discovering Bitcoin is simpler, and more people will be motivated to mine, keeping the system afloat. When mining Bitcoin gets too difficult; however, only the most efficient miners remain on the market. This indicates that when the price of Bitcoin rises, hash power rises as well—more value, more computer power, and greater security.

16.10 Creating New Bitcoins

Bitcoin is a currency, and contributing to its creation and upkeep allows you to earn Bitcoin in exchange for your efforts. Every four years, the compensation for blocks is halved. After ten years of unbroken activity, we are at 6.25 Bitcoins every 10 minutes. Aside from the Bitcoin prize, a successful miner also receives any commissions associated with the individual transactions.

As you can see, the quantity of new Bitcoins continues to decrease; at the time of writing, the total number of Bitcoins produced since 2009 is about 18 million.

Continuing the mathematical series, around the year 2140, 21 million Bitcoins will have been mined.

16.10.1 The Concept of Decentralization

Miners are components, nodes of the network, with the special duty of producing blockchain blocks and releasing new Bitcoins, ensuring security against double spending attempts.

The notion of decentralization, or, to put it another way, the fact that you don't need a central coordinator to verify that all parties behave correctly, is perhaps one of Bitcoin's most revolutionary features.

How does Bitcoin's decentralized coordination work? The answer is "proof of work," a new approach for reaching an agreement on the state of balances. The job entails gathering transactions, generating candidate blocks, and computing hash with zeros in front, as stated. Proof of work is nothing more than a cunning ruse to compel the system to coordinate every 10 minutes on the status of Bitcoin balances.

The incentive mechanism draws new miners who are ready to spend resources to discover Bitcoin, and none of the participants in the game are interested in acting against the Bitcoin network's interests.

Miners make significant investments in order to earn Bitcoins, and they will never attempt to compromise the protocol's resilience because doing so would result in them losing the whole worth of the Bitcoins in their possession. Miners seldom sell their Bitcoins for less than the cost of manufacturing. This means that Bitcoin has a minimum price, determined by the cost of mining a single Bitcoin successfully.

Miners are honest because deceiving the system costs a lot of money initially; it is predicted that rearranging blockchain history to attack the system would cost $5 billion. Second, all hacking efforts would be futile since each node has the option of accepting or rejecting updates to its blockchain copy. Blocks with a double expense will never be accepted by honest nodes. In reality, the attacker would be on a blockchain other than the main one, a blockchain that has no value since it includes fraudulent data.

16.11 Summary

This chapter discussed the future scope of blockchain technology and distributed systems and touched on how you can achieve secure transactions using blockchain. The B-Coin project showed how Bitcoin works and how you can attain secure transactions using the Bitcoin concept.

I am sure that you now understand what Bitcoins are for. The uses of this digital currency, in fact, can be multiple and are not only linked to the speculation that is made on it. The blockchain method is also particularly interesting for its future developments, which could be related to every aspect of our existence. Now that you know how Bitcoin works, nothing can stop you in the discovery of the cryptocurrency!

The next chapter will focus on automated vehicle management systems.

## CHAPTER 17

AI and Blockchain Monitoring Autonomous Vehicles Management Project

The autonomous vehicle management system is the subject of this chapter. This entails operating a vehicle or system in a distributed environment. *Artificial intelligence* and message exchanges (blockchain) are both present in this scenario. Simultaneously, we must prevent catastrophic collapse when it comes to autonomous vehicle management.

17.1 The Connection Between Blockchain and Artificial intelligence

Blockchain and AI are two of the most popular technological developments right now. Scientists have been debating and researching the integration of the two technologies, despite the fact that their development partners and implementations are vastly different. A blockchain, by definition, is a distributed, decentralized, immutable ledger for storing encrypted data. AI, on the other hand, is the motor or "mind" that will enable analysis and judgment based on the acquired information[1].

---

[1] https://blog.goodaudience.com/blockchain-and-artificial-intelligence-the-benefits-of-the-decentralized-ai-60b91d75917b

© Joseph Thachil George 2022
J. T. George, *Introducing Blockchain Applications*, https://doi.org/10.1007/978-1-4842-7480-4_17

AI and blockchain are in a position where they can support and profit from each other. Because both of these technologies may affect data in various ways, combining them makes logical sense and potentially pushes data exploitation to new heights. Simultaneously, incorporating machine learning and AI into blockchain, and vice versa, can improve blockchain's fundamental architecture while also enhancing AI's capabilities. Blockchain could also make AI more logical and intelligible, allowing developers to track and comprehend why deep learning choices are made. The blockchain and its ledger can keep track of all the data and factors that go into a deep learning conclusion (see Figure 17-1)[1].

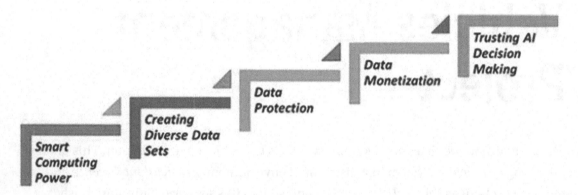

Figure 17-1. *Blockchain and AI*

Furthermore, AI can improve blockchain efficiency considerably more effectively than people or even traditional technology. A glance at how blockchains are now operated on conventional computers demonstrates this, with a significant amount of computing power required to complete even basic activities[2].

17.1.1 AI and Blockchain in Applications

The number of automobiles on the road is rising these days. As a result, preventing traffic accidents is a problem for society. Machine Learning (ML) techniques, for example, are particularly useful in improving the overall performance of the road safety management system. Blockchain uses consensus methods and smart contracts to govern communication between nodes without the need for a third-party intermediary.

---

[2]https://www.forbes.com/sites/darrynpollock/2018/11/30/the-fourth-industrial-revolution-built-on-blockchain-and-advanced-with-ai/#4cb2e5d24242

Simultaneously, AI has the potential to provide intelligent, decision-making robots that are comparable to human minds[2].

Basically, we need to consider the following two aspects when we apply blockchain and AI for application development:

- **Monetization of data.** With consensus algorithms and smart contracts, blockchain manages communication among nodes without the involvement of a third-party or intermediary body. Additionally, blockchain technology facilitates sharing of information on the network, which is decentralized, secure, persistent, anonymous, and trustworthy.[2]

- **Decision making using AI.** Artificial Intelligence (AI) such as Machine Learning (ML) algorithms are very helpful for improving the performance of the overall vehicle safety management system.[2]

17.1.2 AI's Role in Making Real-Time Intelligent and Decision-Making Machines

AI technology enables machines to think for themselves without the need for human involvement. The AI approach is extremely careful in analyzing the collected data via IoT devices that have been placed within a vehicle's driver's cabin. For real-time decision-making operations in vehicles, several machine-learning techniques are significant.

The system evaluates the driver's unfit or uncomfortable state based on the system's training. Then, first and foremost, it communicates with the driver. After that, if it detects the vehicle's uncomfortable body expressions, it sends a report to the pre-programmed network. This chapter explains how to implement AI in vehicle system management[3].

---

[3] A. Sharma, Y. Awasthi and S. Kumar, "The Role of Blockchain, AI and IoT for Smart Road Traffic Management System," 2020 IEEE India Council International Subsections Conference (INDISCON), 2020, pp. 289-296, doi: 10.1109/INDISCON50162.2020.00065.

17.2 Blockchain for Information Sharing and Exchange

Blockchain is critical for sharing and transferring data across IoT device endpoints. It manages the wireless communication network between the various network control locations, systems, and servers using BC. BC is an IoT backbone technology that collects data and distributes it to endpoints or final nodes. As is generally known, BC offers IoT nodes and stakeholders with traceability, trust, privacy, security, and transparency when sharing information.

Blockchain allows providers and Internet firms to share data and approve interoperability based on customer privacy data. It also shares data sharing records in order to authorize data access. Data traceability is also important to guarantee that data exchange is legitimate, controlled, auditable, and regulated[3].

The information should be communicated among the endpoints with trust, security, and transparency via this blockchain system. To achieve data access permission, blockchain shares data sharing records. Vehicle drivers have their own private access control mechanisms and the ability to share or sell their data, as shown in Figure 17-2. Here, the carrier or communication service provider (CSP) provides benefits such as (1) no private data is sent out, (2) confirmation information may be verified and modified, and (3) traceable and tamper-proof information.[3]

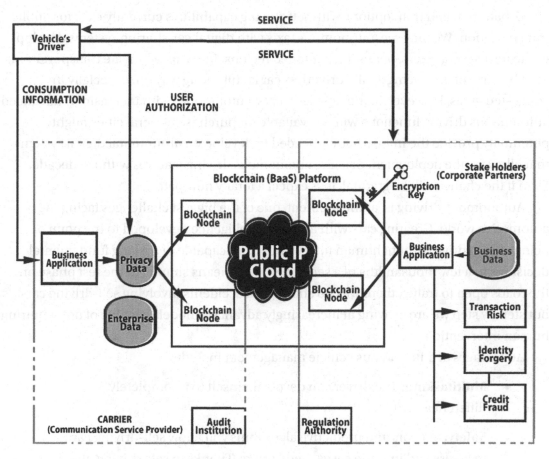

Figure 17-2. *Data transfer via blockchain technology in the vehicle management system*

Note   In this chapter, we created a project (autonomous vehicle management) that combines artificial intelligence and blockchain technology. The goal is to focus on artificial intelligence because the previous chapter talked a lot about blockchain technology. This is a combination of most trending technologies such as artificial intelligence, blockchain, and IoT. There are lots of examples in Western countries where both technologies are implemented in application development.

In all Western countries, self-driving vehicles are now one of the primary axes of mobility development. The European Commission is dedicated to supporting any connected and automated mobility solutions that can help meet the previously established sustainability and safety goals in its smart and sustainable mobility plan.

Urban tram and train options with self-driving capabilities currently exist for public transportation. We may see autonomous taxis with digital car-sharing systems develop in the next several years, operating in limited regions. In terms of private transportation, the objective of producing a fully driverless car is still a long way off, especially in congested areas. However, in the next few years, automobiles with increasingly advanced autonomous driving functions will be available for purchase. Several cities might potentially provide the infrastructure needed to develop environmental digital systems that allow for the deployment of some autonomous driving features within a decade. Even if the change will be gradual, let's expect a totally new path.

Autonomous driving is, at the moment, one of the biggest challenges facing the automotive world. Creating cars with artificial intelligence developed to the point of being able to drive without human intervention and capable of making fundamental decisions in a few thousandths of a second is by no means simple. In the test phase on the roads open to traffic, there was no shortage of accidents involving self-driving cars, but step by step we are arriving at increasingly advanced models capable of not requiring human intervention.

Advantages of autonomous vehicle management include:

- **Multitasking:** The driver can devote themself to a completely different activity.

- **Safety:** Sensors and predictive algorithms will allow self-driving cars to assess and in some cases predict risks. Thanks to safe driving, the number of road accidents would decrease.

- **Efficiency:** Abrupt braking and sudden acceleration can be avoided, thus optimizing fuel consumption.

- **Less traffic:** Once on the road, vehicles would continuously communicate with each other, exchanging data on position, driving speed, and other useful and traffic-compliant information.

- **No one excluded:** Self-driving cars can also be used by disabled people. In fact, they do not require particular physical skills. Just indicate the destination to your driverless driver and that's it.

Computers now play a crucial role in our culture. These systems are today utilized for a variety of applications in a variety of fields, ranging from medicine to avionics, this also includes the comparatively recent emerging technology called artificial intelligence.

Because of the new fields in which these technologies are utilized, the idea of "computer systems" has to be redefined. Most of these systems must meet strict timelines in order to complete their jobs, otherwise catastrophic repercussions may occur, including widespread destruction, injuries, and even fatalities.

We refer to systems as *crucial systems* when they must adhere to strict time frames. When a system's failure might be catastrophic, inflicting serious harm to the environment, infrastructure, or persons, we refer to it as a *safety critical system*.

In certain situations, these systems are used in a physical context. An automated automobile is an example of such a system: it consists of a computer system that performs the computations required to complete the given job and a physical component that interacts with the environment by changing both the environment's and the platform's state.

Since these systems are so widespread and yet so hazardous if they fail, meeting and ensuring their (typically) ultra-high reliability criteria during the design and development process is critical. A system's dependability is a gauge of how "trustworthy" it is, or its capacity to offer accurate service.

A breakdown is an occurrence that causes the given service to be disrupted. A critical system's *dependability* is described as a collection of theoretical and practical indicators. Let's look more closely at the most significant indicators.

17.3 Dependability and Safety

A critical system's *dependability* is described as a collection of *quantitative* indicators. Here are a few of the more important ones:

- *Availability* is a metric that compares the frequency of right versus faulty service.

$$A(t) = \begin{cases} 1 & \text{if a correct service is provided at time } t \\ 0 & \text{otherwise} \end{cases}$$

  $\mathbb{E}[A(t)]$, the expected value of the availibility, is the probability that the system is providing a correct service at time t

- *Reliability* refers to a system's capacity to deliver consistent service.

- *Safety* is defined as the absence of catastrophic effects in the event of a failure.

  Because safety standards necessitate a quantifiable measure, the safety of a system is frequently described by integrating additional metrics like the Mean Time to the Next Catastrophic Failure.

    $S(t)$: probability that **no failure** occurs in the interval $[0, t)$

    MTTF: Mean time between the recovery from a failure and the next failure.

- *Maintainability* refers to the ability to maintain and restore a system after it has failed. This factor has an impact on availability.

- *Coverage* is a metric for how effective the system's fault-tolerance measures are at preventing, avoiding, or correcting problems.

A *risk* is something that threatens the system's reliability: it's an "event" that causes the system to offer erroneous service. Threats can take various forms and originate from a variety of places, such as incorrect specification or incorrect execution of a requirement, or disasters.

When it comes to system reliability, we want to make sure that the service is always right. A failure occurs when a service transitions from being accurate to being wrong. The requirement of minimizing probable transitions from a stage of suitable service to a stage of false service leads project deployment while building a critical system. (See Figure 17-3.)

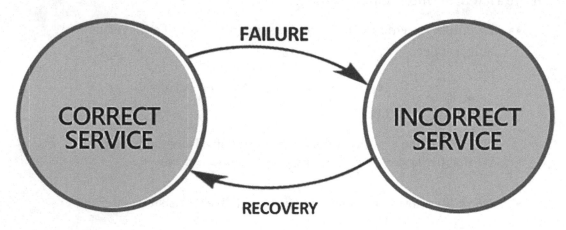

Figure 17-3. Correct vs. incorrect services

We should differentiate between benign and catastrophic failures when assessing the reliability of safety-critical systems. With benign failures, the system may not provide the best service possible, but it will remain safe. In instances when these systems and people operate in close proximity, unsafe service can have disastrous effects such as environmental damage, disturbance of the system's infrastructure, or even fatal accidents. Consider a self-driving automobile as an example. Consider a situation in which the automobile is traveling under "regular" conditions when an obstruction appears in front of it.

Despite the fact that a screeching halt and subsequent ride interruption is a failed state, it is considered a benign failure because nobody was injured. Apart from this, a scenario in which the vehicle accelerates toward a barrier (and eventually collides with it) is deemed a dangerous failure since the occupants may be seriously injured. (See Figure 17-4.)

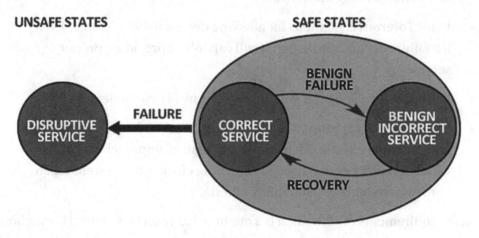

Figure 17-4. States

We want to discover all probable failures to assess the reliability of safety-critical systems. The researchers used the faulty mistake failure chain, which is well-known among academics and policymakers alike, to accomplish their goal:

- A fault is an error with an adjudicated or speculated cause.

- Error: A portion of the system's condition might result in the failure.

- Failure: The circumstance in which a mistake enters the service interface, causing the entire system's service to be disrupted. (See Figure 17-5.)

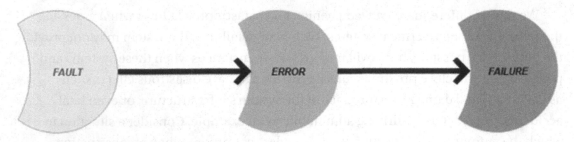

Figure 17-5. *Fault, error, and failure*

When a mistake has progressed to the point that it can no longer be corrected, a system's dependability is determined by a collection of four approaches aimed at preventing or mitigating the impact of potential failures:

- **Fault Prevent the Occurrence:** Methods of preventing failures from occurring or being introduced.

- **Fault Tolerance:** Methods for allowing defects to be tolerated. Even if a failure occurs, the system is still capable of providing proper service.

- **Fault Rid:** Lowering the quantity or severity of system defects.

- **Fault Predicting:** Estimating the current number, future occurrence, and potential effects of defects using statistical approaches. The validation procedure is used to assess the efficacy of the steps taken to meet a system's dependability criteria.

System requirements confirmation is a method that must be followed throughout the development phase, including at the start of the design process. For each stage of the system development process, there are a number of validation techniques to choose from:

- **Numerical Modeling:** Methods for modeling system capabilities using numerical models with a simple analytical solution. In other words, a quantitative analytic function may be used to express changes in the system. These models include the Sequential model and the State-Based model.

- **Simulation:** In a simulated environment, there is an empirical estimate of system reliability. This approach allows you to test if a certain fault-tolerance mechanism operates without causing damage to the real system.

- **Measurement:** Once a prototype of the system is ready, it may be monitored in action and the relevant metrics produced.

It's important to note that these techniques aren't mutually exclusive, and that all of them should be considered during the validation process.

As previously mentioned, validation must take place throughout the lifecycle of a project, beginning with the modeling phase and continuing after implementation. In certain periods, some of the approaches described in this book are more appropriate:

- **Specification:** Validity is accomplished by the description of reliability criteria, which may be verified using numerical techniques. To identify the failure criteria for the system's components, use approaches such as combinatorial designs. Failures are thought to be separate from each other.

- **Design:** It's appropriate to use State-Based models to represent the system's state space during the design phase. Markov Chains and Petri Nets are examples of these models.

- **Implementation:** When the project is far enough along, it may be possible to build a prototype model that can be closely monitored to see how effective fault-tolerance approaches are in improving system dependability.

- **Functioning:** It is possible to test the system in a real-world setting after it has been installed.

17.4 Tracking the System

Monitoring the system is a technique that involves seeing a system operate in its surroundings and collecting data and evidence regarding its features. Currently, it's seen to be a useful way to assess a system's dependability, and many techniques to do so have been presented in the research. We use the approaches presented in these books in this chapter.

This method seeks to continuously monitor a system in its end environment, ensuring that the observed behavior and performance fulfill the specific needs. Validation of the data acquired during the monitoring activity is required:

- **Offline:** While the system is functioning, data is gathered and saved someplace, then evaluated afterward.

- **Online** (or in real time): Data is evaluated as it is obtained. All of these factors must be considered while developing a monitoring strategy:

  - Identifying the system's important events, measures, and qualities that must be evaluated in order to determine the system's dependability.

  - Data labeling in order to add more information to raw measurements.

  - Data collection and transfer to the analysis node for processing.

  - Data filtering and classification based on the metrics of interest The entire system is referred to as target system in the description of a monitoring process. When the tracking activity is linked to a specific H/w or S/w or piece of the system, an aimed component or final application is employed. The professionals and academicians are full in agreement that these diametrically opposed techniques are effective:

    - Analysis in a black-box setting.

    - Analysis in a white-box setting.

The strategy you choose is determined by how much command you have over the target system, particularly its inner implementations.

A black box approach can be used when the implementations are unknown, such as when the ability to monitor action is performed by a third-party system. After defining a workload, the task is offered to the system, and its outputs are noticed. (See Figure 17-6.)

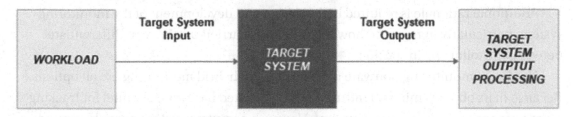

Figure 17-6. *Target system output processing*

It is possible to study the target machine "on the inside" by attaching a probe directly to the computer and viewing the system's intermediary outputs while it runs, if the internal characteristics of the target system are known and easily available. Because these probes are directly connected to the system's internal components, they can offer considerably more information than simply observing the system's outputs can.

On the one side, this technique gives a lot more information on the system's behavior, but it also necessitates more caution in terms of monitoring and system probing. These two principles, in particularly, must be followed:

- **Representativeness of choices:** In order to execute a successful monitoring activity, the probes should be able to get a sufficient number of relevant facts.

- **No intrusiveness:** Probing must not alter the system's behavior; otherwise, the acquired data will be useless.

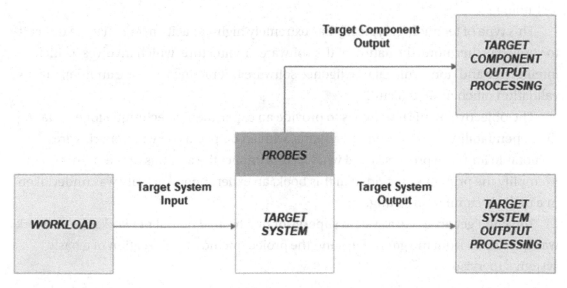

Figure 17-7. *Probes*

Additional rationale is required in the design and development of the monitoring system, particularly in regard to how the probing is carried out. We can differentiate between the following in specific.

Hardware monitoring, software monitoring, and hybrid monitoring are all options. Because of its obvious minimal intrusiveness, a devoted hardware channel for tracking is the best approach to observe a system. However, as systems get more sophisticated, installing hardware probes becomes increasingly difficult, if not extremely difficult. (See Figure 17-7.)

Software probes are more powerful than hardware probes because they have access to more relevant data and can establish the context in which a specific output was created. Data extraction and measurement instructions can be included in the procedure, the operative system, or a new probe process can be created. In a hybrid technique, equipment/software probes might be utilized simultaneously, with specific emphasis devoted to reducing the disadvantages of each technology.

17.5 Motivation and Goal of This Work

A *neural network*, which is in charge of driving the automobile, is pitted against a system supervisor, which offers fault-tolerance mechanisms to prevent catastrophic failures. In relation to the effects autonomous automobiles may have on future system advancements, they are among the most current and promising safety essential technologies.

This type of technology typically has extremely high-capacity needs that are difficult to verify. Furthermore, the nature of the software architecture, which involves artificial intelligence and non-artificial intelligence software interacting with one another, makes validation much more difficult.

The objective of this research is to provide an experimental technique for evaluating the dependability of such complex systems, with an emphasis on what metrics are acceptable for these processes and what factors impact the analysis process. To exemplify the principles provided in this book, an experimental activity was undertaken in a realistic simulation setting.

You can't get access to a system supervisor or a trained neural network. The network was developed from the ground up, and the project included the creation of a basic system supervisor.

It's crucial to note that the goal of this work isn't to provide a complete treatment of the argument; rather, it's to begin a period of exploration of these notions and difficulties, which will need additional validation and research in future designs.

17.6 Automotive Applications

One of the popular trends this decade is self-driving cars. AI that have been actually trained to drive using machine learning techniques have shown that a computer can drive a car. However, if these systems fail, individuals might be hurt or killed. Simultaneously, certifying the ultra-high dependability specifications demanded is proving difficult. Today's modern problems with self-driving vehicle safety are reviewed in this chapter.

17.6.1 Autonomous Cars as Cyber-Physical Systems

A car's ability to drive itself necessitates the use of appropriate technology and software. As a result, autonomous vehicles are classified as *cyber-physical systems* (CPSs), with the potentially devastating effects of a failure in/of these systems placing them in the important systems category.

The system gathers data from various sensors to perceive and map the local environment. Here are some of the most significant sensors and their functions:

- **Highly accurate GPS sensors:** These sensors are useful for monitoring change in the status of the automobile and objects in the surroundings over time.

- **Cameras:** Face recognition software and cameras are generally used to process recorded images.

- **Lidars and Radars:** Lidars are the next step in the evolution of traditional radars. The information gathered from these sensors is used to map the surroundings and detect obstacles and objects in the vicinity of the vehicle.

These sensors' results are integrated and sent into the car's control system. Figure 17-8 depicts a simplified version of the software architecture.

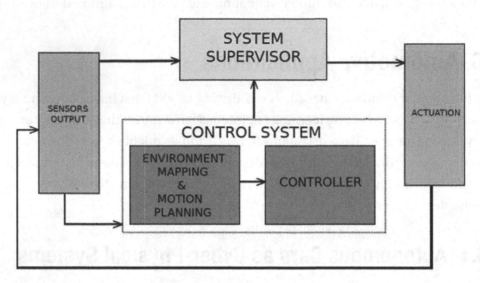

Figure 17-8. *The software architecture of the system is abstracted at a high level*

Sensor data are inputs to the management system, which are divided into two parts. One input collects data straight from the sensors, processes it to create an occupancy grid1 to map the nearby region, and generates a physical model of the system in terms of following the appropriate path to a final stage without collapsing. The other input collects data from the sensors, processes it to create an occupancy grid1 to map the nearby area, and generates a physical model of the system to get the correct path to a final stage without collision.

A car's activities include accelerating, braking, and steering. Because of the importance of their job, a system supervisor is required. This system is in charge of detecting potential hardware faults or erroneous process control outputs for and, if required, executing a right action.

The system administrator is the key part of such systems and prevents breakdown. Without a doubt, certain checks may be performed when data is analyzed, but the final decision rests with the system's monitor, and underestimating its importance might have disastrous results, such as the 2018 Arizona tragedy in which a lady was killed by a self-driving car during a practice run.[1]

Additional examination found that the vehicle's radar and Lidar sensors detected the victim around six seconds before impact, and that it took four seconds to infer that there was an impediment on the road requiring an emergency stop. During testing for "smoother rides," however, this safety-checker was deactivated, resulting in tragedy.[4]

The high complexity of these systems raises issues among specialists, including the need to develop a new perspective for studying and testing their safety, as well as the need to raise awareness about safety.

17.7 Safety and Self-Controlled Vehicles

The amount of automation may be split into six categories, ranging from 0 to 5, by an SAE International proposal to categorize self-driving cars' autonomy. Level 0 implies no autonomy: the car is operated only by a person; level 5 means that no human involvement is necessary, and the vehicle must be capable of not just driving safely on the road, but also avoiding catastrophic failures that may seriously injure people. The greater the reliability criteria for an automobile to be used on open streets, the more autonomous it is.[4]

Demonstrating a device's dependability is a difficult undertaking in and of itself, but it becomes considerably more difficult with ultra-high dependability systems like these. In addition to the problem at hand, showing the dependability of autonomous vehicles has two additional challenges: how do you test the system efficiently and safely, and the presence of neural networks, and as such it is difficult to explain why it produced the output y given the input x.[1]

Several studies have shown that road testing vehicles is impossible. One of these, dubbed the RAND study, considers how many miles of driving it would take to demonstrate autonomous vehicles' accuracy using traditional statistical inference, estimating that if autonomous vehicles' fatality rate was 20 percentage points lower than humans', it would take more than five centuries with "a fleet of 100 driverless cars being test-driven 24/7 a day, 24/7/365 a year."[1]

The confirmation of ultra-high dependability criteria for safety-critical systems is a well-known topic in the safety literature, and autonomous cars haven't been added to it. In actuality, the RAND research is just one example of the problem described in Littlewood & Strigini's paper from 1993, in which the same ideas are examined and extended for any ultra-high dependability system.[1]

---

[4]rcl.dsi.unifi.it

The fundamental flaw in the RAND study approach is that the frequency of future failures cannot be anticipated only based on the observed one. Not only because of the quantitative findings of its impossibility, but also because this method is ineffective: a failure rate that was observed. This technique cannot function, not only because of the quantitative approaches of its impossibility, but also because an observed frequency failure of zero would lead to optimistic (and potentially dangerous) forecasts. Fortunately, as Zhao et al. demonstrate, this dilemma is solvable.[1]

Validating the reliability criteria of an autonomous vehicle appears to be a difficult challenge in and of itself. The fact that these automobiles are controlled by neural networks makes things much more difficult.

The area of machine learning has seen a rise in attention in recent years, resulting in important scientific advancements. As a result of these advancements, autonomous automobiles appear to be a reality, as AIs have achieved astounding results with their abilities, and large businesses such as Amazon and Alibaba are investing even more in artificial intelligence related research. The way people interact with computers is changing dramatically thanks to this new wave of AI research, and neural networks have produced surprising results.

While neural networks have shown promise and appear to be the only method to reach objectives like automated vehicles, it has been proven numerous times how weird a network's forecast may become when the inputs are skewed and how wide the confidence level can be when the inputs are skewed. The absence of established standards and certifications for this sort of software, as well as the need to comprehend neural networks fully, has prompted worries about how reliant these systems may be. With advanced AI businesses lobbying for more limitations, there is now a growing awareness of the problem.

17.8 Controller: The Problem with the Checker

The connections between the control sys and the sys admin are at the heart of the vehicle's motions. The control sys, often known as the *primary factor*, is the software that conducts the system's major computations, which are required for the vehicle to run. To avoid catastrophic failures in this situation, fault-tolerance measures such as the system administrator are required. Due to high-reliability demands of these systems, this type of architecture is required in order to attempt to cover all conceivable failures. (See Figure 17-9.)

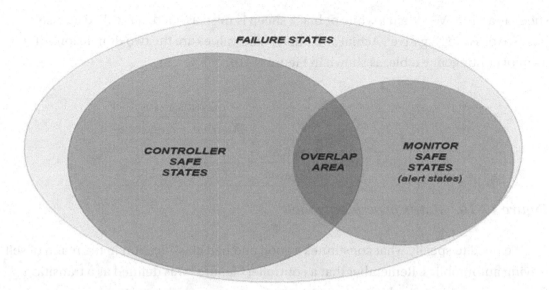

Figure 17-9. *The system's secure states are depicted in this diagram*

A safe condition is one in which the control sys generates an output that doesn't cause the vehicle to crash. The system's degree of safety may be represented as the union of the controller's and supervisor's failure regions, with an overlap region where the supervisor is truly damaging to the system's performance.

Consider a self-driving automobile on the road when an unexpected stumbling barrier arises. If the primary identifies the barriers properly, it should take a self-protective action to prevent going into alert mode.

If the controller fails to detect the obstacle or detects it but continues to throttle, the controller is judged to have failed, and the fault features kick in, the controller switches from a safe to an alert state. It is now the sys administrator's obligation to take remedial action to put the system into fail-safe mode. As a result of the failure of both elements, an administrator mistake will definitely force the system to fail, resulting in a failure state.

The *clustering algorithm,* a unique table arrangement that allows visualization of a classification system's performance, may be used to show the system supervisor's probable actions. This is achieved by dividing the world into two categories: positive and negative.

Assume we're trying to tell the difference between white and black sheep in a flock. The Positive Class will be the black sheep's class. A black sheep that has been identified as such is known as a True +Ve. White sheep make up the -Ve class, and each white sheep is a True -Ve. When a white or black sheep is misclassified, it is called a False Positive or False Negative[1]. Actual and anticipated values are the two dimensions of this form of contingency table, as shown in Figure 17-10.

		Actual Value	
		Positive	Negative
Predicted Value	Positive	TP	FP
	Negative	FN	TN

Figure 17-10. *Matrix of perplexity table*

We need to specify what constitutes a good and bad classification in the realm of self-driving automobiles. Remember that a controller "failure" was defined as a transition from a safe position, in which the supervisor can manage the ecosystem without collapsing, to an alert state, in which the system would eventually collapse without the administrator.

As a result, the +ve class represents the set of events that will ultimately cause the controller to fail, whereas the negative class represents the set of events that the controller successfully controls. We'll put the administrator's choice to distinguish between safe and alert statuses to the test. To accomplish this, we used the following definitions for positive and negative forecasting:

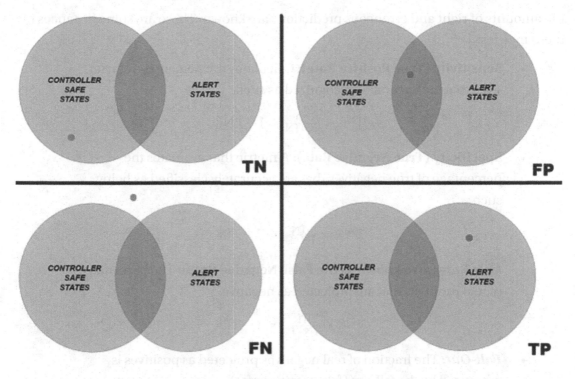

Figure 17-11. *True and erroneous predictions are represented graphically in the sys's state space. The system's present status is represented by dots. A blue dot indicates that no alert has been raised, whereas a red dot indicates that an alarm has been triggered by the monitor*

- **True Positive (TP):** Due to a controller failure, the system went into alert mode, which was correctly recognized and stopped by the controller.

- **True Negative (TN):** The sys is in good working order, and the controller does not sound an alert.

- **False Positive (FB):** Although the sys is safe, the monitoring signals an alarm.

- **False Negative (FN):** The sys is on high alert, and the controller is unable to identify the threat.

These raw numbers are just a starting point for more sophisticated and valuable measurements, which are generally given as rates and linked together using statistical laws, making them statistically comparable and straightforward to compute provided the amounts of right and erroneous predictions are known. These are some instances of these metrics:

- **Sensitivity (True Positive Rate):** Calculates the percentage of true +Ves that are accurately recognized as such.

$$TPR = \frac{TP}{TP+FN} = 1 - FNR$$

- **Specificity (True Negative Rate):** A metric that evaluates the percentage of true negatives that are accurately classified as being such.

$$TNR = \frac{TN}{TN+FP} = 1 - FPR$$

- *Miss Rate* **(also known as the False Negative Rate):** The percentage of real positives that are projected as negative.

$$FNR = \frac{FN}{FN+TN} = 1 - TPR$$

- *Fall-Out:* The fraction of real negatives projected as positives is measured by the fall-out (false positive rate).

$$FPR = \frac{FP}{FP+TN} = 1 - TNR$$

These four rates can also be coupled to provide a variety of other metrics that indicate the model's forecast performance.

Here are a few of the much more commonly utilized metrics:

- *Accuracy* is a metric for quantifying systematic mistakes in forecasts. Disparities between such a prediction and its "actual" value are caused by inadequate precision.

$$ACC = \frac{TP+TN}{TP+TN+FP+FN}$$

- *Precision* is a measure of statistical variation in the model used for forecasts that is used to describe random mistakes in forecasts.

$$PREC = \frac{TP}{TP+FP}$$

- *Fβ-score* is a combined accuracy and sensitivities measure of a test's reliability. This runs from 0 (worst value) to 1 (best value), and it is directly related to the true positive.

$$F_\beta - score = (1 + \beta^2) \cdot \frac{PREC \cdot TPR}{\beta^2 \cdot PREC + TPR}$$

Matthew's Correlation Coefficient is an indicator of overall forecast quality that considers every cell in the confusion matrix. This measure runs from 1 (worst value) to 1 (highest value), allowing for a more comprehensive assessment of model correctness.

$$MCC = \frac{TP \cdot TN - FP \cdot FN}{\sqrt{(TP+FP) \cdot (TP+FN) \cdot (TN+FP) \cdot (TN+FN)}}$$

The *ROC5 Curve Plot* is a graphical representation of a binary classifier's effectiveness, with the x-axis indicating false positive rate and the y-axis indicating true positive rate, with the plot divided by the y = x line.

Values above this line indicate "excellent" forecasts, while values below this line indicate "worse-than-random" forecasts, and values on the line indicate arbitrary guesses.

All of these indicators may be computed and connected to one another if the real number of positive and negative expectations is known, making switching points of view of the analysis simple. We want to show that by utilizing this technique, we can estimate all of the quantities needed to compute complicated extra metrics like Threat Score and False Discovery Rate, which are reliant on the assessment's needs.

This is just a safety-related extension of the asymmetric fault-tolerant architecture for computer systems, with a primary component doing the major calculations and a primary checker detecting (and correcting) any primary defects. The challenge of determining the reliability of these simpler systems is well-studied in the publications.

The chance of a system failing on a given input (or collection of inputs) is demonstrated to be tightly dependent on both the coverage of the primary checker and the coverage of the secondary checker in a paper released by Popov and Strigini in 2010.

We want the primary to cover as much ground as possible in the case of self-driving cars. This is achieved by putting the neural networks that will drive the car through extensive training. The control sys must be able to manage the bulk of potentially hazardous occurrences if the network is "fully trained." It's feasible that, at some time, the controller learns to manage the system supervisor's "alert states," diminishing the supervisor's total contribution to the software's safety. (See Figure 17-12.)

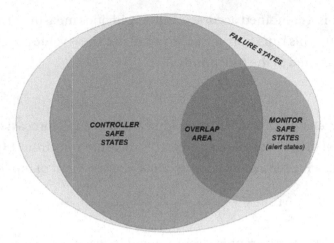

Figure 17-12. *The controller now captures all of the covered states in the past, as well as several that were previously only covered by the monitor*

Another scenario is that a part of the failure region covered by the controller becomes exposed during the training. This might lead to a scenario where certain formerly safe conditions are no longer safe.

Because the system supervisor's coverage area cannot vary without modifying its implementation, a transition to one of these states will invariably end in a failure. (See Figure 17-13.)

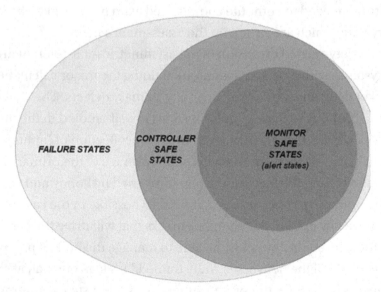

Figure 17-13. *Although some of the states covered previously in the training are no longer covered, the controller now captures all the states covered in the past by the monitor*

When it comes to self-driving cars, we want the main to cover as much ground as possible. This is accomplished by rigorously training the neural networks that will control the vehicle. The management system should be able to handle the bulk of potentially harmful occurrences as long as the network is "fully educated".

The creation and execution of an experimental approach to examine these elements is presented and discussed in the following sections.

17.9 System Analysis Method

17.9.1 Preliminary Rounds and Introduction

The objective of this research is to provide a preliminary testing approach for monitoring emergence-related traits that arise in a controlled environment when a control system interacts with a system administrator. An antiviral program's software design was reduced to just two components:

- **A controller:** A neural network that has been taught to control the automobile using reinforcement learning methods.

- **A safety supervisor:** A system supervisor submodule that uses data from a Lidar sensor to determine if the vehicle is approaching an object too rapidly and applies an emergency brake if necessary.

The goal of this study is to take a fresh look at the problem and assess its feasibility in a controlled, simulated setting. Because the system is made up of two constituent systems—controlling and monitoring—we believe that a point of view based on emerging behavior emerging from the interplay of the systems might increase the standard of the evaluation.

This section explains and explores a strategy for investigating the safety level of an autonomous vehicle over time, which includes observing the emergent behavior of a neural network operator and evaluating it safely in a virtual environment.

The suggested framework is focused on investigating the emergence that occurs as a result of the interplay of these two constituent networks.

We are focused on how a monitor's efficacy changes as the neural network learns and the effects of training techniques on a safety monitor's efficacy.

The ability to enhance neural networks by training them on datasets is one of their most appealing elements. One step of training involves gathering data across n stages and revising the weights of the prediction function.

The weights of the function indicate the network's status at epoch after the training phases. A neural net should produce satisfactory results after "enough" epochs. As the number of epochs required grows, the task gets more difficult. Driving a car is a difficult task, and saving the weights of every period is impossible.

As a result, we define a breakpoint for a neural network N as a generic epoch of N. Assume N has completed thousand epochs of training. If we save the weights of the usually suppose every 100 epochs, we'll have ten checkpoints:[1]

Checkpoint1 < checkpoint2 < : : : < checkpoint10

where checkpoint1 represents the channel's weights at epoch 100, checkpoint2 represents the network's weights at epoch 200, and so on.

Take a look at a self-driving car that is undergoing testing on the road. Its objective is to stay in the car as long as possible without crashing. As the automobile progresses on its journey, the world around it will alter. It is possible that the chance of a subsequent accident increases dramatically in specific system states, such as when a person unexpectedly crosses the road. If and only if the controller's action results in the pedestrian being struck, will we consider it a failure. If the pedestrian is genuinely identified and the automobile strikes something else while attempting to avoid it, the same logic applies.

Any action taken by the controller that might cause a crash is deemed a failure. When a potentially damaging event occurs, such as when the chances of seeing a crash are higher than normal, the controllers is destined to fail if and only if its attempts to prevent the coming failure are unsuccessful. In this sense, we don't distinguish between climatic changes that enhance the chance of an accident (e.g., a passenger strolling down the street) and the controller's harmful actions at this stage of the project.

It is the sensor's job to run security to prevent a system failure if the controllers fails.

If the controller fails, the monitoring must not only identify whether it succeeded or not, but also run a security routine to keep the entire system from failing. We believe the monitor's actions to always be safe in this initial step of analysis. That is to say:

- The network will be in a safe condition if the controller completes all of the stages in the safety routine.

- One of the following might cause the safety monitoring to fail:

- The obstruction has not been found.

- The barrier is identified, but the routine's execution is not completed. If both the administrator and the safety monitor crash, resulting in a failure, we evaluate the system to have failed.

We may separate the system states into three groups based on this concept:

- **Safe States:** States in which the controller does not require the monitor's assistance.

- **Alert States:** Situations that necessitate the monitor's intervention. The safe state space would be reentered if the impending mishap was correctly detected (and prevented).

- **Failure States:** Areas where an accident has occurred. It's vital to keep in mind that the monitor can't identify every circumstance. There are some incidents that cannot be avoided and for which no monitoring can save the system, resulting in a straight shift from a safe to a failure state. (See Figure 17-14.)

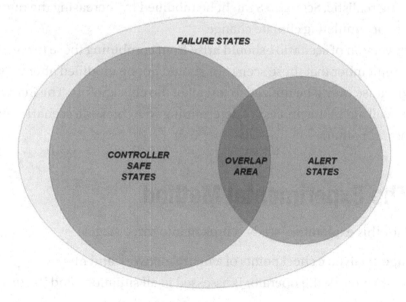

Figure 17-14. *The phase space of the system is shown*

What's important is discovering the likelihood of a system failure and figuring out how to reduce it. Simultaneously, we want to see how the efficacy of the safety monitor evolves over time as the controller learns.

This is beneficial not just for ensuring that the network improves during the learning, but also for the controller to get a better knowledge of the monitor's use as they gain experience. Because several checkpoints of the very same system are evaluated under the same exact circumstances to discover how the operator's behavior changes over time, this is necessary for the experimental activity.

Multiple checkpoints are required not just to ensure that the connection is developing, but also to track how the efficacy of the monitor changes over time. Furthermore, as you'll see in the following section, if multiple checkpoints from the same system are tested in the same situations, it can obtain relevant metrics and compare the behavior of two checkpoints in the same circumstance.

Several scenarios must be established before the analysis can begin. A scenario is a collection of beginning conditions under which the automobile is to be tested (for example, the car's spawn position, seeds used in random number generators: : :). The difficulty level for the given example is represented by the pedix h. The rationale for this is that we want to test the car in the same beginning settings as previously, with the exception of one aspect, so that we may learn more about what causes the system to fail more frequently. The h variations should become more complicated as time goes on while remaining realistic. Scenario S might be modified by increasing the number of cars in the scenario or simulating climate change.

A tougher version of scenario1 should arise from combining these two versions. It's crucial to remember that these scenarios should not be modified after they've been established because they'll be utilized to test all of the checkpoints. The information gathered here will aid in the process of determining what makes a scenario "harder" for some systems than others.

17.10 The Experimental Method

The method for this exploratory study is broken into three stages:

- **Stage 1:** Given c checkpoints of a neural network and nh circumstances, the operator is assessed in all situations and its runs are logged.

- **Stage 2:** The security monitor is verified once it has been connected to the system by repeating the tests that were performed in Stage 1.

- **Stage 3:** The network is retrained using various techniques to enhance its efficiency from the previous checkpoint. After that, the updated controllers and the safety monitor are evaluated in all of the specified situations.

We're interested in determining the neural network and monitor's quality in the first phase. This is accomplished in two phases. The controller's m checkpoints are tested in all circumstances in the first stage. We're primarily interested in seeing how the controller's reliability varies in relation to these checkpoints in this phase.

The issue of repeatability is one of the most difficult aspects of evaluating a neural network. It's quite improbable that the same neural network would act in the same way in numerous runs if the beginning circumstances were the same.

Because of this network characteristic, it's feasible that the mode of failure indicated in one of the scenario runs may never happen again, or that the time necessary to do so would be unreasonably long. Because it is hard to foresee all conceivable failure scenarios, we believe that this type of situation approach may help in resolving this issue by creating more challenging operating conditions in which the variables that cause a crash may be examined.

To address the issue of repeatability, a black box was built for each test scenario that was run. This method keeps track of the operator's actions so that the particular run may be looked at further to discover whatever went wrong with the controller. These data may then be utilized to find out which dangerous circumstances the controller safeguards at checkpoint j, and whether or not these scenarios are still protected when the network is reviewed at checkpoints --:j + x.

17.10.1 Controller Test

The controllers are assessed in solitude in each situation, at each difficulty level, until a crash occurs. It's still conceivable that there won't be any failures recorded. Acceptable acting criteria are outside the scope of this study, although they remain a source of debate in academia; nevertheless, as mentioned in the previous section, this issue may be resolved.

Some of the difficulties that occurred during the method development phase prompted the decision to isolate the controller in order to test it. The primary challenges are consistency and non-intrusiveness. As previously mentioned, the neural network's repeatability problem is handled by creating a black box that saves information about the car's condition in every frame. Because a safety-brake enforced by the monitor would almost certainly modify the ambient circumstances for the duration of the simulator, we wouldn't be able to calculate controller performance metrics, we can't test the entire system (controller and monitor) at the same time.

Testing the controller in isolation aids in the resolution of these difficulties and serves as a warmup for the second step. In all cases when the controller has been tested for each complexity, the following must be computed at a minimum:

- $MDBF_{i,j} = \frac{\#\,of\,faults}{meters\,travelled}$

    - Mean Distance Between Failure for the ith checkpoint, at the jth level of difficulty

- $MTBF_{i,j} = \frac{\#\,of\,faults}{operational\,time}$

    - Mean Time Between Failure for the ith checkpoint, at the jth level of difficulty

- $FR_{i,j} = \frac{1}{MTBF_{i,j}}$

    – Failure Rate of the ith checkpoint at the jth level of difficulty

- $R_{i,j}(t) = e^{-FR_{i,j} \cdot t}$

    – Reliability Function of the ith checkpoint at the jth level of difficulty, i.e. the probability that the Controller C_i is not failed at time t when operating at difficult j

- All these measures are aggregated to compute overall performance metrics of a Controller i, without being specific to the difficulty level, but still computed separately for deeper examination of the Controller's behaviour in different environmental conditions

One of the most important metrics for assessing a system's dependability function R(t) is the Median Time to Failure, which is simple to compute under simulated conditions and is used to determine the rate of the exponential function. Statistics in the automobile sector, on the other hand, are frequently expressed in terms of traveled distance, such as average distance to failure, collision incidence per kilometer, and so on. If the parameters and simulation hardware are powerful enough to conduct the computations at a defined time-step, it's very simple to flip the point of view on the data using this approach.

We expect the following inequation to continue as long as the neural network is fully trained: Ri(t) 6 Rj(t), where I and j are two checkpoints, and I j. This may be easily confirmed using the data collection method described previously.

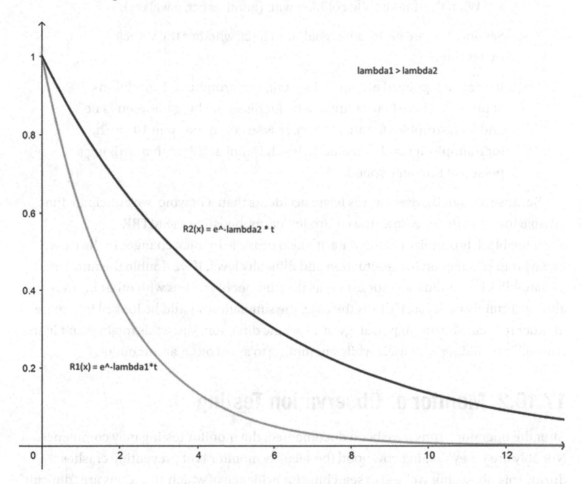

Figure 17-15. *The reliable function determines the likelihood that the system will continue to work at time t. We anticipate that more experienced drivers will be able to complete longer runs than less trained networks*

- Other information should be recorded as well, if the simulator used for testing permits it, in order to improve knowledge of the controller's behavior, such as :

  - The car's instantaneous velocity and acceleration vector.

  - What the automobile collided with (another car, a walker).

- Set one or more destination goals and track whether the vehicle meets them.

- If a crash happened at time t, determine environmental conditions at time t-x. These figures are crucial for distinguishing between "safe" and "catastrophic" failures. If a fence is struck at less than 10 km/h, for example, it may be deemed a less harmful accident than striking a person at the same speed.

Because a trained driver causes fewer accidents than a newbie, we anticipate the reliable function to increase as the controller learns, boosting the MTBF.

If the black box utilizes better data, it's also possible to track changes in the car's behavior in connection to the situation and difficulty level. If we double the number of automobiles in the situation, for example, the number of crashes with other barriers will almost certainly increase. If this is the case, the simulation should be looked into more in order to focus the training strategy in a specific direction, since this might result in the controllers colliding with walls while attempting to avoid other automobiles.

17.10.2 Monitor or Observation Testing

After the operator's runs have been documented, the monitor testing may commence. Not only are we evaluating how good the security monitor is at preventing crashes during this phase, but we're also searching for evidence of which situations are "difficult" for the monitoring and which are "easy" for the controller.

Because the controller now encompasses all of the failures previously disclosed by the screen, and the risks posed by its novel behavior are too great for the watch to detect, its behavior may evolve to the point where the monitor is no longer capable of detecting impending failures as the internet backbone matures.

On the other hand, the opposite is a viable option. In the early epochs, the controller, for example, would drive "crazy," making a lot of abrupt, high angle steering and ride at high speeds. Because the controller's behavior is unexpected, the monitor will have a harder difficulty anticipating the future state. The network will move more smoothly as it learns, making it simpler for the monitor to see potential accidents.

The main issue is that the monitor's effectiveness may diminish as the network learns, resulting in a completely pointless component that may even be harmful to the system's performance: the operator may grow sufficient to cover all of the damage covered by the screen at a previous checkpoint, resulting in a useless component. The system's overall safety may not be jeopardized if we believe the monitor's activities to be completely safe, but the safety monitor's security will result in fewer smooth trips.

The monitor is put to the test by repeating the runs that were produced during the controllers testing step. The beginning conditions must also be the same, and they must be kept in the black box from the previous stage. The controller's prior runs are now repeated, with the monitors linked to the systems and the warnings raised throughout the run recorded, as well as whether it was able to avoid the previous crash.

The main issue at this point in the investigation was non-intrusiveness. We cannot consider rerunning the simulations just by adding the safety monitor and watching how things proceed for the reasons stated above. If an alarm is triggered, the safety monitor overwrites the controller's action, altering the next section of the run. This isn't an issue in theory if you can tell the difference between false and real positives. However, without developing software sensors monitor and mapping the environment, we won't be able to predict what a technical error will be.

Because this is a safety monitor, there will be false +ves, even if they are extremely low, thus this method will not solve the problem.

The goal is to maintain track of the warnings that occur during the operation while also avoiding the safety procedure from being initiated. Because we'll be repeating the runs from Phase 1, we'll be able to pinpoint the exact time t when the switch to the alert state happened before the crash. Because we know t, all prior alerts to t are false +ves or false reports, based on this information. Coverage can be approximated by allowing the Monitors to start the safety procedure after this point in time.

As mentioned in the previous chapter, we use the confusion matrix to show the predicted values of a model in comparison to real values to see how good it is at classifying tasks. However, measuring all of them for real-time critical systems is difficult, if not impossible. It's especially difficult to comprehend when the operator averted a collision, but the monitor did not sound an alarm.

This makes calculating the number of real negatives exceedingly difficult since, in most cases, such instances can only be recognized when an operator reviews each individual run, presenting a degree of arbitrary nature into metrics like true negatives.

For example, a safety monitor input is made up of a series of timed input that may be thought of as the development of the environment while the system is running. As a result, it's impossible to predict whether another state will be alerted or secure since we don't know when the collection of inputs that would ultimately lead to a crash will begin.

Because the monitor requires a certain number of true negatives, the metrics and rates that may be calculated are limited. Simultaneously, the security monitor classifies the condition of the system in each frame, collecting Lidar data, assessing it, and deciding whether or not a safety brake is required. Due to the system's real-time nature, we may regard any frame in which the monitors does not raise an alarm as a true negative. We can compute all of the widely used metrics in statistical classification models using this method.

We must combine genuine and false pluses and minuses, such as precision and accuracy, to achieve large benefits since the vast quantity of real negatives is likely to be far greater than the other metrics for the reasons previously stated. Because the false positive rate is stated as FP/FP+TN, numbers with numerous zeroes before the first significant digit result. Furthermore, in order to give an intelligible rate measure for false positives, the quantity of false positives was computed over the distance traveled in a session.

The rates of correct and wrong operator predictions were determined as previously mentioned and may be used to compare checkpoints:

- Miss rate and awareness

- Specificity and consequences

- Correctness

- Precise

- Matthew's Factor of Connection

- Percentage of false positives per meter

- Precision recall curves reduced

An ISO standard was used to choose accuracy and reliability. The notion of accuracy has been superseded by the concept of prediction trueness, with accuracy being explained as a representation of a mix of random mistakes needing large precision and accuracy. The most helpful metric for assessing a confusion matrix is Matthew's Correlation Coefficient, which is calculated as the total of all forecasts and has been found to offer more accurate overall data than the F-score.

We chose not to use Fi since it does not function well with imbalanced datasets in general, resulting in conclusions that are either overly optimistic, depending on the size. We opted to utilize MCC as a measurement of the monitor's performance because of the large number of True Negatives and our interest in the monitor's overall utility.

The False +Ves per Meter is used to predict how the system would behave if the controllers and the security were both turned on and operating together, as well as to quantify the impact of the latter's faulty safety-brakes. The ROC2 curve, a graphical representation of a classifier tool's diagnostic abilities, might have offered a fast visual representation of the sensor's efficacy, however this method was not possible. The x-axis is determined by PR, whereas the y-axis is determined by TPR.

The figure would be flattened on the left side due to the significant imbalance of our dataset, where the number of false is likely to be lower than 10-2, based on how genuine negatives were classified. As a result, based on data obtained for each checkpoint in each difficulty, we used highly precise cropped to produce a graphical mean, a curve generated by defining the x-axis by recall and the y-axis by accuracy.

We couldn't construct a test-set to evaluate the monitor while altering the cutoff for choosing whether to brake and presenting the whole curve since the monitor only defines states as safe or dangerous in real time depending on data provided by the Lidar sensor. As a consequence, past data for each degree of complexity was computed, and these values were displayed to explore the link between difficulty and monitor efficacy, cropped to the region containing the anticipated value.

When testing the monitor, it's a good idea to put it through its paces in order to gather additional data and develop links between the data. This element is unconnected to the level of difficulty mentioned above, since it is anything linked to the environment that may provide proof as to when the monitor is operating well and when it is not, and it is more involved with fault injection at a higher level.

The ways by which a security monitors' settings may be modified are mostly defined by how it's implemented, and the development team is in charge of selecting what problems to include and how many to include. Reduce the amount of data read by the sensors or add noise into the observations are two easy options. This stage will teach you how to change the software's internal settings to get the "ideal" version, which will be utilized throughout the controllers retraining process.

17.10.3 Controller Retraining

At this point, we've gathered information on the monitor's and controller's actions. Whenever the neural network is saved from the latest checkpoint, we will investigate how much these values differ depending on the learning technique used.

We're looking at a controller constructed up of a neural network that has been trained using reinforcement learning techniques, as described at the start of this chapter. In these methods, a reward function is utilized to inform the network whether it is functioning GOOD or BAD, and it is calculated for each prediction step.

The essential parameters are required by the training function and are reevaluated at each algorithm's iteration:

- Response of the network.

- The current state of the system where the action was performed.

- A prize given for completing a task in a specific manner.

In this phase, we'll look at how different neural network training techniques impact the overall behavior of the system, with a focus on the security monitor's efficacy.

To begin our investigation into this issue, we identified four techniques as well as the expected consequences when the training is done. These results are "predicted" in the sense that we don't know how the network will react to a modification in the training method or if the observed behavior will be the same as the one predicted.

The strategies created using this technique are mostly dependent on the reward function and the channel's actions:

> S1) When the automobile strikes anything, the reward function is more punitive, but braking is somewhat more rewarded, as long as the car does not stop going.

> S2) The security monitor is connected to the system, and if an alarm is raised, the monitor's response takes precedence over the network's (the safety brake).

S3) If the monitor raises an alarm, the network's activity is substituted by the monitor's. For acting like the monitor, the network receives a good reward.

S4) If an alarm is triggered, the training phase is terminated and the network is given a poor reward.

We estimate the controller's median time/distance among failures to be reduced if we use S1. Giving a higher negative incentive for crashes and a lower positive reward for braking (if the car does not stop driving) should encourage the car to choose braking over swerving (which might result in a new dangerous scenario), thereby increasing the time between failures and the distance traveled.

The goal of S2 is to "train" the network to brake if the monitor raises an alert. As a result, the warring states formerly covered by the Monitor might become safe states.

S3 resembles S2 in many ways. Providing a positive incentive for behaving like the monitors is expected to speed up learning.

S4 is by far the most promising method, and it has the potential to provide the most intriguing outcomes. When the security monitor raises an alert, regardless of whether it's a true or false positive, a negative reward and a change in the training step should compel the network to totally avoid instances where the monitor intervenes. Essentially, we expect the safety component's efficacy to be significantly decreased.

The new devices are tested as in Phase 1 when the four controllers have been sufficiently educated. For the controllers and monitor, the same measurements are estimated, and the results are compared to the actual checkpoints.

17.11 Method Implementation and Results

The tools utilized, the software architecture and technique implementation, as well as the data gathered throughout the analysis, are reviewed in this chapter. A DDPG Agent1 was taught how to drive in a city setting. During the training, checkpoints of the network's status were recorded for comparison. To provide a unique view on AV behavior, these network checkpoints were tested with and without a simple safety monitor.

17.12 The Tools and Software

17.12.1 CARLA Simulator

CARLA[5], an open-source simulator created by University of Barcelona researchers, was used to construct a realistic environment with accurate physics simulation and data sensors. The objective of this simulator was to provide an environment in which AI agents could be trained to drive, with a high level of control over simulation settings and the simulation of real sensors that could be modified to improve or diminish data quality or insert mistakes.

CARLA is designed to work in a client-server environment. The server is essentially a game created in C++ using Unreal Engine 4. C++ speed is unquestionably critical to the server's functionality: not only must the surroundings be simulated (including pedestrian/vehicle movements, climate modeling, etc.), but also all of the data required from the sensors linked to the system

CARLA is now at version 0.9.7, and each release brings significant improvements, earning further attention from experts for its realism. Unfortunately, CARLA 0.9 had just been released when our study began, and the tools we needed were not yet available online[5].

Version 0.8.4 was utilized at first due to the number of jobs completed for the previous stable version of CARLA.

Version prior to 0.9 have limitations on the amount of control you have over the simulation's parameters and the data it collects. This does not obstruct our study, but it does limit the useful information about the surroundings and system in some way. Some of these flaws still exist in previous simulator editions, but the bulk of them were fixed after the upgrade from version 0.8 to version 0.9[2].

One of the most severe difficulties was revealed to be coordinate systems. Prior to version 0.9, developers utilized UE4's default coordinate system, which is left-handed despite the standard being right-handed. This looks to be a minor issue, since the problem may be easily solved with the use of a transformation matrix. However, due to time constraints, it was decided to stick with the developers' method and modify the data mostly at the analysis stage.[2]

---

[5] http://carla.org/

This version of CARLA includes four sensors, which were all used in the experiments. Because of the Python APIs, they're straightforward to learn:

- Cameras

  - A picture of the scene is provided by the final camera.

  - To understand depth in the surroundings, the depth map camera assigns RGB values to items.

- CARLA (see `http://carla.org/`)

  - A semantic segmentation classifies distinct items in the view by presenting them in various colors based on their class.

- Lidar based on raycast

  By lighting the object with laser beams and measuring the time it takes for the reflected light to return to the sensor, Light Detection & Ranging (LDR) is a technique for detecting the environment and estimating the distance between objects.

The three cameras were utilized throughout the network's training phase. Three scene final cameras are mounted on the automobile to allow the driver to observe the surroundings.

The vehicle may acquire a color-map of the distances between objects in the scene thanks to the depth map camera. Semantic segmentation provides picture categorization features by contacting the server for ground-truth information. This is undeniably a simplification of a real system, in which the most powerful photo software is essentially other neural networks that have been trained independently. A misclassification can also be viewed as a control system error.

If a possible threat is detected, the safety monitor will not "fix" the misinterpretation; instead, it will react promptly and safely to avoid the consequences; hence, this simplification will have no influence on the entire approach.

The other accessible sensor for this version of CARLA is a raycast based Lidar. This sensor's parameters may be readily tweaked to mimic actual Lidars like the Velodyne Lidar or flaws like low data quality, noisy data, or data loss. The Point Cloud format was used to produce the data.

Because high hardware resources are required to mimic a genuine Lidar in the simulations, a significantly modified version of the Velodyne64 Lidar is used with the given criteria:

- Number of channels = 64

    - The system's total number of laser beams. These lasers are spaced evenly along the y axis. The more lasers there are, the more precise the scanning will be.

- The range is 75 meters.

    - The range of lasers in meters

- Frequency of rotation = 15 Hz

    - These settings define the scanning beams' rotation rate (in Hz)

- 1.000.000 scores per each second

    - The quantity of points produced by the sensor for each picture

- FOV vertical boundaries (high = 24m, lower = -2m). Distances are measured in relation to the sensor's location.

    - Scanning's min and max heights

The simulator has Python APIs for modifying sensors as well as a lot of control over what's being emulated, such as seeding places for spawning, pedestrian and vehicle behavior, and the status of "actors" in the scene, such as their position and velocity.

All of this information, as well as ground-truth values, is provided by the simulator. Simulation-related measures, such as simulation time-steps or frames per second, might be used. Metrics connected to actors include vehicle speed, collision severity, and the 3D acceleration vector.

During the testing of this tool, an issue with the Lidar sensor data was discovered, which has yet to be rectified. The issue caused the bounding boxes of the cars to be warped when they moved, resulting in very poor data. Following considerable investigation, an updated version of the simulator was discovered, with the bounding boundaries for each vehicle being modified to produce correct data. Developers are currently working on this problem, but it cannot be fixed without human involvement in the source code.

17.12.2 Controller Settings

The neural network that will select what action to take to move the automobile is the most essential element for the controller implementation. We required a framework with the following features.

- A code for training.

- There are no significant flaws in the codebase.

- Create an atmosphere in which the network can communicate with CARLA.

- Make a default training approach available.

We chose Intel AI Lab's reinforcement-learning platform Coach after analyzing all of the device applications for CARLA.

This framework fulfills all of the following criteria: it is distributed as a Python package that may be edited. The project's development team assures us that the product will be of high quality. There are also numerous settings to choose from as a starting point. Two of these choices include a CARLA simulator interface and a preset training strategy, which is precisely what we needed.

The Deep Deterministic Policy Gradient method, introduced in 2015, is implemented in these settings. As demonstrated in the original work, this method performed well in tasks such as vehicle driving.

- P1: The first setup perceives the environment using a single front camera as well as the additional data enhancement cameras given by CARLA. This preset's agent will very definitely lack any sense of depth provided by the regular camera, instead depending only on the depth camera.

- P2: Because the automobile is equipped with three conventional cameras as well as all of the data augmentation cameras described in the preceding section, this setup employs all of the cameras accessible in CARLA and has a much more fascinating design.

The usage of data augmentation cameras allows us to ignore object misclassifications as well as other benefits such as estimating distances between objects. This is a simplified form of a true architecture, in which object recognition units are neural networks that must be educated and assessed differently, as stated in the prior section.

A misclassification, on the other hand, would very definitely cause the controllers to act in unexpected ways, which the security monitor would have to be able to detect and perhaps correct. Sadly, even if the vehicle is being rewarded positively, the initial setting has a flaw that causes it to stop throttling. It would have been interesting to test this setup as well, to see how it impacts the safety monitor's efficacy in terms of network data access.

It's crucial to note that our objective isn't to create the "ideal" agent or autonomous vehicle. The codebase was examined, but owing to time constraints, we were unable to examine all of the specifics of the given implementation. This framework served as an illustration of the ideas discussed in this book.

17.12.3 Safety Monitor Implementation

To begin the research, we required software that could read Lidar data and map the environment as well as detect impediments. This software must also be real-time and capable of communicating with CARLA. The latter is self-evident: the CARLA server must receive the "brake" order whenever an alert is triggered. The first required some thought: one might envision capturing the Lidar data ahead of time and then conducting the simulations using this data. Unfortunately, this method will not work since we are concerned not only with having a 100% accurate forecast, but also with the quality of monitor's security measures.

If the same measurement is made in two separate simulations and the results are somewhat different, the monitor may respond in a completely different way than it would have if the real-time data provided during the model had been used. If the precision of measurements is solely relevant to the research simulator, we can't disregard the impact that a brake has on a particular experiment.

A survey of the best "non-neural network" approaches, as well as an evaluation of the open-source instruments available, were done in order to build an appropriate security monitor. To process point cloud data, the Point Cloud library was chosen as the open-source library. It was written in C++ to achieve those objectives while processing large amounts of data. This library was initially released in 2011, and each successive version has enhanced it, due in part to the large community that has helped with testing and debugging new features.

This package contains a set of methods that implement the most common Point Cloud processing techniques. The steps for creating an object-detection module are outlined here:

- **Down sampling:** With a considerable degree of redundancy and noise, a single check can produce 100,000 records. As a first step, a down sample is generally required to eliminate all of the "useless" data. The Voxel Grid Filter was selected for this stage after considerable consideration.

- **Ground segmentation:** The first required step after downsampling (if necessary) is to filter out data that is worthless for object recognition, such as points relative to the ground. To distinguish the ground from the things we want to identify, these points must be filtered. In our implementation, we use the RANSAC2 algorithm, which is a mechanism for distinguishing between "inliers" and "outliers."

- **Clustering:** This last stage is necessary to properly define what constitutes a scene item and which data points are linked to that item. Clustering techniques based on point proximity can be used to accomplish this. Because it is a range-finding approach calculating the Euclidean distance between points and the premise that dense points indicate the same item, the Euclidean Clustering Technique was chosen.

- **Tracking and Avoidance of Objects:** Items identified in the first three components must be watched throughout time to determine if two objects observed in two sequential stages are the same entity. This is usually done by combining a failure safety procedure with physical models, such as the Kalman Filter, that anticipate their behavior over time.

However, developing a Kalman Filter for such a complex model would have taken much too long, forcing us to put our study on hold. As a result, we streamlined the object identification and failure avoidance procedure as follows:

- Only data from in front of the automobile is saved. This is a significant improvement to the concept, since the monitor can now only identify obstructions in front of the vehicle. However, while this will undoubtedly affect the safety monitor's efficacy, the ideas discussed in the preceding section remain valid.

- The failure prevention procedure used is based on Mobileye's Responsibility-Sensitive Safety paradigm, which was proposed by Intel. When an item is detected, the speed of the object in relation to the system is calculated. If the system's distance traveled in one second plus the distance is greater than the object's distance traveled plus the space between the systems and the objects, a safety brake is engaged.

Because the safety monitor is written in C++, an architecture to communicate data with CARLA was created, both to use the Point Cloud library and for performance considerations.

The CARLA client's point clouds. This data is analyzed in the same way as the previous phases, and if necessary, an alarm is given back to the client. If the monitor receives an alarm message, the controller's operations are overridden, and a brake is applied. The object identification module was influenced by Engin Bozkurt's open-source project. To adjust the detection algorithm settings to our purposes and to interface with CARLA, the software was heavily changed.

17.13 Experimental Activity

This part explains how the approach created in the preceding chapter was put into practice, as well as the technical issues that arose during the process.

Coach's default technique was used to train the Controllers in an urban context in order to produce four checkpoints that were then assessed.

CARLA offered 152 spawn points, which were used to create scenarios. A basic configuration and three variants of it were created for each spawn point:

> h0-Default Setting: With 30 people and 15 automobiles, the map is produced using the same circumstances as when the controllers were trained.

> h1- Setting for Pedestrians: The map is created with the number of pedestrians increased from 30 to 60.

> h2- Setting Vehicles: The map is produced with the number of cars in the environment increased from 15 to 30.

> h3- The map is made by merging h1 and h2, resulting in a scenario with 60 pedestrians and 30 automobiles.

152 pairs of unique seeds were produced for consistency and reproducibility throughout the variations, each with its own beginning point. You may use the same seed for many iterations of the same starting spot this way.

The automobile is also assigned a destination goal to attain, which is likewise documented for repeatability, to supplement the information regarding the system's overall performance. If the goal is met, the achievement is noted, and the sys is assigned a new target to pursue.

In normal cases, a crash might take an extremely long period to occur. As a result, a maximum operating duration of 15 min was set to show the principles presented in this work, after which the system's mission was regarded as complete.

Four checkpoints were developed and evaluated in the first part of the investigation using the technique outlined in Section 3. The coding was publicly available because the Coach project is open-source.

We were able to utilize software probes to monitor the controller's activities as a result of this. The source code was changed to include instructions for writing all required data into a separate file for every run:

- The situations' starting position and seeds

- Actions that the controller has taken

- What will happen if there is a collision?

- If a target is met, make a note of it as well as the new target coordinates

In general, altering the source code may result in a reduction in overall performance and outcome accuracy. The CARLA simulator, thankfully, allows you to run simulations at a specific time step. To guarantee that all data received from the server is correct and timely, this was set to the minimum: ten frames per second. Because we have no control over the variable time-step, it may introduce unpredictability into the data. This also serves as a baseline for testing repeatability. It took roughly a month and a half to finish the initial training portion, as well as the Controller test.

In the second step, the security monitors were assessed at each checkpoint. The source code was changed once again to establish two autonomous, parallel processes: one takes Lidar data from the CARLA server and sends it to the security monitor server, while the other waits for the security monitors to decide whether or not a brake is required.

Each frame, the CARLA system creates Lidar data. Because the burden for data creation is completely dependent on the CPU, execution times are significantly slower. Unfortunately, if FPSs are less than ten, CARLA has a problem that causes data to be incorrect. To guarantee the lowest constraint of ten frames per second, a powerful machine was necessary. Software probes were added to the codebase to gather information regarding the monitor's alarms, and the source code was modified once more. While the safety-behavior monitor is being watched, the first step's runs are now repeated. During the test, all of the alerts that were generated were false positives.

To assess the quantity of true positives, the emergency brake is activated two seconds before the accident. This method allows us to assess the safety-performance monitor in its operating context.

Following the completion of the first phase, the data obtained is processed to computerize the measurements stated in the preceding chapter.

Checkpoints for the controller:

- Average time among failures

- Interval between failures (MTBF)

- Rate of failure

- Stability

• Security Inspector:

- Matrix of predictions confusing

- Positives/negatives rates (true/false)

- Perfection details

- Matthew's Correlation of Coefficient

- Percentage of false positives

Training is continued from the previous checkpoints using the previously mentioned techniques, and the measuring procedure is performed in the same manner.

Some of the approaches mentioned need security monitor training, leading in exceptionally fast execution times. Because of the high processing load required to create Lidar data, this stage took roughly three months, after which the training was stopped. The data collected may be compared to evaluate if the network is learning correctly as well as how the security-efficacy monitor evolves over time.

Data was gathered and analyzed using Python scripts to aggregate data and provide metrics for the controller and the safety-overall monitor's functionality. For this type of work, data aggregation is essential. However, due to the complexity of these systems and the infrequency of many detrimental occurrences, individual runs must be evaluated and compared before data can be aggregated.

Due to the large quantity of data obtained, we offer the collected results primarily in aggregated form in the following part. Other issues about "raw" data, which were not included in this research but were provided separately for evaluation, exist.

17.14 Results

17.14.1 Testing the Controller (Phase 1)

The collected data is kept in different files for each run, and the measures specified in this chapter are computed using Python code. The obtained data is compared to determine the controller's goodness and modifications in the safety-efficacy monitor's across the neural network's stages.

The distances traveled for each circumstance were plotted to determine whether the number of meters walked was increasing and if there were any scenarios that were particularly "positive" or "challenging" for the system.

This is the first step, which aids testers in distinguishing between significant and minor scenarios. If the distance covered by the controller in scenario x is less than the usual distance traveled in all checkpoints, there are two options:

- There may be a danger that the controller has not learned to handle if the controller always goes the same distances in all checkpoints before exploding.

- If the distance traveled varies in a brief interval, the likelihood of a collision may be determined by the initial conditions. In any event, using this method, it's easy to figure out which situations lead the controllers to crash rapidly, and each one may be investigated further.

It's important to remember that if a pattern arises when testing various checkpoints, such as when the controller regularly works exceptionally well or exceptionally poorly, in both cases, a study of the particular instance is necessary.

For these reasons, the rationale for "poor" runs is self-evident. It may sound counterintuitive but doing many "good" runs in the same circumstance necessitates more care. An examination of the relationship between performance and beginning conditions is required, and it may be shown or refuted using this method.

When the sys recognizes a "good pattern," like a run in which the car just repeats the very same sequence without encountering any other cars on the road, a more complex problem arises.

The order of magnitude differs significantly between Checkpoints 1 and 4 at normal difficulty, and in a few situations, the maximum length set for these tests has been achieved. Another fascinating feature of this method is that the bottom constraint on distance traveled for C2 : : 4 remains constant throughout the challenges, remaining at 22 meters.

A closer look at the travel distances and running times indicates that there are runs in which the controller makes no progress, implying that the event that triggered the crash was of a sort that the controller couldn't handle. These types of results are undoubtedly intriguing in terms of determining whether the shortest runs share any environmental variables that might cause the controller to perform poorly. (See Figure 17-16.)

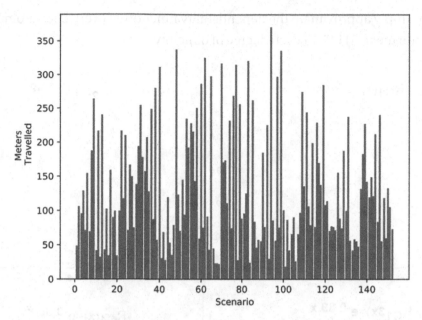

Figure 17-16. *At normal difficulty, controller C1 moves in meters at every situation*

The time gap between two consecutive activities is known because the simulation time that has elapsed between two stages of the simulation is specified and understood: the true total length of a single run may be estimated by counting how many actions the controller has performed. (See Figure 17-17.)

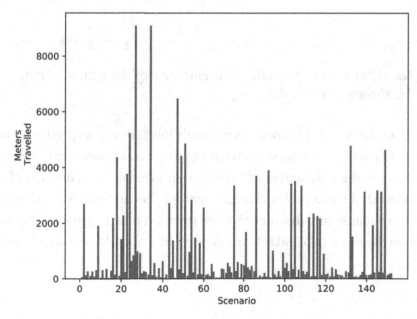

Figure 17-17. *Controller C4's distance traveled at every scenario at normal troubles*

We can simply approximate the dependability function of every checkpoint in this way, using the mean MTTF in each degree of difficulty.

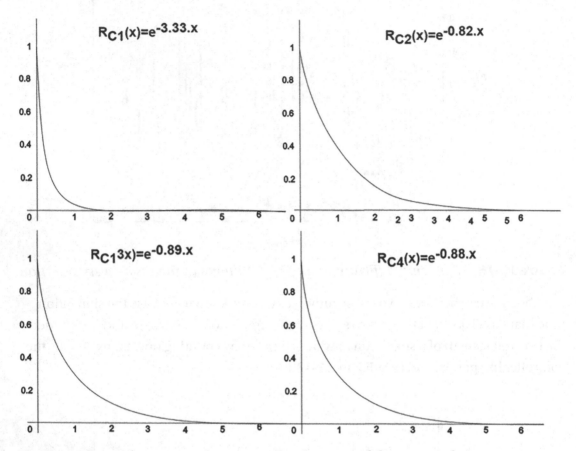

Figure 17-18. _After x min of reaction, the chance y of the systems being operational is shown graphically_

The MTTF of the initial checkpoint is relatively low (20 sec), as predicted, and grows as the number of checkpoints rises. Interestingly, the second checkpoint appears to perform better than the third and fourth checkpoints. Despite this, analysis of a portion of the runs in which the second checkpoint accomplished extremely good results in terms of time to collapse and distance traveled revealed that its driving is far more dangerous than the other two and is likely to result in a poor driving style in which the car prevented a crash almost every time by steering at the last possible moment. Another indication that C2 isn't always superior to C3 and C4. C3/C4 indicates that the apparent increased safety is most likely due to "fortunate patterns" in the sense indicated above.

Fortunately, as the findings from Phase 3 will demonstrate, the controller was able to overcome this issue.

Checkpoint distances follow a similar pattern: longer runs are really trips in which the automobile travels more meters. This guarantees that the system isn't "cheating": if the car isn't moving at all, the execution time will be greater. We may estimate the durability function in terms of km traveled prior to crashing by computing the average distance traveled by each checkpoint in each level of danger.

Furthermore, the observed advances in the distance to failure tend to coincide with the progress for a while to failure, implying that the two metrics are linked.

Because CARLA permits the kind of item with which a collision happened to be recorded, rates of the type of object collided in relation to total collisions are calculated for every checkpoint, for each risk category. This method is beneficial for a number of reasons: (See Figure 17-19.)

- To see whether the automobile slams into walls, lamp poles, or fences, indicating that it is going off-road.

- To see how the automobile reacts to different levels of difficulty; for example, if the number of people is raised and there are fewer pedestrian collisions, the system may be capable of preventing human accidents.

- To recognize the system's capacity to prevent failures when interacting with certain things.

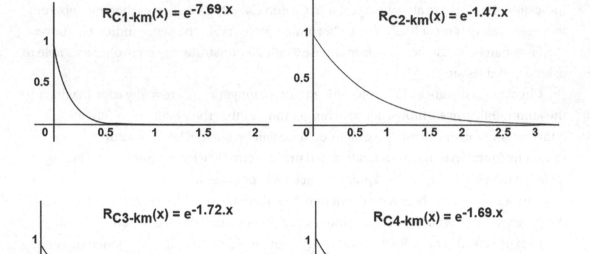

Figure 17-19. *After x km, the chance y of the system becoming operational is shown graphically*

Charts that shows $\frac{\#\,kind\,hit}{Total\,Collisions}$ for Checkpoints 1…4, in each difficulty level

Those diagrams may be used to see how the system performs as the scenario's complexity is increased while it is being trained, as well as to see whether there are any correlations between the types of collision and the security checks. The first checkpoint, as expected, collides with off-road objects, showing the controller's weak driving abilities. (See Figure 17-20.)

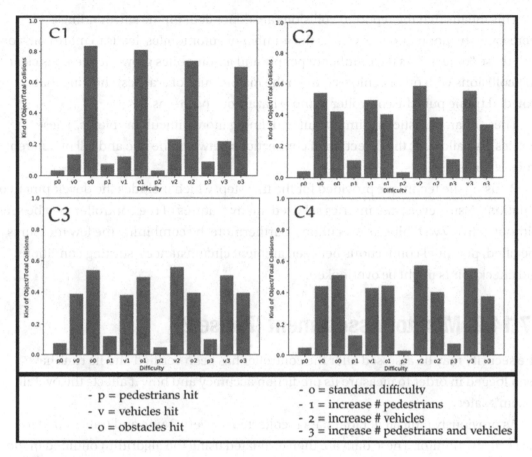

Figure 17-20. *Charts*

It also appears that the ratio of collisions with generic barriers has a tendency to follow the total checkpoint achievement. When comparing this graph to the contributing, it can be seen that C1 has the largest ratio of collisions against barriers, whereas C2 has the lowest ratio. C3 increased the frequency of these impacts, which was accompanied by a decrease in the MTTF/ MDTF, which was later decreased by C4.

Even though the four degrees of difficulty described were fairly simple, they proved to be an effective means of evaluating the system's performance in situations other than the training environment. In problems three and four MTTFs and MDTFs are significantly lower, indicating that situations with high traffic are more difficult to manage. At the similar time, the elements of the difficulty chosen influence the increase/ decrease in hit percentages with a certain type of object.

This means that the reported collisions are dependent on the surroundings. Increasing the population, as well as the number of automobiles, leads to more collisions with these "objects." As the number of people and automobiles grows, it becomes clear that collisions with other vehicles remain the major cause of crashes, showing that crowded traffic puts the controller in more hazardous positions.

These characteristics are important in defining more difficult problems. These metrics also allow for the detection of connections between the rise and fall of different types of collisions.

By using the technique provided for the first step, which includes the development of situations, issue levels, and metrics selected, many features of the controller may be seen without actively watching its executions. Furthermore, by combining the few measures specified, potential connections between ambient circumstances, starting conditions, and checkpoints might be overlooked.

17.14.2 Monitor Assessment (Phase 2)

The security may be assessed after the controller has been verified and its runs have been logged in order to measure its prediction accuracy and how it affects the overall system's safety.

As previously indicated, Lidar data is collected at every frame and transmitted to the security monitor. These data are then evaluated using the algorithm outlined in the Sensor Development sections, and a message with specifics on whether the vehicle is braking is sent back to the control system. There is no coordination between these two components, as there is in real-world systems of this type: Because this would result in choppy runs, the controller would be unable to wait for the security monitor at every frame.

The following technique is used to calculate the quantities of real positives, real negatives, fake positives, and false negatives:

- The control system runs recorded in the initiation section are replicated after attaching the Safe operation to the automobile.

- The Safe operation is permitted to issue alerts, but the safety brake is not applied until the period t has passed since the system entered an alert state, as described in Chapter 3.

- Because a choice of a "early" t may induce a brake for an activity that the processor managed, and a choice of a "late" t may cause the safety monitor to fail merely because the safe stop was activated too late, t is an important parameter for the observation's dependability. When a vehicle transitions from a secure to an alert condition, the safety brake should be activated as quickly as possible. Unfortunately, understanding when this transition occurred is not always feasible (if not impossible in complicated runs).

- All warnings produced before t are considered false positives, based on the average speed of the automobile in relation to the velocity limit and the time required to analyze Lidar data and obtain an answer from the security monitor, which was set at two seconds in this study.

- True negatives are any frames for which the monitor reaches a prediction but does not issue an alarm.

- If the system lives for the maximum duration set for a single mission, but the safety issues an alarm after time t, a false positive warning is raised.

- An effective avoidance of an accident (if one occurs) as a result of the Safety-brake Monitor's is regarded as a real positive.

- Regardless of whether the Safe operation triggered an alert or not, if a collision occurs, it is classed as a false negative.

- After determining the amounts of genuine, fake, affirmative, and negatives, they can be combined in more exact measures.

The technique proposed in this study looks to be a good strategy to understand and verify the controller's behavioral assumption as well as monitor the monitor's behavior. The monitor's efficacy appears to be impacted by the controller's dependability. While the True Positive Rate remains steady around 0.75, we can observe how the monitor's precision decreases after C2, raising some questions about the safety monitor's long-term efficacy.

The decrease in precision indicates an increase in false positives, which leads us to believe that the monitor is unable to accurately identify the system's states owing to the controller's new behavior. The MCC of every checkpoint supports this notion, exhibiting the same accuracy behavior that the controller is taught. We're interested in seeing if the MCC lowers in phase 3 once the controller is restrained because it's a measure of the monitor's performance overall.

As expected, this monitor creates a large number of false positives. This has no effect on the efficacy of the surveillance approach outlined, but it does assist to understand how the system would behave if both parts functioned together, i.e. with a lot of "false" security produced by the safety-false monitor's alerts.

Viewing the accuracy-recall curves offers a fast visual representation of the safety-performance monitor's decline, which works well with a "dumb" controller but becomes nearly disruptive with better trained controllers.

Figure 17-21 demonstrates that, despite its low efficiency, the monitors perform best at the highest difficulty setting, i.e. when the number of people and automobiles in the scenarios is doubled. The controller's second-best performances are shown with the second-most difficult difficulty, i.e. the level when the number of vehicles is increased, after C1. Although the link between something "hard" for the controllers and something "hard" for the observer cannot be completely examined in this study, charting these pictures revealed unexpected behavior, leading us to look into this more in future studies.

	C-1	C-2	C-3	C-4
TPR	0.711	0.81	0.76	0.78
FNR	0.25	0.15	0.28	0.24
FPR	0.0027	00.009	00.250	0.0036
TNR	0.91	0.997	0.998	00.931
ACC	0.995	0.991	0.664	0.991
PREC	0.64	0.15	0.18	0.15
MCC	0.69	0.37	0.36	0.34
FPPM	0.52	1.13	1.02	1.12

Figure 17-21. *The safety monitor forecast rates for control points 1 to 4*

These findings are in line with the data collected and analyzed, as the security performs well with C1, while C2 to C4 produce almost identical outcomes, with C2 producing somewhat superior results.

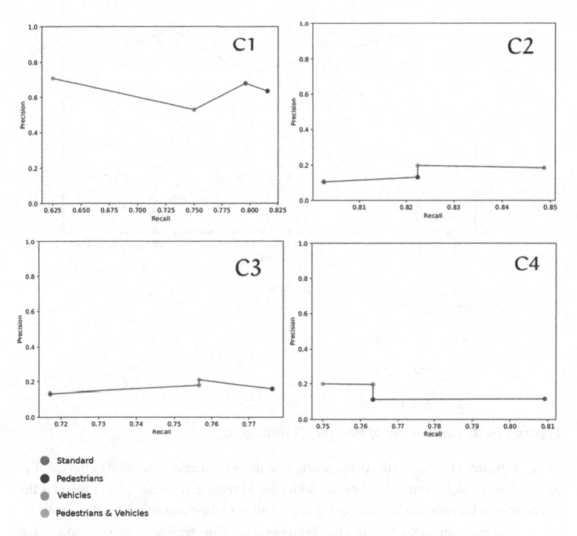

Figure 17-22. *Accuracy recall curve for checkpoints C1–4 based on observed values at every level of complexity*

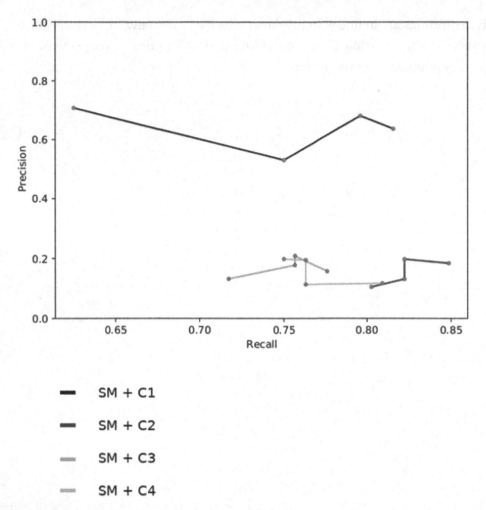

Figure 17-23. Comparing of PRC for C1 through C4

To comprehend the results of the safety monitor's predictions, we had to personally perform and watch some of the best runs for Checkpoints 2 in phase 1. High speed is the major reason for monitor failures for C2.7, according to the percentage of false-positive causes shown in the table. Another intriguing aspect of this type of data collection is that it appears that as the network learns to handle new situations, the security produces more false alarms, and, more importantly, the scenarios that will eventually result in a crash are of a new type that the watch is unable to detect.

The table in Figure 17-24 shows how this approach works and how a great quantity of information and proof about the system's behavior can be gathered using only a few observations. Depending on the real hardware available and the simulation model, further measurements can be acquired and combined to supplement this information.

	C-1	C-2	C-3	C-4
SM ERROR	80 %	41%	40 %	58 %
SUDDEN STEER	0.01 %	10 %	25 %	12 %
FAST SPEED	20 %	49 %	37 %	29 %
SLOW SPEED	0.99 %	1 %	1 %	1 %

Figure 17-24. *C1 generates a high percentage of false - negative: : : C4*

The monitor's effectiveness appears to be impacted by how the controller acts, as we anticipated at the start of this project. Most significantly, evidence shows that the monitor's prediction accuracy is unrelated to the length of time the controller has been taught. Retraining the network with various techniques and using the same monitoring approach for the operators may confirm or refute this finding.

17.14.3 Retraining and Rechecking (Phase 3)

If Phase 2 suggested that the efficiency of the same security varies when applied to different checkpoints, restructuring with different strategies and comparing the performance of controllers trained in these methods to the one we used as the default approach will be critical in confirming or refuting this theory. In this phase, we retrained C4 using the five techniques listed here:

S0) The Coach framework's basic technique, which was used to train C1... 4, with the optimization method calculated depending on the total neural network quality.

S1) When the automobile strikes anything, the functional form is now more severe, but braking is somewhat more rewarding, as long as the car does not stop going.

S2) The security monitor is connected to the system, and if an alarm is raised, the sensor's response takes precedence over the network's.

S3) If the monitoring raises an alarm, the network's activity is substituted by the monitor's. For acting like the monitors, the network receives a good incentive.

S4) If an alarm is triggered, the training phase is terminated and the system is given a poor incentive.

The result is {C5S0, C5S1, C5S2, C5S3, C5S4}.

On the failure of the S2, S3, and S4 techniques, regrettably, the safety monitor-based methods did not yield the expected results. S3 and S4 stop the controller from moving, while S2 causes it to stop after a few meters if there is something in front of the vehicle, even if it is a considerable distance away. Because not moving is a poor reward, none of these checkpoints receive an unintentionally large reward for their behavior. As a consequence, the scenario in which the neural net becomes stuck between a local minimum and maximum may remain a theory, but we feel the training time was too short.

The monitor's extremely large false positive rate is probably certainly to blame. Extended training in this manner taught the vehicle not to move in order to avoid the safety alarms and monitors. Even though these techniques account for the possibility of the car not moving by penalizing it with a -ve benefit, it was not sufficient to keep the automobile from remaining still.

We think that the DDPG algorithm's reward function is well-defined, in the sense that it accounts for all good and bad behaviors, and that immediate rewards are well-balanced, as there are no inadvertently huge payments. However, adjusting all of the reward factors to prevent results like the one we witnessed is exceedingly tough owing to the difficulty and diversity of circumstances that a network should be allowed to drive a vehicle. Most important, we have no way of knowing if this behavior is a product of the reward function's design or if it requires more training to observe intriguing behaviors.

The most important issue with training is the time commitment; it is difficult to teach n agents using n techniques and then wait for them to be taught before determining which approach produced the best results.

The tuning of the network's parameters is primarily dependent on regulations and heuristic approaches, as demonstrated by many publications. These methods, on the other hand, have shown to be time-consuming and error-prone.

Furthermore, at this time, trial-and-error appears to be the sole way to measure the reward function's efficiency. Because training data is still being investigated and there are no defined laws for self-driving vehicles, this problem, which is unique to these algorithms, remains unresolved. In academia, the design of the reward function for these relatively new algorithms is a hot issue, with academics trying to find out how to offer an appropriate learning model.

Simultaneously, as previously said, AV training needs a huge amount of data, which is frequently inaccessible or insufficient as compared to traditional training methods. There are several frameworks for designing decision-making rules for relevance feedback, but most of them seem to focus on how to speed up the learning process rather than how to add learning factors to these networks.

Creating probabilistic models to aid in the calibration of reward system parameters prior to the controller's retraining phase would be a fascinating approach. Because the protection performance measures were effectively approximated, the technique presented in this book would have a substantial impact on the construction of these models.

In reality, the reward function has no means of knowing ahead of time what value each state should be assigned. Keep in mind that we are in a full spatial condition, which is difficult to depict and makes it hard to evaluate all potential events and transitions, making our task much more difficult.

Unfortunately, because of the complexity and uniqueness of these systems and techniques, more research is required to address these issues, and the development of a simulation process to aid fine-tuning will be critical in future work.

17.15 Summary

This chapter looked at how to do a checking activity on self-driving automobiles managed by a controller and a sys admin.

Such systems demand special attention due to their complexity and the main problems of the ecosystem in which they function. This research is meant to be a first step in defining how such systems should be monitored. Because they are regularly employed in military activities, automatic vehicles are not a novel sort of equipment. However, because self-driving cars will be operating in close proximity to humans and in an urban environment, greater caution will be necessary in coping with the wide variety of events that may occur.

We also questioned if there were any links between the efficacy of the relative safety and that of the control element when the latter was taught for long periods of time using various approaches. We covered the basic principles of these activities in the initial parts, such as:

- The definitions of reliability and safety, which are both critical components of safety. In the context of self-driving automobiles, critical systems were examined.

- Problems that prohibit us from deploying self-driving automobiles in metropolitan areas at this point in time.

- How an incorrect/poor/optimistic evaluation of these systems' reliability might have catastrophic repercussions when they are implemented.

- Problems in analyzing observed emerging behavior as a result of the interaction of two main constituent components.

Is the efficacy of the safety monitor impacted by the controller's behavior, and if so, how? By the duration of the training and the strategies used throughout the training.

The instruments accessible for this type of activity were considered in the creation of this initial technique. We have to seek open-source alternatives because most solutions in this sector are private and proprietary, indicating that performing these studies in non-professional contexts is difficult.

The Lidar sensor issue would have rendered our study unfeasible, and it could have been impossible if it hadn't been for Zhuang's effort, because our only alternative would have been to rely on ground observations, which would have been useless for our research.

While the Coach framework was created by Intel AI Labs, it has the usual problems that plague open-source projects, the most notable of which being the failure of one of the two CARLA agents to move after a few rounds of training in Phase 1. This problem makes us question if there were other flaws in the training algorithm's architecture that contributed to the C5S2:::4 behaviors.

Another issue that obstructs the framework's use is that the memory is not properly released, leading it to overflow and crash the running processes. As a result, we had to maintain a close check on the training process and redo it after each mishap.

The monitoring activity was created with the following major characteristics in mind:

- **Consistency:** By saving the controller's activity in each frame, as well as the RNGs1 seeds, goal objectives, and the environment variable of every circumstance in files.

- **The ability to be unobtrusive:** Because of the client-server design, code instrumentation may provide non-real-time data or incorrect measurements. This difficulty is solved by CARLA, which allows users to conduct simulations at a set time step. But the h/w should be capable of achieving the specified time step.

- **Adequate representation:** One of the main issues with monitoring self-driving cars is the representativeness of test cases, because dangerous occurrences might be so complicated and numerous that it is difficult to evaluate them all. In this regard, defining scenarios and difficulty levels helps provide a variety of scenarios based on the same situation. Concerns regarding the dataset's nature arose from the predictive value of the metrics generated for the security monitor. The selection of the metrics to be utilized in the confusion matrix, as well as the exclusion of the others, were explained and justified.

- **Availability:** The search for the appropriate tools to employ for this task was difficult owing to the large number of options presented, many of which had significant practical constraints. However, the technologies we utilized in this project allowed us to complete this task.

At the same time, we cannot overlook the problems that these initiatives have. This approach has shown to be a helpful tool for analyzing the performance of the entire system, with a focus on well-known metrics for evaluating a system's reliability and the security monitor's effectiveness.

The creation of situations and problems is essential for establishing whether external factors impair performance of the system and for creating and evaluating "uncommon" circumstances that cannot always be covered when building ad hoc safety cases.

The main hypothesis that inspired us to start this study was to examine if the performance of "static" error-checkers was impacted by neuronal network performance, and if ad hoc training approaches had an impact as well.

According to the data gathered, the monitor's efficacy with expert agents is expected to alter, encouraging us to further investigate this hypothesis. The failure of those methods (S2, S3, S4) that employed the safety monitor to direct the training did not provide us with proof of this reality, and this issue was highlighted at the beginning of the chapter. There are two possible causes for this failure:

- A reward function that isn't defined.

- The training duration was insufficient.

We believe the neural net required more time to comprehend what the security was attempting to educate since the trained agents did not receive an accidentally huge reward for keeping motionless. A bigger simulation time step would have allowed us to run simulation time faster than real time, which would have helped us save time.

We were unable to train the models for extended periods of time or retrain the networks by altering the reward parameters since this required hyper hardware. Around the same time, the security proved to be less effective when used in conjunction with the checkpoint that produced the best results, which was obtained from Checkpoint C4 by modifying the training method, whereas and it has the same TPR (0.75) when used in conjunction with the security checks trained with method S0, except perhaps Checkpoint C2.

While Checkpoint C2 was unquestionably a unique instance for the reasons outlined in earlier chapters, the same theory cannot be ruled out for C5S1. We want to continue training C5S1 in the future to validate this reality. This study demonstrated the benefit of analyzing self-driving automobiles in a simulated environment, taking into account and overcoming many of the difficulties that emerge when calculating relevant metrics for such systems, as well as usual monitoring concerns.

The next chapter wraps up the book and gives a broad overview of blockchain technology and distributed system environment.

CHAPTER 18

Summary

The primary conclusions from this examination of blockchain technology and its cross-sector applicability are summarized in this chapter.

The blockchain is built on a unique set of properties, including decentralization, tamper-resistance, transparency, security, and smart contracts. Because there is no central authority to control the system, it is very resistant to single-point faults. The records in a blockchain are tamper proof in this regard since it is extremely difficult to alter or delete transaction records. All transactions in public or open blockchains are transparent and observable.

All transactions are timestamped, which implies that information like payment details, contracts, ownership transfers, and so on are publicly connected to a certain date and time.

However, there are still a number of unresolved difficulties, such as public blockchains' restricted scalability and performance, which is primarily due to low transaction volumes or excessive power consumption when using existing PoW consensus techniques. Other concerns include the possibility of a majority of participants colluding to infiltrate the network, as well as the network's significant reliance on a small number of players.

The extra responsibility for key management, which can be as simple or as significant as losing a phone or a backup of credentials, is another major source of security vulnerabilities.

Another key subject that requires more investigation is how to safeguard personal, sensitive, or confidential information.

If certain records do not need to be transparent then transparent data in a blockchain could be a problem. Data that's publicly accessible or needs to be updated because of mistakes or inconsistencies is a problem for blockchain.

© Joseph Thachil George 2022
J. T. George, *Introducing Blockchain Applications*, https://doi.org/10.1007/978-1-4842-7480-4_18

18.1 Blockchain in the Policy Context

The EU (European Union) has taken notice of the growing popularity and interest in blockchain technology. The focus was first on the advent of cryptocurrencies and virtual currencies like Bitcoin. On the EU website, several initiatives concentrating on the cross-cutting impact of blockchain are now being researched.

The EU has established the Blockchain Observatory and Forum, and the Anti-Counterfeiting Blockathon Forum as significant projects in close partnership with industry stakeholders, start-ups, governments, international organizations, and civil society as part of its recent efforts.

The EP (European Parliament) has also actively participated in previous and ongoing discussions on blockchain's cross-sectoral potential, having previously enacted a resolution on virtual currencies, which sparked the formation of the FinTech task force.

Since then, the Research Service of the European Parliament has issued studies and other materials on the subject. In addition, there are two resolutions titled "Distributed Ledger and Blockchain Technologies: Building Trust Through Disintermediation."

18.1.1 Avoiding the Tragedy of the Commons

Blockchain is more than simply an ICT breakthrough; it also allows new forms of economic structure and government. The author proposes two approaches to blockchain economics: innovation-focused and governance-focused. The governance method, which is based on new institutional economics and public choice economics, is the most promising, according to the author, since it represents blockchain as a new technology for forming spontaneous organizations, or new sorts of economies.

A case study of the Ethereum-based infrastructure protocol and platform is used to demonstrate this.[1]

In the light of these arguments, the idea is that blockchain allows you to record, so irrefutable, permanent and shared, the access of each individual in the common and the relative use of its potential benefits in each period of time, giving at the same time all the information of their availability in the same or other periods of time.

The possibility of access could then be conditioned a priori, on the basis of a protocol that equiripartisce among the subjects, the availability of the resource over a specific period of time and thereafter, on the basis of the common knowledge of the

---

[1] *Davidson, S., De Filippi, P. and Potts, J., 2016. "Economics of Blockchain." Available online:*

periods of peak usage and the possible enhancement of the same resource in the periods of time where it remains unused. This enhancement could take place in two ways:

- By means of an individual decision to defer, provided that this can be done with equal utility, their consumption habit in off-peak periods.

- Reentering into play for the benefit of the community (thus in fact producing common value), free of charge or behind an established reward (in the form of tokens called tokens), the part of the resource to which it would be entitled but which it would have no possibility or contingent interest to use.

The second point deserves further consideration. The greater the external incentives to the production of commons the greater the likelihood that the platform will polarize toward market logics in which *extrinsic* motivations to action prevail or at least significantly distort the *intrinsic* motivations to the logics of the community. This is the case for example of Backfeed, an innovative decentralized commons production platform based on blockchain, which provides sophisticated functionality to develop incentives associated with financing outside the user community and expressed through cryptocurrencies that can be spent toward other goods. In this way, participants are aggregated and coordinated according to a mechanism similar to that of exchanges based on individual interest.

The assertion of a truly alternative logic, however, should then be one whereby tokens should be "minted" within the community with an exchange value between the benefits of the same common or of different common that could be determined based on the amount/time of work required for their production/utilization. The information regarding the origin of the value (work) would be recorded, in an unmodifiable way (unless of course rather complex hacking activities) in the token data which could be accepted and increased in value according to the preferential priority of the request.

For example, suppose Antonio and Francis both want to buy an apple using blockchain cryptocurrency. Vittorio grows and sells apples and needs to have tokens to buy water. Antonio owns tokens for water while Francesco has tokens for visiting museums. Suppose that collecting apples and water takes the same time, while visiting the museum of the place takes half the time it takes to produce the first two. Antonio's exchange has priority because Vittorio, as an apple grower and seller, prefers tokens to buy water. While in fact Antonio only needs to spend one token to get an apple, Francis must first spend two of his tokens to buy the water token from Antonio, then he can spend his water token to compare the apple from Francis.

The mechanism would create an additional demand for two water tokens (by Vittorio and Francesco) that correspond to the offer of two museum tokens (by Francesco) and an apple (by Vittorio). This would increase the value of water tokens by increasing the community's interest in preserving the resource.

We note in general that the system provides full transparency to all users, as all behaviors that are admittedly consistent with the common goal are subject to peer-to-peer evaluation, which further determines the actual perceived value of the network/community. We also note how this type of transaction validation protocol is based on a sort of proof of value (Proof of value) instead of on the solution of a mathematical puzzle (Proof of Work), as occurs in the so-called mining activities of the Bitcoin blockchain, with obvious savings in terms of computing power and energy consumption.

In the hypothesized system, all activities can be clearly monitored and therefore visible to the entire community, and behaviors inconsistent with the logic of the community itself can in fact be identified and sanctioned and the related marginalized bearers. Although anonymous and almost fictitious, trust can be built within the user community.

The hypothesis implicit in the concept of tragedy of commons, i.e. the problem of the lack of communication between those who share the resources, can be rejected and the breadth of the telematic network can extend the scale of cooperation far beyond the simple local level. Obviously, even for blockchain, as for any other telematic activity, it is not possible to completely avoid the risks associated with the improper use of sensitive data, their general protection and their sovereignty, which can significantly inhibit the effective dissemination of this. technology.

We observe that the usefulness of blockchain in overcoming the tragedy of the commons does not derive from being a "new" technology, but from its ability to be functional to the qualitative resolution of the decision coordination problems implied by the use of common resources.

Therefore, only the awareness of these problems and the willingness to deal with them, combined with the affirmation among the users of the common culture of communication, reciprocity, and sharing, can ensure that the technological solution provided by blockchain is of real help to the construction of a self-organized ecosystem, capable of leading to a "happy resolution of conflicts" on common goods. Obviously, the property of blockchain to simultaneously guarantee a reward mechanism would not be extraneous to the feasibility of this construction.

18.2 Transforming Industry and Markets

Blockchain technology is projected to benefit a variety of industries, businesses, and firms that are now experimenting with it or whose industry or enterprises may be touched by its existence in the near future. For example, blockchain-based solutions could make it easier for untrustworthy actors like manufacturers, retailers, distributors, transporters, suppliers, and consumers to connect in global and distributed supply chains.

From farm to fork, traceability and quality control that extends to cultivating, storing, inspecting, and shipping food could improve all stakeholders' accountability. Proof of origin and adherence to environmental rules, as well as organic labeling, fair trade, and other aspects, could assist consumers in making informed decisions and help businesses transition to more sustainable business models.

18.2.1 Government and the Public Sector

The potential to provide personalized services to specific citizens, raise trust in governments, and improve automation, transparency, and verifiability are all advantages of blockchain technology for the public sector. In some cases, adopting blockchain technology to perform public services can result in significant additional benefits. Increased security is one example.

A government-issued identification on the blockchain, for example, can save citizens, businesses, and governments time and money when it comes to developing, managing, and accessing IDs for specific services. Public benefits, such as pensions, contributions, subsidies, and other monies, can benefit from a decentralized network powered by blockchain to conduct transactions without the need for additional third parties or intermediaries.

Blockchain can be utilized in the education sector to register digital credentials, allowing for quick verification and validation while cutting red tape for educational institutions and businesses.

For the most part, blockchain has yet to be integrated into current systems to create new features that give citizens better protection. When it comes to supplying property data or linking to specific individuals or entities, this technology still relies on input from centralized or government systems.

Furthermore, there are concerns about how to assure the external coherence of statements sent electronically without the involvement of a court. The large volume of transactions that must be processed with smart contracts, in particular, is a significant difficulty. Finally, the capacity to set, resize, and maintain collaboration among many different firms is critical to the adoption of blockchain technology.

18.2.2 Data Management

Most firms and industries already use digital data management, and this trend is likely to continue in the near future. Who processes, stores, and owns the data, as well as how and why they do so, are or will be critical concerns for any company. A blockchain could provide extra tools to assure the validity and dependability of data as a tamper proof ledger.

18.3 Secure Recommendations

If properly managed, blockchain can significantly reduce costs and improve efficiency in IoT systems. However, technological integration into IoT-enabled contexts is far from perfect. Only 10% of blockchain ledgers in production, for example, are expected to include IoT sensors by 2021. Furthermore, most IoT systems have a long way to go before they are computationally capable of handling. Blockchain implementations on a large scale.

While the single point of failure has yet to be eliminated, IoT security is based on the provision of security for all connected devices on a continual basis. IoT users, both individuals and organizations, should seek multi-layered security with end-to-end protection that spans from gateway to endpoint and is capable of preventing potential network breaches and compromises. This includes the issues covered in the following sections.

18.3.1 Privacy Policy

Security and privacy attacks can be exploited on blockchain networks. This topic is covered in several chapters, which characterize attack surfaces, identify vulnerabilities in consensus protocols, discuss security and privacy threats to blockchain without and with required authorization, identify methods to defend against duplicate spending, either developed by blockchain technology or proposed by researchers to mitigate the impact of these attacks, and explore what can be done to mitigate the impact of these attacks.

Through cryptography, blockchains document ownership of all existing coins inside a cryptocurrency ecosystem at any one time. A transaction is recorded in a "block" on the blockchain once it has been validated and cryptographically verified by other network members or nodes. The timing of the transaction, preceding transactions, and transaction details are all stored in a block.

Transactions are kept in chronological order and cannot be modified once they have been entered as a block. Since the launch of Bitcoin, the initial application of blockchain technology, this technology has accelerated the development of new cryptocurrencies and applications.

The data is not checked and handled by a single body as in traditional systems due to decentralization. Rather, every node or computer connected to the network verifies the legitimacy of transactions. Cryptography protects and authenticates transactions and data in blockchain technology. Data breaches have become more widespread as the usage of technology has increased.

Personal data and information are retained, mishandled, and misused, posing a threat to privacy. Many people want blockchain technology to be widely used because it can increase user privacy, data security, and data ownership.

18.3.2 Smart Contracts

Another area in which it is important to fix the spaces and expectations related to the blockchain is that of smart contracts. Smart contracts based on blockchain can bring enormous benefits to companies, organizations, and public administrations.

The prospects are unquestionable and sectors such as insurance, logistics, and procurement are already reaping important benefits. Here too there remains a point of utmost attention in the transition phase from the real, physical, and digital world, in the certainty of providing correct information by subjects, persons, or companies, and correctly identified.

18.3.3 Distributed Computing Systems

These are used to tackle computationally intensive problems. There are two broad categories in this area:

- Cluster computing

- Grid computing

Cluster computing involves computers, usually similar and located in the same area, connected by a high-speed data network (LAN). For example, you can use Beowulf, which, through a master computer, is able to distribute a set of processes on a group of Linux machines.

One field of application of cluster computing is the computation of weather forecasts. The European Center for Medium Range Weather forecasts in Shinfield Park, READING, Berkshire, Great Britain, consisted of hundreds of thousands of similar systems, connected with a very high-speed local network (in the order of Terabits).

In the case of *grid computing,* the resources are heterogeneous and can belong to different institutions. Belonging to different institutions, these resources are connected through geographic data networks, usually the Internet.

An example of grid computing is the SETI project for the search for extraterrestrial life. The programming of distributed computing systems takes place using special libraries of some kind, which facilitate the use of the physical infrastructure.

The criteria for choosing between cluster and grid architecture is to evaluate the amount of data to be exchanged between nodes. If the data to be exchanged is a lot, it is necessary to use cluster computing. If the data is sparse, however, it is possible to use grid computing. High-performance computing is a research area in its own right.

18.3.4 Distributed Information Systems

These have the objective of managing distributed information. That is, we have pieces of information about different systems, and we want to manage them in such a way that they appear as if they were all present in one system.

Classic example: distributed databases. There can be implementations:

- Distributed transaction processing (or TPS: transaction processing system)

- Enterprise application integration (EAI)

Distributed transaction processing. In transactional systems, the ACID (Atomicity, Consistency, Isolation, Durability) properties apply to a database.

In particular, atomicity consists of being able to execute a whole block of instructions, or not doing anything otherwise. Consistency means that any constraints imposed are respected. Isolation implies that multiple parallel transactions do not interfere with each other. Durability means that, when the order is committed, the results of the operations are permanent.

Distributed transactional systems have a greater inherent difficulty than centralized ones: they can fall apart. Think of the fact that we are dealing with multiple databases, each in different systems. If the job in an intermediate database fails, it is also necessary to cancel the job already done in all the previous databases, in which it was completed successfully.

A Transaction Processing Monitor (TPM) is normally used to implement transactional distributed systems. Basically, it consists in having a central system that collects requests and distributes them to the different systems, verifying precisely how the individual operations are going. In this way, the information is distributed, but the control logic is centralized.

Instead of integrating databases, one can think of integrating applications, thus approaching the concept of Enterprise Application Integration.

In this case there are a series of servers, equipped with peer-to-peer communication interfaces. The desired information is constructed by accessing the various servers that contain it, and then mounted appropriately. This approach is much more complex than the TPM. For example, think of web servers with service access interfaces. To integrate the related data, it is necessary to work on the responses of the services in question.

18.3.5 Distributed Pervasive Systems

Pervasive distributed systems are part of the environment that surrounds us. The devices that compose them need to discover the services and adapt to the environment.

Examples of pervasive distributed systems are:

- Home systems

- Electronic systems for healthcare and wireless sensor networks

A domestic system is typically:

- Self-managed

- Self-configured

- A personal space

Electronic healthcare systems are composed of sensors that detect health measures from the patient (motion sensors, ECG, ...) and transmit them via a body-area network (BAN) to a hub that collects them and retransmits them to a centralized repository.

An alternative architecture consists of connecting the measurement sensors to an external storage system via a continuous wireless connection. Unlike home systems, healthcare systems cannot be deployed with single server architectures.

Healthcare systems need in-network computing capabilities. Wireless sensor networks (WSNs) are autonomous sensor systems, distributed in physical space, which cooperatively monitor physical or environmental conditions.

They are characterized by stringent limitations regarding:

- Processing capacity

- Amount of memory

- Power supply capacity

These systems are particularly challenging in relation to:

- Energy consumption

- Programming

- Safety

- Routing

- Software engineering

- Middleware

Typically it will be necessary to obtain the information collected from the sensor network. Several architectures are possible.

It can be assumed that the sensors do not cooperate with each other and do not store the collected data, but merely send the data directly to the operator; or you can have sensors capable of processing and storing data. In response to a query, the sensors responsible for the requested data are sent only the answers.

These solutions are not very attractive because:

- Energy consumption is high.

- It is necessary to limit the response data to the operator.

For these reasons, the need to have in-network processing capabilities is considered. For this purpose, pub/sub (publish/subscribe) patterns can be used.

18.4 Client and Server Anatomy
18.4.1 Client

The clients have the function of allowing the users to interact with the servers. This functionality can take place in several ways. The client can provide direct access to the services on the server by giving the user only the interface. In this context, the server does everything. The client is called a *thin* client.

An example is the X Windows machines, where the clients do nothing but display the graphics decided by the server.

It is possible that the client hosts software components that go beyond the pure graphical interface, taking charge of part of the application, to gradually reach extremes such as ATM machines and TV set-top boxes. In these cases, the user interface can become a minority component of the software present in the customer. While local processing and communication support may be predominant component.

So far we have talked about the functional requirements of the software. But there may also be non-functional requirements.

For example, transparency for data access is usually implemented with a software emulator on the client that provides the same interface as the server, masking the differences (data and communication format).

Leasing, migration, and relocation are usually accomplished via naming systems, with the cooperation of client software. For example, consider how your cell phone works. When walking, the mobile phone measures the signal strength of the cell it is working with, and compares it with the powers of the other cells it receives.

When the power of the reference cell drops excessively, the mobile phone (therefore the client) triggers the process to change the reference cell, requesting the connection to the strongest signal among those available.

Similarly when dealing with embedded systems and the multi TCP, this means that a layer 4 (cellular) client opens multiple TCP channels (such as via a radio network and via WiFi). It routes the TCP traffic on the best performing channel. If the signal of the current channel degrades—because you go too far from the WiFi access point—your mobile phone passes the TCP traffic to the radio network. Indeed, if the signals are both good, it can do load balancing on both networks. This is an example of relocation of services. Even the masking of communication errors usually takes place on the client side.

18.4.2 Server

A *server* is a process that implements a specific service used by a collection of clients. There are several ways to organize servers. Iterative servers directly handle requests and respond to clients. Concurrent servers do not handle the request directly, but pass it on to a separate thread/process, after which they wait for the next request.

Concurrent servers are implemented with threads or with processes.

The port on which the server works is either cataloged or is a known port. There are superservers that launch other servers. When a superserver sees a call on the port of competence of a particular server, it activates it. There are UNIX services that do this job. And it is worth using a superserver only toward servers that are rarely called.

It may be necessary to have two channels to the server, one working, and the other out of band to send control information. A classic example is FTP.

Another aspect to consider is the possible need to manage the status of the request. A server with stateless requests is said to be *stateless*, while if the requests have a state to handle, we have *stateful* servers.

A stateless server does not need to store information necessary to perform the client's requested service. It merely responds by sending the requested data. If it stores something related to the past, it is not something necessary for the processing of the requested service. The web server is an example of a stateless server. In this case, if you need to keep status information, you are forced to keep it in the client (as a web or HTTP cookie).

Instead, a stateful server needs to maintain information for the processing of the requested service, for each connected client. For example, a file server needs to maintain the status of requests in progress from each client to prevent concurrent writes to the same file by two different clients.

Whether or not to manage the status of the request for each client has a very significant impact. Stateless server development is much simpler.

Not only because they have less data to keep under control, but mostly because if a stateless server crashes, you can just restart it. You don't need to rebuild the state.

On the other hand, if a stateful server fails, it is necessary to reconstruct the status of the operations in progress for each client: a much more complex operation. On the other hand, a stateful server is usually faster, albeit more complex.

18.5 Questions About Distributed Systems

18.5.1 What Is the Role of Middleware in a Distributed System?

Middleware is a software layer placed between the operating system and the architectural layer. It can provide transparency regarding access to data. For example a client written in C, which must interact with a server written in Java. The Java virtual machine ensures a homogeneous definition of an integer data.

Instead, the C compiler optimizes access to the memory of an integer data, consequently in general it has different structures for different hardware systems. Just as the format between Little Endian hardware systems can differ from Big Endian systems. Middleware can address these differences regarding data access. But it can also provide other services, such as a common API to program other services.

Middleware is used to improve the transparency of the distribution, which is normally missing in the network operating system. That is, the middleware increases the unified vision that the distributed system must have.

18.5.2 What Is Meant By Transparency (of Distribution)?

Distribution transparency means the ability to hide from users and applications the fact that the system has distributed aspects. Examples can be transparency in access to data, transparency in localization, transparency in migration, transparency in relocation, transparency in the reply, transparency to competition, transparency to faults, and transparency to persistence.

18.5.3 Why Is it Sometimes Difficult to Hide the Occurrence of a Failure and Its Recovery in a Distributed System?

Because it is usually not possible to distinguish between a long wait for the response because the server is down, compared to the same wait because the server is slow in responding. Consequently, a system can say that the service is not available, when in fact the server just takes time to respond.

18.5.4 Is It Okay to Have Two Different Programming Languages for the Development of Distributed Systems?

A server program written in C ++ provides the implementation of a BLOB object that can be accessed by a client program written in Java. Server and client may have different hardware, but they are all connected to the Internet. Describe what problems need to be resolved in order for a client to invoke an object method on the server.

There are problems to be addressed at both the hardware and software levels. Hardware can have different types of data storage (MSB vs. LSB), and software use different structures for their management (C++ objects are different from the same objects written in Java). Consequently, in these cases it is necessary to use a framework that takes care of the related implementation details.

Having different hardware means you can have different representations of the data in the request and response messages from client to object. A common standard must be defined for each type of data to be transmitted between client and object and vice versa.

Furthermore, computers can have different operating systems. Therefore, it is necessary to deal with different types of operations to send and receive messages or to carry out method invocations. A common operation will be defined in the C ++/Java program, which will be translated into the particular operation required within the operating system used.

Having two different programming languages, C ++ and Java, you have two different ways of representing data structures. It is necessary to define a common standard for each type of data structure to be transmitted, and a way of interpreting it for each of the languages.

18.5.5 What Is the Difference Between Cache and Replication?

The *cache* copies some of the data, and usually does it on the client. *Replication* copies a node in its entirety and does so on the server. A benefit of replication is system scalability.

A drawback of replication that, in the event of frequent data updates, the data traffic and the time required to update replicas can become unsustainable.

18.5.6 When Is It Appropriate To Use a Cluster Rather Than a Grid Computer?

A *cluster* is used when the communication rate between different computers is high. The servers are connected with a high-speed data network.

Grid computing is oriented toward the execution of client/server type tasks: a task is assigned, and it is executed. Servers are connected via the Internet and can belong to different organizations, and nodes can have different functions.

18.5.7 How Do You Differentiate Between Different Types of Distributed Systems?

The *enterprise information systems* manage different sets of data distributed on different nodes, with the aim of making the total set of data transparent, that is, as if it were all centralized in a single node.

Pervasive systems are sets of autonomous nodes, distributed throughout the environment, which collaborate to achieve a common purpose.

18.6 Advantages and Disadvantages of Blockchain

Note that there are many applications and advantages in the use of blockchain technology, among which:[2]

- Blockchain technology eliminates the need for a third-party middleman in transactions, allowing the parties involved to conduct transactions without the involvement of third-parties who monitor the event, thus lowering the danger of the parties defaulting.

- Because the validity of transactions is confirmed when each block is closed, the data and information are of high quality. The transaction will not be included in the specified block if it is not completed. The information included in each block and throughout the blockchain is found to be consistent, chronological, and credible, ensuring a high level of data quality.

Another important issue to consider is the technology's longevity and dependability, as the network is decentralized and peer-to-peer in nature, with no central point. Due to the talk from a central point, decentralization aids in safeguarding the system when there is a failure or even if it is hacked. Each "peer" has a copy of the data, ensuring that it does not get lost.

Another benefit of the blockchain technology is the process's integrity. Users must ensure that transactions will be completed according to the terms proposed, otherwise the event will be invalidated. Another important aspect for transaction transparency is transparency, immutability, and advertising, which are all connected to public blockchain.

The process of compressing all of the data illustrates the ease of collecting all ledger transactions into a single public ledger while also lowering the cost per transaction. Associated expenditures and trade products decrease without the involvement of third parties.

The adoption of blockchain technology is also good for the environment since it decreases the number of documents printed and file storage space. Every document

---

[2] **Blockchain: the technological revolution and impacts to the economy.** Multidisciplinary Core scientific journal of knowledge. 04 year, Ed. 03, vol. 07, pp. 110-144. March 2019. ISSN: 2448-0959

or transaction may be concealed or converted to code and referenced in the ledger, illustrating the breadth of blockchain technology's uses.

Other blockchain-based applications that are useful are:

- **Creating dispersed and autonomous marketplaces.** According to Z, I, it's similar to a virtual shopping mall, bringing together numerous brands and businesses in one location. As a result, blockchain ensures that assets are transferred in a safe, confidential, and timely manner, while also providing flexibility to the cashier and asset management.

- **The technology is self-contained and does not require the use of third-party middlemen.** Because of the open competition and best prices, if a firm provides valuable products to potential customers with the assurance of authenticity, the connection is beneficial.

- **Commercial transactions have made it easy.** Cost management becomes easier with the use of this technology since it allows companies to build a network of suppliers and partners, automate contracts, and monitor them along the supply chain. Furthermore, because human contacts are reduced, blockchain minimizes transaction mistakes or a lack of knowledge, as well as the implementation of agility between parties.

- **Administer and secure decentralized private records.** Every record is encrypted and needs a unique access key, ensuring absolute data security, especially at educational institutions and enterprises in the human resources sector, without fear of forgery.

- **Monitor the origin of products and materials.** The blockchain can ensure a product's quality and safety, as well as the traceability of its inputs.

According to Garcia, utilizing blockchain technology permits one of the benefits, *auto-soberania,* which allows users to identify and control the storage and administration of their personal data at the same time.

Another intrinsic benefit of blockchain technology is the speed with which assets are sent, considering that certain financial institutions take days to complete a wire transfer and do not operate on weekends. The timezone has a role in international commerce. Transactions may be carried out 24 hours a day, every day, to any place, with quick shipment confirmation, thanks to the adoption of blockchain. What else ails people interested in Blockchain technology and your business application, is the query. According to Wood, there is no difference between permissionless calls on public networks and permissioned calls on private networks.

The structure of the nodes in the peer-to-peer network determines security in private networks when the participants are aware. The members' joint validation of the permitted accounting transaction. Private blockchain operators regulate what each peer may do and how they connect, and each node has a precise copy of the accounting that is continually updated. An active node must have a certain number of active connections in order to be legitimate.

As a result, a node that exhibits flaws in information transmission should be recognized and inhibited in order to maintain the system's integrity. Consensual operation high availability policies are used to avoid locking the system. The proof-of-work is a validation step before granting authorization to construct a new block, which improves process security and dependability.

In the way of public networks, membership validation, also known as consensus, happens at 10-minute intervals on average for selecting a leader node validator to execute the accounting update, a technique known as *data mining*. In this setting, transactions are considered secure after a few hours. Meanwhile, following the new update, the transaction might be invalidated, which is known as a *fork operation*. Run a fork for earlier accounting transactions.

Because of the necessity for mining on public networks, it is assumed that the security percentage does not reach 100%, but the use of alternative consensus algorithms methods might determine who invests as many commodities in blockchain as the proportionate miner invested.

It also serves to highlight some of the problems that blockchain technology deployment may encounter, including:

- **The speed of miners:** They aim to verify with agility for transactions and information entered into the blockchain, which requires income and expensive equipment.

- **Regulation by the states:** It is understood that there is some fear about the regulation of this technology, especially with regard to the criptomoedas that are in the blockchain like Bitcoins. Financial institutions and the state itself lost market share, causing economic and political instability.

- **Power consumption:** Blockchain miners spend time and a lot of computer resources to validate transactions.

- **Control, security, and privacy:** Regulation without state, there is no control or security of data sharing, even with smart contracts, for contracts can be violated.

- **Integration:** Blockchain technology is still new and little used and the creation of a network depends on the acceptance of commitments to develop internal strategies to apply this technology on a large scale. In this context, the scope needs to be broader to consider blockchain as a decentralized network.

- **Cost:** The price and timing of operations is reduced. On the other hand, the cost of initial capital for the application is very high.

- **Complex application:** The application does not have the meeting of different projects which can be a difficult task.

According to Lamonier, 23% of organizations planned to adopt blockchain technology in their businesses in 2018. Financial institutions had the highest percentage, while 43% of businesses were intrigued, but no research had been done on the topic. Although more study is needed before blockchain can be used, it has the ability to manage big companies and alter the economy.

It is necessary to define the notion of POC (Proof of Concept), which is a term used while the blockchain is being tested. According to Lamonier, many firms are prepared to invest in proof of concept for this technology, and 66% of experts and CEOs feel that blockchain will be the next digital revolution, according to a recent poll.

The banking system is the industry with the most successful blockchain implementations, allowing new firms that employ blockchain security to seek investment from established institutions, some of which have already adapted to this technology.

Its use in this sector allows financial services to have more accuracy and security in their financial transactions, allowing them to provide better service to their clients both inside and outside the country with tremendous agility.

Within the realm of financial services, advantages include lower costs, faster settlement times, improved data quality, simple and transparent auditing, and increased security.

18.7 Blockchain Technology and Cost Cutting

Some institutions have begun to investigate digital assets on their own. Recent data suggests that this might raise GDP by lowering real interest rates, distorting fees and monetary transaction costs, and improving central banks' ability to stabilize the economic cycle. Gains in efficiency in payments, clearing, and settlement could be masked by the lack of anonymity.

A UK FinTech firm just issued, approved, settled, and registered the world's first cryptocurrency bond, which was built entirely on public blockchain infrastructure. The fact that this amount was legally recorded as financial activity is another unique feature of it. The sandbox authority was in charge of monitoring.

In terms of the secondary market, it's thought that one of the first transactions involving blockchain technology was an asset management firm purchasing a disaster bond that had been produced using the platform. When compared to typical transaction techniques, the company stated that the accompanying transaction costs were much lower.

The financial sector is taking notice of blockchain's unique properties, with major financial institutions announcing that they are currently experimenting with the technology. For example, 40 of the world's major banks took part in a large-scale trial employing multiple blockchain technology suppliers to test a system for trading fixed-income assets.

In our increasingly interconnected world, blockchain technology has the potential to enable parties who do not have a high level of trust in one another to exchange any type of digital asset (money, contracts, land, medical and educational records, services or goods) on a peer-to-peer basis with few or no intermediaries.

Many possibilities exist with blockchain and distributed ledger technologies (DLT). Aside from these blockchain uses, there are a few fundamental obstacles that are preventing DLT from becoming widely used in the financial sector:

- **Performance and scalability:** The current effectiveness of blockchain technology is limited due to the complexity of application design, which can result in bottlenecks due to the system's latency.

- **Privacy:** The fact that all information is exchanged among participants is one of DLT's primary advantages. However, in financial transactions, this can result in concerns with confidentiality. Cryptography and zero-knowledge proofs are two experimental answers to this challenge.

- **Outdated infrastructures:** Legacy infrastructures must interface with DLTs, which can be difficult to convert due to differences in underlying technology.

- **Updating and maintaining software:** Changing software in the absence of a central authority necessitates participant unanimity, which must be maintained to avoid chain breakdowns.

- **Real-world applications:** A small subset of participants was analyzed in the payment cases. The majority of real-world applications involve cryptocurrency speculation.

18.8 Summary

Although blockchain technology is best recognized for supporting Bitcoins, it is being used in a wide range of applications. This technology is a shared permanent record between parties that demonstrates a security mechanism based on information decentralization, mostly in the financial sector. Its remit has been broadened to include the safekeeping of any document[3].

Globalization is one of the major benefits of blockchain, as it is unaffected by external variables such as data, finance, or even government. Its technology is used to keep track of transaction records, particularly for financial transactions, which are kept in a block with a hash number. When the block is finished, it is hashed, indicating that the block transactions are legitimate and immutable, and a new beginning block is created.

This technology enables participants, whether corporations or individuals, to create contracts, execute transactions, and move values without depending on middlemen to safeguard the event and set business rules.

---

[3] **Blockchain: the technological revolution and impacts to the economy.** Multidisciplinary Core scientific journal of knowledge. 04 year, Ed. 03, vol. 07, pp. 110-144. March 2019. ISSN: 2448-0959

It turns out that banks have investigated the use of blockchain in transactions in order to reduce costs and accelerate the liquidity process. This technology allows cash, shares, bonds, securities, shares, contracts, and other assets to be transferred and kept securely and peer-to-peer.

Defects and cost reduction are the primary reasons why financial institutions, auditing firms, and banks are investing in blockchain-based solutions, since financial middlemen are too expensive.

Secure can decrease the risks of the blockchain application process in the financial context, according to studies conducted by creative companies in the blockchain space.

The reduction in expenses for all actors in the economy would allow for widespread collaboration via a peer-to-peer network, which might impact our current agreements.

The rise in online transactions necessitates a higher level of security for the data that this technology can supply. Despite its novel character, blockchain provides enough assurances for preserving data, documents, and financial transaction records, particularly in terms of security.

Because the disruptive potential of blockchain is larger than predicted given economic, financial, and social conditions, the effects of blockchain on consumers' relationships with financial institutions may be seen in the institutions' shifting emphasis. Blockchain regulation is important to guarantee that legal relationships are created, but it also allows the government to limit the technology's powers.

In the face of this new virtual economy, blockchain technology must continue to develop and earn trust. In this context, fresh research is needed to add value to blockchain and maintain its legitimacy, while also strengthening the network and positively affecting the world's economy.

Index

A

Absolute deadline, 176
Abstract-syntax, 201
Active resources, 176
Agrifood industry, 2
Alert states, 383
Application Specific Integrated
    Circuit (ASIC) mining, 152
Artificial intelligence (AI), 357
    blockchain, 358, 359
    making real-time intelligent and
        decision-making machines, 359
Ask4Bridge mode, 250, 253, 255
Assets, 326
    Hyperledger Fabric, 127
Automated surface observing
    system (ASOS), 287
Automotive applications, 371–373
Autonomous automobiles, 370
Autonomous vehicle management system
    advantages, 362
    controller, 374–381
    data transfer via blockchain
        technology, 361
    dependability and safety, 363–367
    experimental activity, 400–403
    experimental method
        controller retraining, 392, 393
        controller test, 385–388
        monitor or observation testing,
            388–390, 392

method implementation and
    results, 393
results
    controller testing, 403–410
    monitor assessment, 410–415
    retraining and rechecking, 415–417
safety and self-controlled vehicles,
    373, 374
system analysis method, 381–384
tracking, 367–369

B

Behavioral Elements, 202
BFT-based Proof of Stake, 115, 116
Bitcoin
    address, 19, 20
    block, 41–46
    blockchain structure, 45
    decentralization, 355
    digital signature, 20–26
    vs. Ethereum stacks, 56
    history
        distributed consensus, 13, 14
        Linked Timestamping and the
            Merkle Tree, 12
    Nakamoto Consensus (*see* Nakamoto
        Consensus)
    nodes functions, 352–354
    private key, 16
    project
        blockchain into cryptocurrency, 351

© Joseph Thachil George 2022
J. T. George, *Introducing Blockchain Applications*, https://doi.org/10.1007/978-1-4842-7480-4

Printed in the United States
by Baker & Taylor Publisher Services

Printed in the United States
by Baker & Taylor Publisher Services